DOCTOR WHO

PSYCHOLOGY

A MADMAN WITH A BOX

edited by
Travis Langley, PhD

#PsychGeeks #DWpsych
www.sterlingpublishing.com

STERLING
New York

STERLING
New York

An Imprint of Sterling Publishing Co., Inc
1166 Avenue of the Americas
New York, NY 10036

ISBN 978-1-4549-2001-4

Distributed in Canada by Sterling Publishing Co., Inc.
C/o Canadian Manda Group, 664 Annette Street
Toronto, Ontario, Canada M6S 2C8
Distributed in the United Kingdom by GMC Distribution Services
Castle Place, 166 High Street, Lewes, East Sussex, England BN7 1XU
Distributed in Australia by NewSouth Books
45 Beach Street, Coogee, NSW 2034, Australia

For information about custom editions, special sales, and premium and
corporate purchases, please contact Sterling Special Sales at
800-805-5489 or specialsales@sterlingpublishing.com.

Manufactured in Canada

2   4   6   8   10   9   7   5   3   1

www.sterlingpublishing.com

Image Credits
Cover: Shutterstock: © Shelby Allison (box); © AstroStar (supernova);
© DrHitch (abstract graph); © Guingm (man); © khun nay zaw (metal);
© korabkova (flare); © pixelparticle (universe)
Dover: 55
iStock: © Anastasiya_Yatchenko: 7; © David Crooks: throughout (gears);
© DavidBukack: 147; © diumo: 52, 128, 179, 245; © duncan1890: 219, 265;
© ilbusca: 89, 109, 193, 209, 231; © KeithBishop: 33; © Nikola Nastasic: 65,
159; © Ner1: throughtout (gears); © nicoolay: 9, 181; © Aleksei Oslopov: 21;
© Roberto A Sanchez: 131; © Tairy: 77; © traveler1116: 247; © tsaplia: 277
Shutterstock: © javarman: throughout (parchment); © Llama: throughout
(gears); © Lorelyn Medina: throughout (gears)

CONTENTS

Acknowledgments: Our Companions   vii

Foreword: The How, Not Why, of Who | Katy Manning   xi

Introduction: Madness in Who We Are | Travis Langley   1

PART ONE: The Hearts of Who We Are   7

1. Who's Who: Interview with Four Doctors and a
   River on the Core of Personality | Travis Langley
   and Aaron Sagers   9

2. The Compassionate Doctor: Caring for Self by Caring
   for Others | Janina Scarlet and Alan Kistler   19

3. The Moral Foundations of Doctor Who | Deirdre Kelly
   and Jim Davies   31

   Factor File One: The Two Factors—Extraversion and
   Neuroticism | Travis Langley   43

PART TWO: Deep Breadth   51

4. The Unconscious: What, When, Where, Why, and
   of Course Who | William Sharp   53

5. Id, Superego, Egoless: Where Is the I in Who?
   | William Sharp   63

6. Weeping Angels, Archetypes, and the Male Gaze
   | Miranda Pollock and Wind Goodfriend   73

7. New Face, New Man: A Personality Perspective
   | Erin Currie   85

8. Dream Lords: Would the Doctor Run with Freud,
   Jung, Myers and Briggs? | Travis Langley   105

   Factor File Two: The Three Factors—Add Psychoticism
   or Openness? | Travis Langley   119

PART THREE: Hands to Hold   125

9. Who Makes a Good Companion? | SARITA J. ROBINSON   127

10. By Any Other Name: Evolution, Excitation, and
    Expansion | WIND GOODFRIEND   143

11. A Companion's Choice: Do Opposites Attract?
    | ERIN CURRIE   155

    Factor File Three: The Five Factors—Adventures in the
    OCEAN | TRAVIS LANGLEY   167

PART FOUR: Lost Things   175

12. Death and the Doctor: Interview on How Immortals
    Face Mortality | JANINA SCARLET AND AARON SAGERS   177

13. Post-Time War Stress Disorder | KRISTEN ERICKSON
    AND MATT MUNSON, WITH STEPHEN PRESCOTT AND
    TRAVIS LANGLEY   189

14. Behind Two Hearts: Grief and Vulnerability
    | JENNA BUSCH AND JANINA SCARLET   205

15. Boys to Cybermen: Social Narratives and Metaphors for
    Masculinity | BILLY SAN JUAN   215

16. From Human to Machine: At What Point Do You Lose
    Your Soul? | JIM DAVIES AND DANIEL SAUNDERS   227

    Factor File Four: The Six Factors—A Good Man?
    | TRAVIS LANGLEY   235

PART FIVE: Natures   241

17. Getting to the Hearts of Time Lord Personality Change:
    Regeneration on the Brain | SARITA J. ROBINSON   243

18. A New Doctor? The Behavioral Genetics of
    Regeneration | MARTIN LLOYD   261

19. The Time Lord's Brain: Regeneration, Determinism,
    and Free Will | DAVID KYLE JOHNSON AND TRAVIS LANGLEY   273

    Factor File Five: The Further Factors—Aren't There
    Limits? | TRAVIS LANGLEY   287

    File Word: Run! | TRAVIS LANGLEY   293

    About the Editor   297

    About the Contributors   298

    Index   307

ACKNOWLEDGMENTS:
OUR COMPANIONS

Tim Cogburn and Harlan Ellison introduced me to *Doctor Who*, whether they know it or not. When we were kids, Tim told me about this British science fiction program that science fiction author Ellison had praised as "the greatest science fiction series of all time"[1] when relatively few Americans knew it existed. Intrigued, I sought out *Doctor Who* novelizations before I ever saw the show. Who was your first Doctor? For some of this book's writers it was a classic Doctor such as Tom Baker (Fourth Doctor) or Colin Baker (Sixth), while for others it was a twenty-first century Doctor such as Christopher Eccleston (Ninth) or David Tennant (Tenth). Mine was my mental version based on novels that did not indicate which Doctor they featured.

All of us who wrote this book thank the folks at Sterling for letting us explore our relative dimensions in mind on page. My Sterling editors Connie Santisteban and Kate Zimmermann are bright, conscientious, fun people. Each is such a joy to work with. I thank them for all their hard work, wisdom, support, insight, cheesecake, and hot tea. Great people back them up and get these books to print: Ardi Alspach, Toula Ballas, Michael Cea, Marilyn Kretzer, Sari Lampert, Lauren Tambini, and too many more to name them all every time. I want to add a special "thank you" to publicist Blanca Oliviery.

This ambitious book series would be impossible without our writers. Different conventions created opportunities for many of us to meet and share ideas: the Comics Arts Conference (Peter Coogan, Randy Duncan, Kate McClancy), San Diego Comic-Con International (Eddie Ibrahim, Laura Jones, Sue Lord, Karen Mayugba, Adam Neese, Gary Sassaman), New York Comic Con (Lance Fensterman), many Wizard World cons (Christopher Jansen, Peter Katz, Donna Chin, Shelby Engquist, Danny Fingeroth, Tony Kim, Mo Lighning, Madeleine McManus, Jerry Milani, Alex Rae, Katie Ruark, Brittany Walloch), and more. The best part of any convention is making new friends and visiting with friends I don't normally see elsewhere, including many of our writers and my editorial assistants on this volume (Jenna Busch, Mara Whiteside Wood). I couldn't cosplay as John Hurt's War Doctor without the right coat, which I got from chapter co-author Matt Munson (who wore a TARDIS jersey when I met him at Adam S.'s Comic-Con party). Because I also discovered some of our writers through their blogs, mostly at PsychologyToday.com, I thank my *Psychology Today* editor, Kaja Perina.

I am truly fortunate to teach at Henderson State University where administrators like President Glen Jones, Provost Steve Adkison, and Dean John Hardee encourage creative ways of teaching. Our faculty writers group (Angela Boswell, Matthew Bowman, Vernon Miles, David Sesser, Suzanne Tartamella, Michael Taylor) reviewed portions of the manuscript. Librarian Lea Ann Alexander and the Huie Library staff keep our shelves full of unusual resources. David Bateman, Lecia Franklin, Carolyn Hatley, and Ermatine Johnston help me and my students go all the places we need to go. Millie Bowden, Renee Davis, Sandra D. Johnson, Salina Smith, Connie Testa, Flora Weeks, and other fine staff members help us all make sure things can get done. My fellow psychology faculty members show great support and encouragement: Rafael Bejarano, Emilie Beltzer, Rebecca Langley, Paul Williamson, and our chair, Aneeq Ahmad—most of all Rebecca as my best friend and so much more in this life.

Through specific classes and clubs, our students helped me merge the academic and nerdy sides of my life into becoming the same thing. Without leaders like Robert O'Nale, Nicholas Langley, Tiffany Pitcock, Dax Guilliams, and Randy Perry, we would have no Comic Arts Club and I would not have attended my first San Diego Comic-Con. Without founders Ashley Bles, Dillon Hall, Coley Henson, and Bobby Rutledge, we would not have one of our largest and liveliest campus organizations, the Legion of Nerds, which leaders Olivia Bean, Steven Jacobs, and John McManus keep going strong. And while I cannot begin to name the many leaders of our student psychology organizations (the Psychology Club and Psi Chi), I applaud them all.

Phil Collingwood, Kristen McHugh, Chris Murrin, and many others weighed in on social media to help point me in the right direction when I've needed to confirm quotes. (Just because a lot of websites attribute a quote to a specific person doesn't prove the person really said it. Cite sources, people!) While we always check original sources as best we can, online databases like TARDIS Data Core (tardis.wikia.com) sometimes help us find the right episode, movie, audio play, comic book, or novel in the first place. The folks at OuterPlaces.com (Kieran Dickson, Louis Monoyudis, Janey Tracey) join us in our excursions, and everybody at NerdSpan.com (Dan Yun, Ian Carter, Ashley Darling, Keith Hendricks, Iain McNally, Alex Langley, Lou Reyna, Garrett Steele, and more) deserves a salute.

My literary agent Evan Gregory from the Ethan Ellenberg Literary Agency handles more details than readers probably want to know. Sons Nicholas and Alex each played roles in paving the path that led to this series of books. Family-not-by-blood Renee Couey, Marko Head, and Katrina Hill helped pave it, too. We thank Daniel Thompson, FirstGlance's Bill Ostroff, and others for our author photos. Vic Frazao, Jeffrey Henderson, Chris Hesselbein, Jim and Kate Lloyd, Sharon Manning, Dustin McGinnis, Ed O'Neil, Nick Robinson, Bethany San Juan, Fermina San Juan, Niki Wortman, and "more Dax" serve as our writers' muses, mentors, devil's advocates, founts of knowledge, and ground support. Eric Bailey, Austin and Hunter Biegert, Christine Boylan, Lawrence Brenner, Peter

Capaldi, Carrie Goldman, Grant Imahara, Maurice Lamarche, Matt Langston, Paul McGann, Naoko Mori, Adam Savage, and Ross Taylor deserve mention for reasons diverse and sometimes paradoxical.

More than half a century ago, Sydney Newman and Verity Lambert gave us *Doctor Who* (created with C. E. Webber and Donald Wilson), and showrunners Russell T. Davies and Steven Moffat have hurled it into the current millennium for new generations to enjoy. Ron Grainer composed the original *Doctor Who* theme, but it was Delia Derbyshire (assisted by Dick Mills) whose arrangement transformed the music into something eerie, haunting, and unforgettable. We owe a great debt to the thousands of people who have worked on *Doctor Who* over the years—so many actors, writers, directors, producers, designers, and more. *Doctor Who* audio play star Chase Masterson is a fine friend. We cannot say enough to thank television stars Peter Davison, Michelle Gomez, Alex Kingston, Sylvester McCoy, Matt Smith, and David Tennant for speaking with Jenna Busch and Aaron Sagers while we were writing this timey wimey book.

The world met the Doctor in the form of actor William Hartnell (First Doctor), but it was Patrick Troughton (Second) who showed us how greatly the character could change and then Jon Pertwee (Third) who brought the Doctor to our contemporary world. This book's foreword by Pertwee's companion Katy Manning, who worked with all of the first three and several who came later, is a special treasure. Thank you, Katy.

Thank you, all.

Let the madness begin.

Reference

Ellison H. (1979). Introducing Doctor Who. In T. Dicks (Author), *Doctor Who and the Day of the Daleks*. New York, NY: Pinnacle.

FOREWORD:
THE HOW, NOT WHY, OF WHO

KATY MANNING

I have never been a "why" questioner—there lies a path to unanswerable conjecture—but rather a "how" questioner. "How" takes you down the path of logic, learning, and understanding.

Being involved in television in the late '60s/early '70s as a young actress was a stimulating and exciting path of technological experimentation, especially in a program like *Doctor Who* that I had watched from its conception in front of and from behind the sofa! It required space travel to other planets, aliens, electronic music, and "otherworldly" sound effects. The hero was a nomadic two-thousand-year-old man with two hearts who traveled in time and space via a blue police box! A genius concept, allowing limitless adventures and possibilities into the world of fantasy and imagination. Computers were in their infancy, entire rooms of massive machines looking somewhat like Boss in *The Green Death*.[1] Cameras were big and cumbersome, so to achieve what they did during the '60s in black and white was all due to the remarkable creativity of the enthusiastic, dedicated technical teams with a great deal of trial and error and a very small budget—often with little time and difficult, barren winter locations. Last-minute lines like "freak weather conditions in Dungerness" covered the problem of two days of snow, rain, thick fog, and bright sun! I even had hot water poured around my thin suede boots to unfreeze them from the ground. Once we were in the studio for recording, there was a very strict 10 p.m. curfew, and, with special effects to be done in the studio, it was always a tense time where actors had to be sure of achieving performances in one take. When Barry

Letts took over as producer in 1970, he fought relentlessly with
the powers that be to obtain a little extra money to experiment with the development of special effects and really take
this unique program forward. Alien masks were given from
the makeup department over to the special effects department,
using anything and everything to achieve this end.

The Earthbound Doctor

When I joined *DW* in 1971,[2] it was the beginning of many
new things but very importantly the first year of *Doctor Who* in
color. Color separation overlay, too (now green screen), was in
its infancy and would add so much possibility. (I was put in front
of three different-colored screens while it was being perfected.)
Barry also wanted to open up *Doctor Who* to a wider audience
and age group, which he did with resounding success, building a cult following and soaring ratings. Barry Letts and his
right-hand man, the incorrigible scriptwriter/editor Terrence
Dicks, introduced the Doctor's Moriarty in the shape of the
Master, played to perfection by Roger Delgado. Real members
of the army and navy were used in several episodes. Richard
Franklin was introduced as Captain Mike Yates to strengthen
the UNIT team led by Nicholas Courtney as the quintessential
Brigadier ("chap with wings, five rounds rapid"),[3] and John
Levene as Sergeant Benton. It was a risk to banish the Doctor
to the planet Earth by the Time Lords. However, it really gave
UNIT a solid part to play. After all, in our limitless imagina-
tions, aliens are to be expected on other planets, but it takes
a whole new twist when a policeman rips off masks to reveal
faceless Autons, troll dolls come to life and kill, or a man is
even devoured by a blowup black plastic chair.[4] Completely
nonhuman Daleks lurking beneath our cities[5] or the summon-

ing up of the Devil in a picturesque country village church[6] is perhaps more frightening and unexpected on the planet we inhabit. Story lines followed subjects like the slow destruction of the planet Earth through chemicals and financial greed.[7] Interesting to me and indeed perhaps the Doctor was that all the scientific progress we make is useless without moral progress on any planet.

Jo Grant and Her Doctor

The casting of Jon Pertwee as the Third Doctor was inspired— an actor known mostly through radio and light entertainment, a master of character voices, and a real adventurer in his private life. All these talents added to the depths of character Jon brought to "his" Doctor, his first truly dramatic role: a swash-buckling dandy with a wonderful ethereal quality, a dark secret side, and a desire for justice and peace, but always an other-worldly twinkle in his eye. A man we could trust. It was an honor to be cast alongside him, as I had grown up admiring his work. We instantly became fast friends and I learned so much about everything from this wise and wonderful man. This played out onscreen. I was working on a series (my first role out of drama school) for ITV and I was not available during the original auditions, so by the time I appeared, the role of Jo Grant had been shortlisted to three. After a lone improvised scene, I was cast! A nineteen- or twenty-year-old niece of a high-up member of UNIT, who was hired not because of her ability but because of nepotism, she had done a short training course with UNIT, escapology, Sanskrit, and some very dubi-ous GCE (HSC)* results! Jo could ask the questions on behalf

*General Certificate of Education (Health & Social Care).

of the younger viewers and non–sci-fi boffins, and appeal to the teenagers as a trendy miniskirted, platform-booted, beringed girl of the '70s. She was foisted onto the Doctor. She was resourceful, brave, cheeky, disobedient, and a little clumsy; didn't scream much; did not always agree with the Doctor, but (as in *The Daemons*) was prepared to lay down her life for the man she learned to love and respect. In turn, she brought out the nurturing side of the Doctor's character and she grew up onscreen in our living rooms, ending her tenure by marrying a Nobel Peace Prize–winning echo warrior—a younger version of the Doctor, a professor played excellently by my then-real-life-fiancé Stewart Bevan. In a beautifully crafted script, her meeting with her professor mirrored Jo's first clumsy meeting with her Doctor.[8] There was no other part I could have played where my powers of imagination were so deeply tested, where I could have learned so much from both the technical teams and my fellow actors, or where I could have done stunts in the safe hands of the incredible and patient boys from Havoc, led by Derek Ware. Jon insisted on doing the majority of his own stunts and I was never far behind! He was an absolute joy to spend every day with and was a strong, committed team leader.

The First Three

When *The Three Doctors*[9] came about, a first in bringing their past regenerations together, I felt extremely privileged to be working with the Doctors I had grown up watching. Sadly, William Hartnell, who set the bar very high as the First Doctor and who I believe created some of the traits given to the future Doctors, was very ill and his filming was done without us. Patrick Troughton as the Second Doctor was a very different actor than Jon. Pat was what we used to call a classical actor, with a huge career in theater behind him and a wonderfully naughty sense of humor. He liked to improvise around the script, whereas Jon liked to know exactly what was going to be said and what he was going to respond to. Their differences were soon overcome with respect for each other's choices in playing the Doctor. Watching these two very contrasting but great actors weave their magic was a master class. Pat's Doctor may have seemed discombobulated, but this cleverly concealed the twinkling genius beneath the surface. The clothes that each actor wears as the Doctor help define his take on the character.

New Doctors

This pioneering show prompted so many to enter the world of acting, producing, writing, and directing—way too many to name. For others, *Doctor Who* brought a magical, trustworthy hero into their lives and living rooms. The genius Russell T. Davies, a massively keen boy fan, was the champion who regenerated *Doctor Who* back onto our screens after a well-deserved rest—bringing with him all the modern technology, along with brilliant scripts and casting. Amongst this, he also created marvelous spin-offs, including *The Sarah Jane Adventures* with the unrivaled Liz Sladen. So, after forty years, I had the privilege of working with a young Matt Smith's Eleventh Doctor, yet again putting a totally unique and delightfully physical stamp on the character of the Doctor. Though a younger actor, there was something extremely comforting and familiar about him as my Doctor. He was so warm and generous, and allowed me great freedom in our emotional scenes together. An unforgettable time shared with Liz and a script that encompassed Jo's life forty years on—perfection.

On audio I have played Jo Grant with Sylvester McCoy's Seventh Doctor, a lighter and enjoyably clownish take on the character. I played Iris Wildthyme with Peter Davison's Fifth Doctor—a younger, more gentle Doctor—and Colin Baker's more bombastic Sixth Doctor, and talked with Peter Capaldi, the Twelfth Doctor, about his inspired performance and layering of the Doctor. More recently, I have worked with the incomparable Tom Baker, the Fourth Doctor. I could not ask for more! It seems to me, watching all the actors who have brought their innovative expertise to our screens, that one of the Doctor's two hearts belongs to the character and the other to all the brilliant actors who brought the Doctor so strongly and believably into the hearts of the viewers, now seen and loved in more than one hundred countries around the world.

So the question of why *Doctor Who* is still so popular after all these years is impossible to answer. All *Doctor Who* fans will have their own take on that and indeed who their favorites are. But, for me, "why" or even "who" matters not at all. I shall just continue to watch, enjoy, and marvel at the phenomenon of the *Doctor Who* kiss, the love that everyone who has ever been involved or watched *Doctor Who* has.

 Katy Manning's career has spanned nearly fifty years and three countries. Her extensive television work began with John Braines's groundbreaking series *Man at the Top*. During this time, Katy was given the role of Jo Grant in *Doctor Who* alongside the unforgettable Third Doctor, Jon Pertwee, a role she revisited some forty years later in *The Sarah Jane Adventures*, starring Elisabeth Sladen with Matt Smith as the Eleventh Doctor. Katy's theater credits extend from London's West End to Sydney's Opera House. She returned to the UK with her critically acclaimed one-woman show about Bette Davis, *Me*

and Jezebel. Katy has voiced numerous cartoons, including the award-winning *Gloria's House* as the ten-year-old Gloria. She has hosted her own interview show and directed two major musicals and several other plays. For over a decade, she has recorded for Big Finish as Jo Grant in *The Companion Chronicles* and as Iris Wildethyme in her own series, and guested on *The Confessions of Dorian Gray, Doctor Who Short Trips, Dracula,* and *The Lives of Captain Jack Harkness*. Katy wrote and performed *Not a Well Woman* in New York and LA, now recorded by Big Finish. More recently, Katy appeared on *Casualty* and for Bafflegab recorded *Baker's End* with Tom Baker.

Notes

1. Classic serial 10–5, *The Green Death* (May 19–June 23, 1973).
2. Classic serial 8–1, *Terror of the Autons* (January 1–23, 1971).
3. Classic serial 8–5, *The Daemons*, pt. 5 (June 19, 1971).
4. All in the classic serial 8–1, *Terror of the Autons* (January 1–23, 1971).
5. Classic serial 9–1, *Day of the Daleks* (January 1–22, 1972).
6. Classic serial 8–5, *The Daemons* (May 22–June 19, 1971).
7. Classic serial 10–5, *The Green Death* (May 19–June 23, 1973).
8. Classic serial 10–5, *The Green Death* (May 19–June 23, 1973).
9. Classic serial 10–1, *The Three Doctors* (December 30, 1972–January 20, 1973).

INTRODUCTION: MADNESS IN WHO WE ARE

TRAVIS LANGLEY

"I thought—well, I started to think—that maybe you were just, like, a madman with a box."
—Amy Pond[1]

> *"A possible link between madness and genius*
> *is one of the oldest and most persistent of cultural*
> *notions; it is also one of the most controversial."*
> —psychologist Kay Redfield Jamison[2]

Think outside the box. No matter how deceptively large your box might be, no matter how many swimming pools and libraries and strikingly similar corridors it might hold, and no matter where it might take you or when, be ready to step outside and look around. This kind of thinking takes the Doctor away from Gallifrey[3] and carries him from one adventure to another instead of merely observing history and the universe from a place of greater safety inside. Rather than stick with the tried-and-true, the Doctor tries something new. Copernicus, Galileo, Mozart, and countless others down through the millennia have been called "mad" for making novel claims, challenging established ideas, and trying something new. When the TARDIS (embodied in a woman) calls the Doctor the only Time Lord "mad enough"[4] to run away from Gallifrey with her, is she calling him insane or is she talking about his unconventionality?

What is madness? Psychiatrist Thomas Szasz has repeatedly accused the mental health profession of perpetuating myths about mental illness by describing any aberrant, disconcerting, outrageous, or otherwise unconventional behavior as "illness" or "disease."[5] Diagnosticians evaluating whether clients' behavior is bizarre or unhealthy must take into account what is considered normal for each client's environment, social class, or culture.[6] The Doctor's supposed madness does not refer to regeneration-induced chaos in his memories and personality because that's normal for Time Lords; he's even thought to be "mad" by their standards.[7] The qualities deemed inappropriate by their standards, however, may be heroic by ours. Scientific and artistic originality are not the only forms of unconventionality to get someone slapped with a label of madness. Standing up for what's right can, too, and the Doctor's fellow Time Lords are not known for doing what's right for others.

By any standards, the Doctor is an unconventional hero. His thinking may be divergent, convergent, deductive, inductive, logical, and illogical—or at least unconstrained by anyone else's rules of how to follow a logical train of thought. He engages in a lot of *heuristic* thinking, taking mental shortcuts because he often lacks the patience for more methodical, meticulous, *algorithmic* analysis.[8] Taking shortcuts in decision making leads to more mistakes but, to be fair, his heuristics are based on foundations more solid than ours tend to be. He charges in with little or no plan,[9] tries something, tries something else, and continually adapts to circumstances because he has the sheer ability and experience to make it all work out in the end (most of the time) and a personality that simply lacks patience.

What *is* the Doctor's personality? Given how many different incarnations he has taken, can we even say he has "a" personality? Throughout this book, that question keeps coming up. Every book in this *Popular Culture Psychology* series covers a wide range of topics, whichever areas in psychology seem appropriate and interesting to nearly two dozen authors each time, and yet some specific subject emerges as the most prominent every time. *Star Wars Psychology: Dark Side of the Mind* stresses the importance of looking past the surface when considering the complexities of good and evil; *The Walking Dead Psychology: Psych of the Living*—trauma; *Game of Thrones Psychology: The Mind Is Dark and Full of Terrors*—motivation; *Captain America vs. Iron Man: Freedom, Security, Psychology*—heroism; *Star Trek Psychology: The Mental Frontier*—the growth of the human race. As it turns out, *Doctor Who Psychology: A Madman with a Box* looks repeatedly at the nature of personality, the *Who* in it all.

How can an unconventional hero with an unconventional personality (or personalities) help us look at human psychology, and can we really use our own psychology to look at him? The Doctor, of course, is not just any ancient, time-traveling alien. He is an ancient, time-traveling alien who finds himself fascinated with us. We can use our sense of psychology to look at this character and we can use this character to look at our psychology, because this character judges himself by looking at us. If there's a bit of bedlam in us all, then letting it out can sometimes be creative, constructive, and good for us—a kind of madness or passion that is not a mental disease at all.

> *"There's something you better understand about me, 'cause it's important and one day your life may depend on it: I am definitely a madman with a box."*
> —Eleventh Doctor[10]

> *"The madman is a waking dreamer."*
> —philosopher Immanuel Kant[11]

References

Eshun, S., & Gurung, R. A. R. (2009). *Culture and mental health: Sociocultural influences, theory, and practice*. New York, NY: Wiley-Blackwell.

Freud, S. (1900/1965). *The interpretation of dreams*. New York, NY: Avon.

Jamison, K. R. (1993). *Touched with fire: Manic-depressive illness and the artistic temperament*. New York, NY: Free Press.

Kant, I. (1764/2011). Essay on the maladies of the head. In P. Frierson & P. Guyer (Eds.), *Observations on the feeling of the beautiful and sublime and other writings*. Cambridge, UK: Cambridge University Press.

Ross, L., & Anderson, C. A. (1982). Shortcomings in the attribution process: On the origins and maintenance of erroneous social assessments. In D. Kahneman, P. Slovic, & A. Tversky (Eds.), *Judgment under uncertainty: Heuristics and biases* (pp. 268-283). New York, NY: Cambridge University Press.

Sue, D. W., & Sue, D. (2016). *Counseling the culturally diverse: Theory and practice* (6th ed.). New York, NY: Wiley.

Szasz, T. (1960). The myth of mental illness. *American Psychologist, 15*(2), 113–118.

Szasz, T. (1973). *Ideology and insanity: Essays on the psychiatric dehumanization of man*. Harmondsworth, UK: Penguin.

Szasz, T. (2007). *The medicalization of everyday life*. New York, NY: Syracuse University Press.

Notes

1. Modern episode 5–1, "The Eleventh Hour" (April 3, 2010).
2. Jamison (1993), p. 50.
3. Classic serial 6–7, *The War Games*, pt. 10 (June 21, 1969); modern episode 9–11, "Heaven Sent" (November 28, 2015).
4. Modern episode 6–4, "The Doctor's Wife" (May 14, 2011).
5. Szasz (1960, 1973, 2007).
6. Eshun & Gurung (2009); Sue & Sue (2016).
7. See, for example, anniversary special, "The Day of the Doctor" (November 23, 2013); modern episode 9–12, "Hell Bent" (December 5, 2015).
8. Ross & Anderson (1982).
9. "Talk very fast, hope something good happens, take the credit. That's generally how it happens."—Eleventh Doctor in Christmas special, "The Time of the Doctor" (December 25, 2013).
10. Modern episode 5–1, "The Eleventh Hour" (April 3, 2010).
11. Kant (1764/2011), quoted by—and often misattributed to—Freud (1900/1965), pp. 121–122.

Pickup By:
May 12, 2017

5
6
1
2

WI

37131184956639

On the Air:
Doctor Who Television History

Classic series debuted November 23, 1963. First classic serial: *An Unearthly Child* (originally the title of the first episode in the four-part serial, retroactively assigned as the title of the complete serial), introducing the First Doctor. Classic series ended December 6, 1989. Final classic serial: *Survival*, featuring the Seventh Doctor. Television movie (1996): *Doctor Who*, introducing the Eighth Doctor. Modern series debuted March 26, 2005. First modern episode: "Rose," introducing the Ninth Doctor.

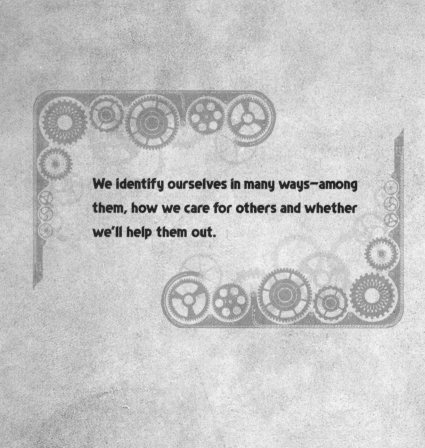

We identify ourselves in many ways—among them, how we care for others and whether we'll help them out.

PART ONE

The Hearts of Who We Are

While other areas of psychology might stress how and why we do what we do, personality psychology builds a foundation upon the first question: Who are we?

CHAPTER ONE

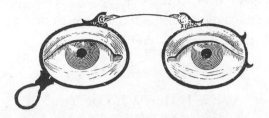

Who's Who: Interview with Four Doctors and a River on the Core of Personality

TRAVIS LANGLEY
AND AARON SAGERS

"Doctor who? What's he talking about?"
—First Doctor[1]

"Things do not change; we change."
—author Henry David Thoreau[2]

Stability versus change, one of the classic debates in the psychology of human development, concerns the permanence of "who" we are.[3] Do basic personality traits formed early in life persist through an entire lifetime, or are they all flexible? The person you are at age thirty may be very different from who you were at thirteen, and yet you still seem likely to have more in common with who you were back then than with some other individual then or now. The Doctor changes more extremely and more abruptly than most of us might, but as the

Eleventh Doctor points out to Clara Oswald right before he becomes the Twelfth, we all change.[4] His changes reflect ours. The debate is not over whether change occurs at all; instead it is more about whether a person has core traits that will remain deeply ingrained despite all other fluctuations over time.

What Is the Who of You?

Gordon Allport, known as the founder of personality psychology,[5] described individuals in terms of *personality traits*, specific predispositions to react in consistent ways.[6] He observed that some traits tend to go together (*trait clusters*, a.k.a. *personality factors*, covered in this book's Factor Files).[7] He concluded that traits can be what he called cardinal, central, or secondary, depending on how *pervasive* (infiltrating most aspects of life) and persistent they might be.[8]

Cardinal Traits

A *cardinal trait* is pervasive and powerful. Most people do not have this kind of ruling passion that guides everything. Even a particularly friendly person, for whom friendliness is a defining characteristic, probably does not worry daily about finding the friendliest way to brush teeth or eat ice cream. Allport offered sadism as an example of a cardinal trait. Nearly everything the Dominators[9] and Angel Bob[10] do seems aimed at hurting others, so in their cases, the cruelty seems cardinal. Fiction often depicts villains as having cardinal traits such as sadism or lust for power, but even they tend to pale in comparison to the single-minded Daleks, driven as they usually are by sheer, murderous hate.[11] When a single trait is all-consuming, the individual with that trait may have a personality disorder because it may interfere with functioning in key areas of life.[12]

Central Traits

Even if most people do not have one trait that affects almost all behavior, each person has a handful of characteristics that each affect a lot of behavior—that person's *central traits.*

In the 2014 documentary *The Ultimate Time Lord*, psychologist Mike Aitken told actor Peter Davison (the Fifth Doctor) that even though the Doctor has a dozen "well-established personalities," he also shows characteristics that carry over from one regeneration to another: steadiness under pressure, risk-taking, extraversion (covered in Factor File One: "The Two Factors—Extraversion and Neuroticism"), agreeableness (covered in Factor File Three: "The Five Factors—Adventures in the OCEAN"), and possession of an ego that "emerges when a leader is really required" even when he is a more reserved version of himself. According to that assessment, these consistent qualities would be the most central traits.

Secondary Traits

Less stable than central traits are the many characteristics that each affect only a little bit of each person's life—the *secondary traits.* Even if someone's love of chocolate is very stable, it would be unusual for that preference to affect much of what that person does. The Doctor's love of Jelly Babies candy— first shown by the Second Doctor[13] and most associated with the Fourth[14]—does not show up in every Doctor and does not shape his major decisions. It is a quirk, not characterization. These secondary traits are not at the crux of the stability versus change debate. That has more to do with cardinal and central traits, the ones that answer the first question of who we each truly are.

Who on Who

Journalist Aaron Sagers has interviewed many *Doctor Who* writers and performers.[15] Among his achievements, he broke the news that Tom Baker would appear in the *Doctor Who* fiftieth anniversary special, "The Day of the Doctor," thanks to a revelation from the actor who played the Fourth Doctor himself.[16] At various fan conventions, Sagers has moderated question-and-answer sessions for different *Doctor Who* stars. To help us get to the hearts of "who," he asked five of them about Time Lord identity issues, starting with how they get inside the head of someone so unlike any real human beings.

> **David Tennant (Tenth Doctor)**: I think the process is the same, whatever it is. Every character is a different set of circumstances. Some of them may be based on historical fact or some of them may just come from a script or some might come from your imagination or other people's imagination. With anything, you start with a script and see what else is out there, and hopefully it coalesces into something that makes a recognizable human being/alien time traveler.
>
> **Matt Smith (Eleventh Doctor)**: Weirdly, with the Doctor, you have got a real person to go on because of fifty years of people doing it and fifty years of stories and fifty years of events. There's a lot of material there.
>
> **Sagers**: What are the core personality traits of the Doctor? What are the key traits that are shared across regenerations?
>
> **Peter Davison (Fifth Doctor)**: I always thought I wanted to bring a certain naïve recklessness back to the Doctor, a certain vulnerability. I grew up

Roll Call

Peter Davison (Fifth Doctor)
First appearance: Classic serial 17–7, *Logopolis*, pt. 4 (March 21, 1981).

Sylvester McCoy (Seventh Doctor)
First appearance: Classic serial 24–1, *Time and the Rani*, pt. 1 (September 7, 1987).

David Tennant (Tenth Doctor)
First appearance: Modern episode 1–13, "The Parting of the Ways" (June 18, 2005).

Matt Smith (Eleventh Doctor)
First appearance: New Year's special, "The End of Time" pt. 2 (January 1, 2010).

Alex Kingston (River Song/Melody Pond)
First appearance: Modern episode 4–8, "Silence in the Library" (May 31, 2008).

Final appearances might be indeterminable. Time Lords never really go away.

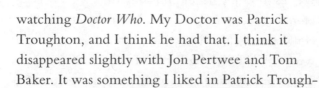

watching *Doctor Who*. My Doctor was Patrick Troughton, and I think he had that. I think it disappeared slightly with Jon Pertwee and Tom Baker. It was something I liked in Patrick Troughton's character, and I wanted to bring that back.

Sylvester McCoy (Seventh Doctor): Funny enough, Patrick Troughton was the first Doctor I saw, but then I lost touch with it because I became an actor. There were no VCRs or ways to record it and keep up with it, and it was never repeated. My distant memory when I arrived in the TARDIS was of Patrick Troughton. Then, I suppose Peter and I are exactly the same!

Matt Smith (Eleventh Doctor): I think we're all slightly mental, really. That is what's nice about it when you look across the board. He's always kind of mad. That was, I think for me anyway, one of the great virtues of playing him. With most other characters—if you're thinking of him as an alphabet—if you're playing a character and something happens to him, you have to go through A, B, C, D, and then you have to go through F and eventually you get to Z. You go through this whole story. Whereas with the Doctor, can leap from A without explaining any other letter. The great thing about playing him is he's always generally the most intelligent person in the room. He's always the cleverest. He knows the most, which allows him to be the silliest.

Alex Kingston (River Song/Melody Pond): I wouldn't call the Doctor a madman.

Tennant: What I always used to love about the Doctor when I played him were the moments where he'd stop and go, "This is brilliant." There was a sort of joy he felt in facing the little unexplored corners of existence—like the fact that he could stop and celebrate the extraordinariness of a werewolf before it bit his head off. Those moments where he would catch himself and be overcome by the marvelous stuff—there was something in that. I guess what appealed to the Doctor in his companions was a sort of passion similar to that.

Smith: And courage, as well. [The companions] were all quite courageous and defiant. And he

needs the antithesis, the balance. He needs someone
to tell him, "No, stay away from the werewolf."

Kingston: And also, he loves humankind. He doesn't
know exactly why he has this affinity with human
beings, but he does. He wants to save them, and
that's very powerful.

Smith: A central character that is essentially the kind
of superhero of the piece, that fixes the world with
a toaster and a ball of string. That's how he saves
the day: through being mad. That's sort of brilliant.

Kingston: He does it with his smarts, not his guns.

Smith: He is a pacifist, really.

The Doctor Defined?

Who does the better job of pegging a character's essence—
actors who played the part or professionals looking on as both
psychologists and fans? The more experts actor Peter Davison
spoke with during his attempt to pinpoint who Who really is,
the more complicated the answer became.[17] All of these answers
are about central personality traits, but they're all complicated
by the issue of stability versus change. The Doctor changes more
dramatically than we do, but we change, too. As several of this
book's chapters explain, drastic personality change can occur
due to changes to our brains[18] with no regeneration required.
Even without traumatic brain injuries, though, we grow and
learn throughout our lives. In this book, we'll explore these
issues of who we are from a variety of perspectives. We'll even
contradict each other at times because some of our most human
qualities are the most abstract and the most difficult to pin
down—none of which means we should not try. The abilities
to imagine abstraction and complexity and also to ask who we
really are may be the most human qualities of all.

As a couple of our Doctors shared, imagination and sheer humanness lie at the hearts of why *Doctor Who* endures.

> **Davison**: It's the endless possibilities, I suppose. I think it appeals to the creative mind, which is why so many people who grew up watching it grew up to work on the show. Showrunners Russell T. Davies, Steven Moffat—huge *Doctor Who* fans. David Tennant—huge *Doctor Who* nerd. It is almost self-perpetuating now. It fires the imagination.
>
> **McCoy**: They say there are only five stories under the sun, and that mankind's genius is to take these five stories and rewrite them. The story of someone coming from outside Earth, down to Earth, taking on human form, and trying to help in the best way possible, being heroic but at the same time being small and human—that is a very, very attractive story. It has been told over centuries and centuries, going way back.

> *"But identity . . . is the foundation of all rights and obligations, and of all accountableness. . . ."*
>
> —philosopher Thomas Reid[19]

References

Allport, G. W. (1937). *Personality: A psychological interpretation.* New York, NY: Holt.

Allport, G. W., & Odbert, H. S. (1936). Trait-names: A psycho-lexical study. *Psychological Monographs, 47*(1), i–171.

American Psychiatric Association. (2013). *Diagnostic and statistical manual of mental disorders (DSM-5).* Washington, DC: American Psychiatric Association.

Carducci, B. J. (2009). *The psychology of personality: Viewpoints, research, and applications* (2nd ed.). New York, NY: Wiley.

Grafman, J., Schwab, K., Warden, D., Pridgen, A., Brown, H. R., & Salazar, A. M. (1996). Frontal lobe injuries, violence and aggression: A report of the Vietnam head injury study. *Neurology, 46*(5), 1231–1238.

Reid, T. (1785). *Essays on the intellectual powers of man.* London, UK: John Bell and G. G. J. & J. Robinson.

Sagers, A. (2012, October 4). *'He doesn't like endings,' but ultimately Whovians don't mind.* CNN: http://geekout.blogs.cnn.com/2012/10/04/he-doesnt-like-endings-but-ultimately -whovians-dont-mind/.

Sagers, A. (2013, November 19). *Exclusive: Tom Baker to appear in 'Doctor Who' 50th anniversary special.* Huffington Post: http://www.huffingtonpost.com/aaron-sagers/ exclusive-tom-baker-to-ap_b_4295773.html.

Sagers, A. (2014, August 14). *Doctor Who in NYC: Peter Capaldi, Jenna Coleman, Steven Moffat talking Time Lord.* Blastr: http://www.blastr.com/2014-8-14/doctor-who-nyc -peter-capaldi-jenna-coleman-steven-moffat-talking-time-lord.

Sagers, A. (2015a, October 9). Exclusive: *Doctor Who writer Toby Whithouse on sonic sunglasses and the bootstrap paradox.* Blastr: http://www.blastr.com/2015-10-9/exclusive -doctor-who-writer-toby-whithouse-sonic-sunglasses-and-bootstrap-paradox.

Sagers, A. (2015b, November 12). *Doctor Who's Mark Gatis teases 'Sleep No More,' his most terrifying episode yet.* Blastr: http://www.blastr.com/2015-11-12/doctor-whos-mark -gatiss-teases-sleep-no-more-his-most-terrifying-episode-yet.

Thoreau, H. D. (1854). *Walden; or, life in the woods.* Boston, MA: Ticknor & Fields.

Watson, D. (2004). Stability versus change, dependability versus error: Issues in the assessment of personality over time. *Journal of Research in Personality, 38*(4), 319–350.

Whitbourne, S. K. (2001). Stability and change in adult personality: Contributions of process-oriented perspectives. *Psychology Inquiry, 12*(2), 101–103.

Young, L., Camprodon, J. A., Hauser, M., Pascual-Leone, A., & Saxe, R. (2010). Disruption of the right temporoparietal junction with transcranial magnetic stimulation reduces the role of beliefs in moral judgments. *Proceedings of the National Academy of Sciences, 107*(15), 6753–6758.

Notes

1. Classic serial 1-1, *An Unearthly Child,* pt. 1, "An Unearthly Child" (November 23, 1963).
2. Thoreau (1854), p. 244.
3. Watson (2004); Whitbourne (2001).
4. Christmas special, "The Time of the Doctor" (December 25, 2013).
5. e.g., Carducci (2009).
6. Allport (1937).
7. Allport & Odbert (1936).
8. Allport (1937).
9. Classic serial 6–1, *The Dominators* (August 10–September 7, 1968).
10. Modern episodes 5–4, "The Time of Angels" (April 24, 2010); 5–5, "Flesh and Stone" (May 1, 2010).
11. e.g., classic serial 12–4, *Genesis of the Daleks* (March 8–April 12, 1975).
12. American Psychiatric Association (2013).
13. Beginning in classic serial 6–1, *The Dominators* (August 10–September 7, 1968).
14. Beginning in classic serial 12–1, *Robot* (December 28, 1974–January 18, 1975).
15. e.g., Sagers (2012a, 2012b, 2014; 2015a, 2015b).
16. Sagers (2013).
17. *The Ultimate Time Lord* (2014 documentary).
18. e.g., Grafman et al. (1996); Young et al. (2010).
19. Reid (1785), p. 113.

Compassion offers advantages for its recipient, but what about the one who shows it? What does science reveal about benefits for the compassionate person?

CHAPTER TWO

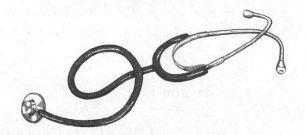

The Compassionate Doctor:
Caring for Self by Caring for Others

JANINA SCARLET
AND ALAN KISTLER

"I'm not sure any of that matters—friends, enemies—so long as there's mercy. Always mercy."
—Twelfth Doctor[1]

"Compassion may have ensured our survival because of its tremendous benefits for both physical and mental health and overall well-being."
—psychology researcher Emma Seppälä[2]

Compassion is witnessing the suffering of another being, feeling empathy toward that being, and experiencing the desire to alleviate that suffering.[3] Throughout his life and his many incarnations, the Doctor displays endless compassion toward his companions and those he is trying to save. The Doctor's many enemies—in particular Davros, creator of the Daleks[4]—argue that compassion makes him weak. Are they blinded by their own cynicism or might they sometimes be right? Is compassion a human flaw or a source of strength? What role does compassion play in people's physical and emotional health?

Compassion and Survival

"Communities, which included the greatest number of the most sympathetic members, would flourish best, and rear the greatest number of offspring."
—evolution theorist Charles Darwin[5]

From an evolutionary standpoint, compassion seems to be necessary for survival. Specifically, compassionate parenting will result in the best care for the offspring, ensuring the best chances of survival for the child. Compassionate caregiving provides physical and emotional stability for the child, ensuring that he or she will grow up and reach the age of reproductive maturity.[6] Compassion is also necessary for marital satisfaction, as well as overall survival of others. When she travels to 1938, River Song intends to kill both Hitler and the Doctor, but is then impressed by the Time Lord's compassion. Convinced to be compassionate herself, she saves the Doctor's life even though she only recently met him (from her perspective) and in doing so sacrifices her ability to regenerate.[7] This is a powerful act of *altruism* on River Song's part, helping another person despite losing something in the process.

When people see strangers suffering, they are less likely to display compassion than they would toward people they care about, like family members and friends.[8] This can be especially problematic if the observers, such as Davros's people, the Kaleds, do not view those who are suffering as human beings or as similar to them. The Kaleds reject and banish any who are biologically and physically "inferior," arguing that they "must keep the Kaled race pure."[9] In fact, the less people view others as similar to themselves, the less likely they are to help them.[10]

However, by recognizing similarities between the observer and the sufferer, such as shared food or music preferences, the observers are more likely to cultivate compassion for the sufferers. The Eleventh Doctor teaches wealthy mogul Kazran Sardick compassion for people of lower classes partly by using time travel to alter the man's childhood, adding experiences that teach Sardick to see them as fellow human beings rather than replaceable resources.[11] These added experiences by themselves do not change Sardick's mind and behavior, but they provide a strong push in that direction. The rest is up to him.

Compassion and Health

Compassion practice helps individuals manage their physical and mental health.[12] Practicing compassion can involve reaching out to others as well as engaging in meditation, such as *loving-kindness meditation* (LKM).[13] Such compassion practice can lower symptoms of depression,[14] anxiety,[15] posttraumatic stress disorder (PTSD),[16] and chronic pain.[17] In addition, compassion practice can improve the quality of social interactions,[18] increase positive emotions,[19] and reduce inflammation.[20]

People who experience as much loss and trauma as the Doctor has may sometimes develop mental health disorders, such as PTSD, anxiety, or depression. Unsure how to cope, some of these people engage in avoidance behaviors by not talking, dwelling on the traumatic event, or connecting with their emotions.[21] When Rose tries to get any answers about who the Ninth Doctor is or where he comes from, he becomes defensive, angrily shouting, "This is who I am! Right here, right now! All right? All that counts is here and now, and this is me!"[22]

When the Doctor experiences that rage and avoids talking about his experiences, he may be struggling with at least some symptoms of PTSD. His experiences are similar to what many combat veterans undergo after exposure to battle. This is especially true when it comes to anger and aggression when encountering a reminder of the war (a Dalek, for example).[23] In addition to PTSD, many veterans and other war survivors experience depression.[24] However, when veterans who struggled with these disorders received a twelve-week compassion training course, they demonstrated significant reductions in PTSD and depression symptoms. During the compassion training, the veterans were taught loving-kindness meditation, which assisted the veterans in cultivating compassionate wishes for themselves, for their loved ones, for strangers, and eventually, even for their enemies.[25]

After the Ninth Doctor is first introduced, he willingly watches Lady Cassandra die, evidently thinking this a just punishment for her crimes. However, after he spends time connecting with Rose, who shows compassion toward friends and enemies alike, he changes. When the Dalek Emperor later threatens all of Earth, this Doctor chooses instead to risk death at the hands of several Daleks (regeneration is unlikely from multiple hits by Dalek weapons) rather than defeat them by committing genocide. This effectively indicates that, through Rose's compassion toward him and others, he grows from the person who ended the Time War.[26]

Compassion Fatigue or Emphatic Distress

Witnessing or experiencing death and destruction, such as the events of 9/11 or what the Doctor witnesses during the Last Great Time War, could negatively affect anyone. After endur-

Hedonic versus Eudaimonic Happiness

Many people are able to find happiness even in the most difficult of circumstances, provided that they are following their core values.[27] The Doctor may be going through many difficult lives, enduring much pain and heartache, but he ultimately stays true to the core value of what it means to be the Doctor—helping people.

Although happiness resulting from *instant gratification* (immediate fulfillment of needs and desires), such as the Daleks gain from destructive actions, may bring some pleasure-based satisfaction (*hedonic happiness*) to a person like their creator Davros, the effects would only be temporary. On the other hand, meaning-based happiness (*eudaimonic happiness*), which the Doctor experiences when he achieves a moral victory and spends time with his friends, has long-term benefits. Pursuing eudaimonic happiness is physiologically and psychologically healthier than seeking hedonic happiness. When companions such as Jo Grant and Sarah Jane Smith end their travels with the Doctor and leave, he is sad to see them go but also proud that they have grown into heroes. Jo and Sarah Jane may feel somewhat abandoned when the Doctor does not continue to visit or check on them, but he explains to each of them (and others) that this is partly because he simply has faith that they will continue to do good work on their own, no longer needing his help, and he sometimes even admires their achievements from afar.[28] Whereas people actively pursuing hedonic happiness may have higher inflammation rates, people leading a meaning-based life (eudaimonic happiness) are more likely to have lower inflammation.[29] Meaning means more to us.

ing such tragedies, even the most compassionate people might occasionally find themselves incapable of empathizing with others (*compassion fatigue*). This usually occurs when someone's mental health or physical resources are depleted, leaving them unable to care for others.[30] By his seventh incarnation, the Doctor decides that too many good people have died and continue to die at the hands of evil forces, and so he becomes proactive, now hunting monsters and setting up traps to destroy or imprison them. These traps sometimes involve lying to his companions or hurting them emotionally.[31] Though scolded for becoming too harsh and manipulative during this time, he believes he is doing what's best. He even voices a fear that his next incarnation won't be willing to do everything necessary to stop evil, even if it means alienating himself from his core principles and companions who once trusted him.[32] By his eighth incarnation, he realizes that he has lost his principles during this time, as well as his compassion, and he eventually gives up master plans and schemes in order to embrace compassion and fun once more.

> "I knew a man . . . a man who became obsessed with the future, with predicting and planning for every variable, who lost himself in the big picture. But the more he planned, the more he gained, the more he realized that he was losing the one thing most precious to him . . . He only wanted to be more human."
> —Eighth Doctor, recalling the Seventh[33]

There are many reasons why someone might experience compassion fatigue—like a stressful job, personal trauma, a difficult work or home environment, or lack of self-compassion.[34] Studies that focus on teaching participants to cultivate compassion for themselves or others find that, after developing and practicing compassion skills, participants are less likely to experience compassion fatigue, as well as demonstrate less stress, less worry, and more resilience against work-related burnout.[35] Some compassion researchers suggest that the term *compassion fatigue* is not accurate and should instead be called *empathic distress* because compassion appears to build resilience while empathy without self-support can lead to burnout.[36]

Empathy, the ability to experience someone else's emotional state, may diminish when an individual is in distress and lacks resources to cope with his or her own struggles. On the other hand, actively practicing compassion for oneself and others might actually aid the observer in coping with his or her own suffering as well as the suffering of others.[37] Soon after the Last Great Time War, the Ninth Doctor is reluctant to speak about the loss of his people and even struggles to talk about this loss with Chem, who is aware that the Time Lords are gone. But after Rose witnesses the Earth's destruction in the far future and explains what that means to her, this Doctor sees that they now have some common ground. They have each lost a home and know their species is gone, so he is finally able to say for the first time out loud to anyone, "My planet's gone. It's dead . . . I'm the last of the Time Lords. They're all gone."[38] Thus begins his journey toward healing and acceptance.

Alleviating Emphatic Distress

Active compassion practice may reduce compassion fatigue for multiple reasons. First, active compassion practice lowers the distress that occurs when individuals see their loved ones suffer. Specifically, compassion practice activates the empathy centers of the brain. Although the Nestene Consciousness is his enemy, the Ninth Doctor apologizes with great remorse that he couldn't save the creature's home planet during the Time War.[39] When the Tenth Doctor realizes that he has inadvertently caused a

Cyberman to experience human memory and pain again, he apologizes for causing the Cyberman any suffering.[40]

Second, this practice reduces the negative effect of stress on the body, typically present when seeing another person suffer. Some negative effects of stress include an increase in the stress hormone *cortisol*. Prolonged exposure to this hormone can lead to poor health,[41] weight gain,[42] and heart disease.[43] Active compassion practice allows the observer to experience both empathy and soothing for the sufferer, reversing the negative effects of stress.[44] For instance, after finding different ways to cheat her death, the villainous Lady Cassandra inhabits the body of a person who has accepted that he will die soon and she finds herself finally understanding such a perspective and making peace with her own mortality. The Tenth Doctor then shows compassion to his dying enemy by bringing Cassandra into her own past so she can see her younger self one last time, an experience that brings her happiness before she dies.[45]

The Compassionate Way

Ultimately, compassion seems to be necessary for survival, allowing for better care of the young, as well as social support.[46] In addition, compassion practices that encourage social connection and meditation promote better physiological and psychological functioning.[47] Specifically, compassion practice can help improve people's mood, reduce inflammation, as well as reduce symptoms of depression and potentially help them recover from traumatic events,[48] such as some of those the Doctor experiences. Although Davros has repeatedly told the Doctor that compassion is a weakness, compassion is one of the Time Lord's greatest strengths. Throughout his adventures and incarnations, he has found that acting compassionately means more to him in the long run than failing to act with compassion, distinguishing him from his enemies and providing the peace of mind that genocidal maniacs will likely never find. In fact, helping people and living life according to one's own moral code is more likely to result in eudaimonic happiness, leading to more life-meaning and satisfaction, compared to a life based on immediate gratification and hatred.[49] It is not an easy path, but it is the right one.

References

Asmundson, G. J., Stapleton, J. A., & Taylor, S. (2004). Are avoidance and numbing distinct PTSD symptom clusters? *Journal of Traumatic Stress, 17*(6), 467–475.

Boscarino, J. A., Figley, C. R., & Adams, R. E. (2004). Compassion fatigue following the September 11 terrorist attacks: A study of secondary trauma among New York City social workers. *International Journal of Emergency Mental Health, 6*(2), 57–66.

Chandola, T., Britton, A., Brunner, E., Hemingway, H., Malik, M., Kumari, M., Badrick, E., Kivimaki, M., & Marmot, M. (2008). Work stress and coronary heart disease: what are the mechanisms? *European Heart Journal, 29*(5), 640–648.

Chapin, H. L., Darnall, B. D., Seppälä, E. M., Doty, J. R., Hah, J. M., & Mackey, S. C. (2014). Pilot study of a compassion meditation intervention in chronic pain. *Journal of Compassionate Health Care, 1*(1), 1–12.

Cole, S. W., Hawkley, L. C., Arevalo, J. M., Sung, C. Y., Rose, R. M., & Cacioppo, J. T. (2007). Social regulation of gene expression in human leukocytes. *Genome Biology, 8*(9), R189.

Darwin, C. (1871/1987). *The descent of man*. London, UK: Penguin.

Epel, E., Lapidus, R., McEwen, B., & Brownell, K. (2001). Stress may add bite to appetite in women: A laboratory study of stress-induced cortisol and eating behavior. *Psychoneuroendocrinology, 26*(1), 37–49.

Figley, C. R. (2002). Compassion fatigue: Psychotherapists' chronic lack of self care. *Journal of Clinical Psychology, 58*(11), 1433–1441.

Fiske, S. T. (2009). From dehumanization and objectification to rehumanization. *Annals of the New York Academy of Sciences, 1167*(1), 31–34.

Fogarty, L. A., Curbow, B. A., Wingard, J. R., McDonnell, K., & Somerfield, M. R. (1999). Can 40 seconds of compassion reduce patient anxiety? *Journal of Clinical Oncology, 17*(1), 371–379.

Fredrickson, B. L., Cohn, M. A., Coffey, K. A., Pek, J., & Finkel, S. M. (2008). Open hearts build lives: Positive emotions, induced through loving-kindness meditation, build consequential personal resources. *Journal of Personality & Social Psychology, 95*(5), 1045–1062.

Goetz, J. L., Keltner, D., & Simon-Thomas, E. (2010). Compassion: An evolutionary analysis and empirical review. *Psychological Bulletin, 136*(3), 351–374.

Hofmann, S. G., Grossman, P., & Hinton, D. E. (2011). Loving-kindness and compassion meditation: Potential for psychological interventions. *Clinical Psychology Review, 31*(7), 1126–1132.

Hutcherson, C. A., Seppälä, E. M., & Gross, J. J. (2008). Loving-kindness meditation increases social connectedness. *Emotion, 8*(5), 720–724.

Jakupcak, M., Conybeare, D., Phelps, L., Hunt, S., Holmes, H. A., Felker, B., Klevens, M., & McFall, M. E. (2007). Anger, hostility, and aggression among Iraq and Afghanistan war veterans reporting PTSD and subthreshold PTSD. *Journal of Traumatic Stress, 20*(6), 945–954.

Jazaieri, H., McGonigal, K., Jinpa, T., Doty, J. R., Gross, J. J., & Goldin, P. R. (2014). A randomized controlled trial of compassion cultivation training: Effects on mindfulness, affect, and emotion regulation. *Motivation & Emotion, 38*(1), 23–35.

Kearney, D. J., Malte, C. A., McManus, C., Martinez, M. E., Felleman, B., & Simpson, T. L. (2013). Loving-kindness meditation for posttraumatic stress disorder: A pilot study. *Journal of Traumatic Stress, 26*(4), 426–434.

Klimecki, O. M., Leiberg, S., Lamm, C., & Singer, T. (2012). Functional neural plasticity and associated changes in positive affect after compassion training. *Cerebral Cortex, 23*(7), 1552–1561.

Klimecki, O., & Singer, T. (2012). Empathic distress fatigue rather than compassion fatigue? Integrating findings from empathy research in psychology and social neuroscience. In B. Oakley. A. Knafo, G. Madhavan, & D. S. Wilson (Eds.), *Pathological altruism* (pp. 368–383). New York, NY: Oxford University Press.

Meyer, M. L., Masten, C. L., Ma, Y., Wang, C., Shi, Z., Eisenberger, N. I., & Han, S. (2013). Empathy for the social suffering of friends and strangers recruits distinct patterns of brain activation. *Social Cognitive & Affective Neuroscience, 4*(8), 446–454.

Ringenbach, R. T. (2009). *A comparison between counselors who practice meditation and those who do not on compassion fatigue, compassion satisfaction, burnout, and self-compassion* [doctoral dissertation]. OhioLINK: https://etd.ohiolink.edu/pg_10?0::NO:10:P10_ ACCESSION_NUM:akron1239650446.

Rockliff, H., Gilbert, P., McEwan, K., Lightman, S., & Glover, D. (2008). A pilot exploration of heart rate variability and salivary cortisol responses to compassion -focused imagery. *Journal of Clinical Neuropsychiatry, 5*(3), 132–139.

Ryan, R. M., Huta, V., & Deci, E. L. (2008). Living well: A self-determination theory perspective on eudaimonia. *Journal of Happiness Studies, 9*(1), 139–170.

Segerstrom, S. C., & Miller, G. E. (2004). Psychological stress and the human immune system: A meta-analytic study of 30 years of inquiry. *Psychological Bulletin, 130*(4), 601–630.

Seppälä, E. (2013). The compassionate mind: Science shows why it's healthy and how it spreads. *APS Observer, 26*(5). Psychological Science: http://www.psychological-science.org/index.php/publications/observer/2013/may-june-13/the-compassionate -mind.html.

Seppälä, E. M., Hutcherson, C. A., Nguyen, D. T., Doty, J. R., & Gross, J. J. (2014). Loving-kindness meditation: A tool to improve healthcare provider compassion, resilience, and patient care. *Journal of Compassionate Health Care, 1*(1), 1–5.

Shapiro, S. L., Astin, J. A., Bishop, S. R., & Cordova, M. (2005). Mindfulness-based stress reduction for health care professionals: Results from a randomized trial. *International Journal of Stress Management, 12*(2), 164–176.

Notes

1. Modern episode 9–2, "The Witch's Familiar" (September 26, 2015).
2. Seppälä (2013).
3. Goetz (2010).
4. e.g., classic serial 12–4, *Genesis of the Daleks* (March 8–April 12, 1975).
5. Darwin (1987), p. 130.

6. Goetz et al. (2010).
7. Modern episode 6–8, "Let's Kill Hitler" (August 27, 2011).
8. Fiske (2009); Meyer et al. (2013).
9. Classic serial 12–4, *Genesis of the Daleks* (March 8–April 12, 1975).
10. Fiske (2009); Meyer et al. (2013).
11. Christmas special, "A Christmas Carol" (December 25, 2010).
12. Seppälä (2013).
13. Cole et al. (2007); Kearney et al. (2013).
14. Ryan et al. (2008).
15. Fogarty et al. (1999).
16. Kearney et al. (2013).
17. Chapin et al. (2014).
18. Hutcherson et al. (2008).
19. Klimecki et al. (2012); Ryan et al. (2008).
20. Cole et al. (2007).
21. Asmundson et al. (2004)
22. Modern episode 1–2, "The End of the World" (April 2, 2005).
23. Jakupcak et al. (2007).
24. Kearney et al. (2013).
25. Kearney et al. (2013).
26. Modern episode 1–3, "The Parting of the Ways" (June 18, 2005).
27. Ryan et al. (2008).
28. *The Sarah Jane Adventures* episode, "Death of the Doctor Part 2" (October 26, 2010).
29. Cole et al. (2007); Ryan et al. (2008).
30. Figley (2002).
31. Classic serial 25–1, *Remembrance of the Daleks* (October 5–26, 1988).
32. Persuasion (2013 audio play).
33. *Time Works* (2006 audio play).
34. Boscarino et al. (2004); Ringenbach (2009).
35. Jazaieri et al. (2014); Seppälä et al. (2014); Shapiro et al. (2005).
36. Klimecki & Singer (2012).
37. Jazaieri et al. (2014); Klimecki & Singer (2012).
38. Modern episode 1–2, "The End of the World" (April 2, 2005).
39. Modern episode 1–1, "Rose" (March 26, 2005).
40. Modern episode 2–6, "The Age of Steel" (May 20, 2006).
41. Segerstrom & Miller (2004).
42. Epel et al. (2001).
43. Chandola et al. (2008).
44. Klimecki et al. (2012); Rockliff et al. (2008).
45. Modern episode 2–1, "New Earth" (April 15, 2006).
46. Goetz et al. (2010).
47. Seppälä (2013).
48. Cole et al. (2007); Kearney et al. (2013).
49. Ryan et al. (2008).

Moral foundations underlie a wide range of behavior, sometimes even the acts other people see as villainous.

CHAPTER THREE

The Moral Foundations of *Doctor Who*

DEIRDRE KELLY AND JIM DAVIES

*"Evil?! No! No, I will not accept that. They are
conditioned simply to survive. They can survive only by
becoming the dominant species."*
—Davros[1]

> *"Moral systems are interlocking sets of values,
> virtues, norms, practices, identities, institutions,
> technologies, and evolved psychological mechanisms
> that work together to suppress or regulate self-
> interest and make cooperative societies possible."*
> —psychologist Jonathan Haidt[2]

Social psychologist Jonathan Haidt proposed a theory of
moral psychology[3] that helps us make sense of the nature of
evil, if that even exists, both in fiction and in our world. His
theory holds that people are born with the capacity to develop
six foundations that each of us cares about to some degree:

harm, oppression, subversion, cheating, betrayal, and degradation. The foundations evolved as a result of various adaptive social challenges that humans encountered. For Haidt, a region's history, traditions, and other socioeconomic factors contribute to the moral development of the moral foundations in those groups.

Each person's level of care for these foundations is like an equalizer that determines his or her moral profile, and the various groups within *Doctor Who* exemplify moral profiles as varied as the cultures themselves. When one or more of these moral intuitions goes too high or too low, a creature can start to believe things to be right that most others will find morally repugnant—it's true for humans, and it's true for the villains of *Doctor Who*.

Doctor Who is full of fascinating villains who vary not only in species but in their fundamental moral outlook on the universe. Rather than being black-hatted, hand-wringing evildoers, bent on spreading chaos and destruction, many of them think they are actually doing the right thing. Their morals just conflict with the Doctor's—and ours.

Care and Harm

The foundation of care/harm supposedly developed as a response to our need to care for children and protect them from being harmed.[4] This foundation was originally triggered in response to suffering or distress in children, but can now be triggered in the presence of harm to things we perceive as less powerful being attacked by something more powerful. For example, seeing an innocent being hurt would generate a response from this foundation.

The human condition is rife with emotion. Many Cybermen

believe that they are helping humans by "upgrading" them to Cybermen,[5] reasoning that there could be no better life than one free of suffering. By this logic, the best and morally right thing to do is to remove people from these emotional bonds. Offering someone a life of logic, free from pain and more or less free from death, can be seen as the purest form of altruism, in the context of Cybermen's underlying moral foundations.[6] Such a care/harm foundation may be the basis for a willingness to sacrifice all other moral foundations, such as liberty, fairness, and sanctity.

In contrast, Sontaran morality is characterized by its complete *lack* of moral harm/care—at least to those who are not Sontaran: They do not mind causing harm to others, and they have a high disregard for those in their society who have to care for the sick or injured. The Sontarans inflict a lot of harm and are, from our current human perspective, acting immorally. Some human cultures have exhibited similar militaristic values. For example, the Greek Spartans believed that being a good citizen required being a good soldier.[7] Based on the Sontarans' moral underpinnings, their actions not only make sense, but are morally appropriate to some degree.

Liberty and Oppression

The liberty/oppression foundation is concerned with how much freedom people have and can exercise. Viewing bullying or people trying to be dominant over others can trigger this foundation. It is the moral center for those with Libertarian political leanings who want the state to have very little authority over their lives.[8]

The Cybermen completely lack the liberty foundation—they are examples of quintessential paternalists. They believe they

Missy, the Good Little Psychopath: A Moment with Michelle Gomez

JENNA BUSCH AND TRAVIS LANGLEY

Actress Michelle Gomez, who plays Missy (the Master regenerated as a woman), told us she doesn't think deceptive, destructive Missy is necessarily a villain. "She has no boundaries. It's just various shades of darkness to Missy. It can get into a sort of morass of blackness. There's a weird sort of perverse justice coming from her. Like any good little psychopath, she believes she's doing the right thing and, for her, the right thing is to annihilate the universe."[9]

Psychopathy is a condition characterized by a lifelong lack of empathy or remorse, missing emotional foundations of morality. Despite its exclusion from the *Diagnostic and Statistical Manual of Mental Disorders* as a separate diagnosis,[10] numerous professionals consider the concept clinically more useful than *antisocial personality disorder*.[11] Whereas antisocial personality disorder's diagnostic criteria depend mainly on antisocial actions, psychopathy is more about the internal qualities that might lead to such actions.

Gomez said that the Doctor and Missy are really the same, except that Missy doesn't mind killing for the greater good, and her greater good is to make the universe disappear. According to her, the Doctor and the Master/Missy are sort of "frenemies." The Third Doctor himself introduces the Master to Sarah Jane Smith as "my best enemy."[12]

know what is best for all other species and will upgrade all others for their own benefit. This has also been shown to be the main motivation of the Cybermen in the new *Doctor Who* series.

Authority and Subversion

The authority/subversion foundation holds that it is morally good to obey those who have authority over you. This foundation developed in the face of having to form societal relationships within a hierarchical group. Interactions with bosses and other superiors, or watching others interact with them, may trigger this foundation. We can see signs of authority among nonhuman animals, too, such as chickens, chimpanzees, and dogs, and many other animals that live in groups. Being subversive is often punished in groups of animals, human and otherwise.[13] Our leaders demand things of us, but we also expect benefits from them (such as protection) in return. We are creatures innately predisposed to hierarchical power arrangements.

When Davros creates the Daleks, mutations of his own species, he removes all traits that he perceives as potential weaknesses, such as compassion and love, and gives his Daleks an incredible loyalty to their cause, that of exterminating outsiders.[14] Human beings have been found to be very obedient, too—the shocking experiments of Stanley Milgram in the 1960s showed that a surprising number of people were willing to deliver severe electric shocks simply because they were told to do so by someone in a white lab coat.[15] This suggests that the authority foundation is present and can be activated in all of us, to some degree.

Davros fails to see the Daleks' desires as evil and insists, "When all other life-forms are suppressed, when the Daleks are the supreme rulers of the universe, then you will have peace. Wars will end. They are the power not of evil, but of good." As psychologist Erich Fromm noted, many people will tolerate great atrocities for the sake of security, stability, and order.[16] The Daleks never question the order or whether becoming the dominant species is the right thing to do, but instead arrange their lives to conform to it.

The Sontarans, too, adhere to the authority foundation. As in all militaristic cultures, the Sontaran Empire presents with a high respect for hierarchy and authority. We see this in human military culture as well. For example, people who join the military tend to be more obedient to authority and more inclined to follow rules.[17] The Sontaran High Command issue orders downward to the rest of the Empire. All Sontarans have a rank and act accordingly. When authority figures call for harm to be done, those who don't have enough of the care/harm foundation may not stop and question the ethics of what they're doing.

Fairness and Cheating

The fairness/cheating foundation (based on justness and equitable rewards without taking undue advantage of others[18]) developed out of a need for people to get what they deserve— good things as well as bad. It may have been triggered by instances of cheating and cooperation. Violation of this foundation leads to people feeling morally outraged at perceived injustice and unfair benefits. This feeling can be triggered by someone free-riding, where they are getting some benefit they are not entitled to, or when someone doesn't get the credit they deserve, or when someone is unfairly punished.

The person who is cheating on a test is deriving an unfair

benefit that those who choose to abide by the rules are not. This kind of free-riding undermines group cooperation and cohesiveness. Additionally, if the cheater is not punished, this can lead to further feelings of resentment and breakdown of group cohesion.[19]

The Judoon, a species who strictly enforce justice (for hire), are so focused on adherence to their goals and rules that at one point they are willing to blow up a whole hospital to punish a criminal.[20] Such a focus on punishing cheaters and disregarding the well-being of those who get in their way demonstrates the danger of having an overly sensitive fairness/cheating foundation.

Loyalty and Betrayal

Loyalty is about being true to others that you have a coalition with. Because human beings are a social species who rely on each other for survival and reproduction, we can see how loyalty would have been an asset for our ancestors. Loyalty can be inspired in single persons (more common among females) or in groups and teams (more common among males).[21] Groups of humans have always competed with groups of other humans, putting an adaptive pressure on preferential treatment to in-group members.[22]

Identifying with an in-group and seeing other groups as outsiders may be inherent to this foundation.[23] An example of this kind of loyalty to one's group is seen in the Sontarans' willingness to only fight for their own species. Those who would fight for others are seen as traitors. This moral foundation underpins a strong sense of loyalty to those they serve with and to the species as a whole. Contributing to this militaristic culture is their high respect for in-group loyalty. The loyalty/betrayal moral foundation developed to promote group support and can currently be seen among fans of sports teams when they rally behind their team. This kind of loyalty is also evinced in humans' choices to serve their country through military and other public service.[24]

While they are not an overly aggressive species, the Silurians have entered into combat with humans on a few occasions when threatened, including when they first appear in *Doctor Who*.[25] When they are revived through underground drilling,[26] they interpret that as an attack and retaliate. The violence comes to a head when Alaya, the sister of the military leader of the Silurians, Restac, is murdered by humans. In revenge, Restac wants to wipe out all humans. This demonstrates the close nature of the loyalty foundation the Silurians feel to their own species. As a group, they are fiercely loyal to one another to the point of being willing to wipe out another species to avenge a fallen sister.

Sanctity and Degradation

The sanctity/degradation foundation evolved out of feeling disgust in the presence of dangerous pathogens in people or objects, such as corpses, excrement, and visible disease.[27] But now cultures can differ in what triggers disgust, and often find out-groups disgusting for one reason or another. (For example, bloody injuries tend to evoke greater disgust in some cultures than in others.[28]) The opposite is purity and sanctity, which is what makes people feel moral outrage when something sacred to them (e.g., a Bible, a flag, a picture of the Dalai Lama) is treated poorly—such as being burned as a part of an art project or political statement.[29] (Many atrocities have been committed in the history of our world in the name of racial purity, including forced sterilization[30] and acts of genocide.[31])

Daleks use species purity to set themselves apart from impure Daleks and from other species: The way in which the Daleks view their species as superior to others can be seen as a form of speciesism.

Understanding the Morality of the Master

How then do we as viewers interpret the motivations of someone who does not demonstrate a developed moral sense, a person who seems to place no importance whatsoever on moral foundations? Is the Master, later known as Missy, devoid of any moral sense or is there another explanation for her amorality? In the purest sense, Missy is an ethical egoist. *Ethical egoism* is the view that the right thing to do is whatever promotes one's self-interest.[32] She can act good when it is in her best interest to do so, but when villainy better suits her ends (and she tends to believe it does), that is the path she takes.[33]

At one point the Master plans to reduce the human population by 10 percent so as to make them more pliant to his will.[34] The massive amount of harm he is causing does not deter the most extreme ethical egoist.

The Moral Foundations of Villainy Explained

The full spectrum of moral foundations can be found in the various villains of *Doctor Who*. Moral development involves a range of views, and morality itself becomes increasingly complex for many individuals. Some of the most heinous acts are committed on the grounds of moral superiority. By understanding moral psychology, we can see how the goals of villains, whether fictional or real, make sense in light of their disparate moral foundations—or, as in the case of the Master/ Mistress, lack of any moral foundation beyond self-interest.

References

American Psychiatric Association. (2013). *Diagnostic and statistical manual of mental disorders* (5th ed.) *(DSM-5)*. Washington, DC: American Psychiatric Association.

Baumeister, R. F., & Sommer, K. L. (1997). What do men want? Gender differences and two spheres of belongingness: Comment on Cross and Madson (1997). *Psychological Bulletin, 122*(1), 38–44.

Black, E. (2012). *War against the weak: Eugenics and America's campaign to create a master race* (expanded ed.). Westport, CT: Dialog.

Boos, M., Franiel, X., & Belz, M. (2015). Competition in human groups—impact on group cohesion, perceived stress and outcome satisfaction. *Behavioural Processes, 120*(1), 65–68.

Buccafusco, C., & Fagundes, D. (2016). The moral psychology of copyright infringement. *Minnesota Law Review, 100*(6), 2433–2507.

Busch, J. (2015, July 9). *Doctor Who: 13 things to know about season 9*. Collider: http://collider.com/doctor-who-13-things-to-know-about-season-9/.

Carruthers, S. L., Lawrence, S., & Stich, S. (Eds.) (2007). *The innate mind* (Vol. 3, pp. 367–391). Oxford, UK: Oxford University Press.

Connolly, P. (2006). *Greece and Rome at war*. Barnsley, MI: Greenhill.

Courtland, L. (2011) Cybermen evil? I don't think so. In C. Lewis & P. Smithka (Eds.), *Doctor Who and philosophy: bigger on the inside* (pp. 199–210). Chicago, IL: Carus.

Daniels, T. (2011, May 1). *Why the BBC tried to . . . Exterminate Nazi Daleks! As Doctor Who's most notorious enemies return to our screens, we reveal what inspired their creator.* Mail Online: http://www.dailymail.co.uk/tvshowbiz/article-1382252/Daleks-Doctor-Whos-notorious-enemies-return-screens.html#ixzz3v52cz2t1.

Delvaux, E., Meeussen, L., & Mesquita, B. (2015). Feel like you belong: On the bidirectional link between emotional fit and group identification in task groups. *Frontiers in Psychology, 6*, 1106.

Fromm, E. (1941). *Escape from freedom*. New York, NY: Holt, Rinehart & Winston.

Fromm, E. (1973). *The anatomy of human destructiveness*. New York, NY: Holt, Rinehart & Winston.

Gal, R. (1985). Commitment and obedience in the military: An Israeli case study. *Armed Forces & Society, 11*(4), 553–564.

Gibson, S., & Condor, S. (2009). State institutions and social identity: National representation in soldiers' and civilians' interview talk concerning military service. *British Journal of Social Psychology, 48*(2), 313–336.

Greene, J. (2009). The cognitive neuroscience of moral judgment. In M. Gazzaniga (Ed.) *The cognitive neurosciences* (4th ed., pp. 987–1002). Cambridge, MA: MIT Press.

Haidt, J. (2001). The emotional dog and its rational tail: A social intuitionist approach to moral judgment. *Psychological Review, 108*(4), 814–834.

Haidt, J., & Joseph, C. (2004) Intuitive ethics: How innately prepared intuitions generate culturally variable virtues. *Daedalus, 133*(4) 55–66.

Haidt, J., & Joseph, C. (2007). The moral mind: How five sets of innate moral intuitions guide the development of many culture-specific virtues, and perhaps even modules. In P. Carruthers, S. Lawrence, & S. Stich (Eds.) *The innate mind* (Vol. 3, pp. 367–392). Oxford, UK: Oxford University Press.

Haidt, J. (2012). *The righteous mind: Why good people are divided by politics and religion.* New York, NY: Pantheon.

Haidt, J., Koller, S., & Dias, M. (1993). Affect, culture and morality, or is it wrong to eat your dog? *Journal of Personality & Social Psychology, 65*(4), 613–628.

Hare, R. D. (1996). Psychopathy: A clinical construct whose time has come. *Criminal Justice & Behavior, 23*(1), 25–54.

Helwig, C. C., & Prencipe, A. (1999). Children's judgments of flags and flag-burning. *Child Development, 70*(1), 132–143.

Hirai, M., & Vernon, L. (2011). The role of disgust propensity in blood injection-injury phobia: Comparisons between Asian Americans and Caucasian members. *Cognition & Emotion, 25*(8), 1500–1509.

Pierro, A., Sheveland, A., Livi, S., & Kruglanski, A. W. (2015). Person-group fit on the need for cognitive closure as predictor of job performance, and the mediating role of group identification. *Group Dynamics: Theory, Research, & Practice, 19*(2), 77–90.

Puurtinen, M., Heap, S., & Mappes, T. (2015). The joint emergence of group competition and within-group cooperation. *Evolution & Human Behavior, 36*(3), 211–217.

Rachels, J. (1995). *Elements of moral philosophy.* London, UK: McGraw Hill.

Richter, E. D. (2008). Genocide: Can we predict, prevent, and protect? *Journal of Public Health Policy, 29*(3), 265–274.

Shelton, J., & Hill, J. P. (1969). Effects of cheating on achievement anxiety and knowledge of peer performance. *Developmental Psychology, 1*(5), 449–455.

Simpson, A., & Laham, S. M. (2015). Different relational models underlie prototypical left and right positions on social issues. *European Journal of Social Psychology, 45*(2), 204–217.

Notes

1. Classic episode 12–15, *Genesis of the Daleks*, pt. 5 (April 5, 1975).
2. Haidt (2012).
3. Haidt (2012).
4. Haidt (2012).
5. Modern episode 2–5, "Rise of the Cybermen" (May 13, 2006).
6. Courtland (2011).
7. Connolly (2006).
8. Haidt (2012).
9. Busch (2015).
10. American Psychiatric Association (2013).
11. Hare (1996).
12. Anniversary special, *The Five Doctors* (November 23, 1983).
13. Haidt (2012), p. 166.
14. Classic serial 12–4, *Genesis of the Daleks* (March 8–April 12, 1975).
15. Milgram (1974).
16. Fromm (1941, 1973).
17. Gal (1985).
18. Buccafusco & Fagundes (2016); Haidt (2012).
19. Shelton & Hill (1969).

20. Modern episode 3–1, "Smith and Jones" (March 31, 2007).
21. Baumeister & Sommer (1997).
22. Boos et al. (2015); Puurtinen et al. (2015).
23. Delvauz et al. (2015); Pierro et al. (2015).
24. Gibson & Condor (2009).
25. Classic serial 7–2, *Doctor Who and the Silurians*, pt. 1 (January 31, 1970).
26. Modern episodes 5–8, "The Hungry Earth" (May 22, 2010); 5–9, "Cold Blood" (May 29, 2010).
27. Haidt (2012), p, 173.
28. Hirai & Vernon (2011).
29. Helwig & Prencipe (1999); Simpson & Laham (2015).
30. Black (2012).
31. Richter (2008).
32. Rachels (1995).
33. All of which the Master demonstrates in classic serial 18–7, *Logopolis* (February 28–March 21, 1981), and Missy in modern episode 9–2, "The Witch's Familiar" (September 26, 2015).
34. Modern episode 3–12, "The Sound of Drums" (June 23, 2007).

Factor File One

The Two Factors—Extraversion and Neuroticism

TRAVIS LANGLEY

We have traits of many kinds. As opposed to *physical traits*, our specific bodily characteristics, *personality traits* are specific psychological characteristics or predispositions to behave in certain ways. Because the Doctor is regularly curious, for example, strong curiosity is one of his enduring personality traits, not simply a momentary state. *Trait theorists* are primarily interested in studying human personality by measuring habitual patterns of actions, thoughts, and feelings—in other words, by measuring personality traits. Gordon Allport, often called the father of personality psychology, identified thousands of terms to describe personality.[1] Personality psychologists trying to detect some order in that chaos observed that certain traits tend to group together in *trait clusters*[2]—constellations of characteristics that are commonly correlated with each other among many people. Sometimes, though, we are simply "seeing patterns in things that aren't there,"[3] as the Eighth Doctor put it—*illusory* *correlations*, variables we mistakenly perceive as related even though they really are not.[4] The Doctor, who looks for "the threads that join the universe together,"[5] would likely appreciate psychologists' search for these coinciding characteristics, up to a point: "Never ignore a coincidence—unless, of course, you're busy. In which case, always ignore coincidence."[6]

Coincidental Characteristics

One reason to ignore some coincidences is because *correlation* (the statistic identifying that variables are related) does not reveal *why* they are related. Even though outgoing people tend to be less fearful than others, that could mean that developing an outgoing nature reduces fear, but the reverse—that fearfulness makes a person less outgoing—is possible, too. In many cases, some other variable (say, brain cell activity levels) causes both with no causal relationship between the things we see as correlated. The Doctor often falls under suspicion for murder, espionage, and a long list of other crimes simply because the TARDIS tends to make him appear at times of crisis. Just as there is a *positive correlation* between outgoing and fearless traits, there is a positive correlation between the Doctor's arrival and states of crisis: As one becomes more likely, so does the other. From a different point of view, though, a *negative correlation* exists between outgoing and fear*ful* traits or between the Doctor's arrival and levels of tranquility while he is around: As one becomes more likely, the other becomes less likely.

Trait clusters are whole groups of characteristics that correlate together in both positive and negative directions, better known as *personality factors* because *factor analysis* identifies the groupings. Sometimes these clusters only show up in certain research samples; that is, the group of people surveyed in those cases show a lot of correlations that other people don't. Just because the Doctor's companions tend to be curious and assertive, that doesn't mean curiosity and assertiveness will consistently correlate among all other people. Personality researchers sought to identify which personality factors are fairly *universal* (meaning the traits will cluster together in any group of people measured) and *orthogonal* (statistically unrelated to each other). Two of the earliest to emerge as universal and orthogonal were the dimensions of extraversion/introversion and neuroticism/emotional stability.

Extraversion

The dimension of extraversion–introversion was first identified and popularized by Swiss psychiatrist Carl Gustav Jung,[7] although he viewed it a little differently from the modern perspective. He saw *extraversion* as a focus on the external world, attending to the environment outside oneself, and *introversion* as an inward focus, paying more attention to one's own internal mental life. Unlike some views that treat people as being either extraverts or introverts, Jung believed that we all have both traits within ourselves, even if we tend to emphasize one more often than the other. Despite the Doctor's amazing awareness of details, he can also become oblivious to his surroundings when lost in his own thoughts. He shows a particular inability to recognize social or subjective aspects of external appearance, like when he tries to compliment River Song's dress but she replies, "Doctor, you have no idea whether I look amazing or not."[8] Factor analyses have shown that many other traits tend to accompany the kind of qualities Jung observed.[9]

Examples of Extraversion Traits
Assertiveness
Boldness

Boredom If Alone
External Focus
Gregariousness
Low Arousal
Outgoing Nature
Risk-Taking
Social Interaction
Talkativeness

We express mixtures of extraverted and introverted traits, depending on the situation, even among those of us who are more prone to one extreme or the other. Some people, *ambiverts*, simply don't tend to go to either extreme.[10] The Doctor and his companions demonstrate many extraverted traits (especially those that lead to adventure), but not all. In his more introverted incarnations, the Doctor needs others to help him come out of his own head, and sometimes—such as when he's the War Doctor—he prefers to be alone.[11]

Neuroticism
Psychologist Hans Eysenck, one of the earliest researchers to study trait clusters, proposed a *two-factor theory* of personality, looking at extraversion and neuroticism as the key personality factors for explaining human behavior.[12] People with characteristic *neuroticism* handle stress poorly, find minor frustrations hopelessly difficult, feel threatened in everyday situations, and are at risk for many nonpsychotic mental illnesses.[13] Named after Freud's term *neurosis*, which refers to nonpsychotic mental illness, this is the personality factor most consistently associated with having unpleasant, negative feelings.[14] However neurotic the Doctor might seem at times, he normally functions well under pressure and does not let lesser frustrations get in the way of focusing on higher priorities.

Examples of Neuroticism Traits
   Anger Proneness
   Angst
   Characteristic Depression
   Emotional Expressiveness
   Envy
   Insecurity
   Instability
   Negative Emotion
   Obsessiveness
   Poor Emotion Regulation
   Vulnerability to Stress

Professionals who focus on the more positive-sounding aspects of these personality factors often call this one by the dimension's less neurotic end, *emotional stability*.[15] Emotionally stable people are healthier both physically and mentally, and yet it is possible to be too stable. Other Time Lords try to make themselves and their society stable to the point of stagnation, resisting change and suppressing emotional life. Given their history of suffering when an unstable tyrant like Rassilon takes charge, wreaking such chaos as to endanger all of reality,[16] their reluctance to indulge in a bit of chaos makes some sense.

Theory Regeneration

As different researchers keep proposing their own personality factor theories, some version of extraversion and neuroticism keeps showing up in theory after theory. Despite their persistence, these factors, named after Jungian and Freudian concepts, are not enough. Eventually, even Eysenck agreed that his theory left out a substantial number of personality traits.[17] When he saw the need to add a third factor, the time came for his theory to regenerate into a form both familiar and new, as we'll see in Factor File Two, "The Three Factors: Add Psychoticism or Openness?"

References

Allport, G. W., & Odbert, H. S. (1936). Trait-names: A psycho-lexical study. *Psychological Monographs, 47*(1), i–171.

Cattell, R. B. (1943). The description of personality: Basic traits resolved into clusters. *Journal of Abnormal and Social Psychology, 38*(4), 476–506.

Cohen, D., & Schmidt, J. P. (1979). Ambiversion: Characteristics of midrange responders on the introversion-extraversion continuum. *Journal of Personality Assessment, 43*(5), 513–516.

Eysenck, H. J. (1947). *Dimensions of personality*. London, UK: Trubner.

Eysenck, H. J. (1966). Personality and experimental psychology. *Bulletin of the British Psychological Society, 19*(1), 1–28

Hettema, J. M., Neale, M. C., Myers, J. M., Prescott, C. A., & Kendler, K. S. (2006). A population-based twin study of the relationship between neuroticism and internalizing. *American Journal of Psychiatry, 163*(5), 857–864.

Jung, C. G. (1921). *Psycholgische Typen [Psychological types]*. Zurich, Switzerland: Rascher Verlag.

Langley, T. (2015). Force files: An OCEAN far away I. Openness and closedness. In T. Langley (Ed.), *Star Wars psychology: Dark side of the mind* (pp. 51–55). New York, NY: Sterling.

Loo, R. (1979). A psychometric investigation of the Eysenck Personality Questionnaire. *Journal of Personality Assessment, 43*(1), 54–58.

Marcus, B., Lee, K., & Ashton, M. C. (2007). Personality dimensions explaining relationships between integrity tests and counterproductive behavior: Big five, or one in addition? *Personnel Psychology, 60*(1), 1–34.

Spinhoven, P., Penelo, E., de Rooij, M., Penninx, B. W., & Ormel, J. (2014). Reciprocal effects of stable and temporary components of neuroticism and affective disorders: Results of a longitudinal cohort study. *Psychological Medicine, 44*(2), 337–348.

Tmka, R., Balcar, K., Kuška, M., & Hnilca, K. (2012). Neuroticism and valence of negative emotional concepts. *Social Behavior and Personality, 40*(5), 843–844.

Wang, L., Shi, Z., & Li, H. (2009). Neuroticism, extraversion, emotion regulation, negative affect and positive affect: The mediating role of reappraisal and suppression. *Social Behavior and Personality, 37*(2), 193–194.

Notes

1. Allport & Odbert (1936).
2. Cattell (1943).
3. *Doctor Who* (1996 TV movie).
4. Previously described in Langley (2015).
5. Classic serial 18–2, *Meglos*, pt. 1 (September 27, 1980).
6. Modern episode 5–12, "The Pandorica Opens" (June 19, 2010).

7. Jung (1921).
8. Christmas special, "The Husbands of River Song" (December 25, 2015).
9. Loo (1979).
10. Cohen & Schmidt (1979).
11. Anniversary special, "The Day of the Doctor" (November 23, 2013); *The War Doctor*, Vol. 1, "Only the Monstrous," (2015 audio plays).
12. Eysenck (1947).
13. Hettema et al. (2006); Spinhoven et al. (2014).
14. Wang et al. (2009); Tmka et al. (2012).
15. e.g., Marcus et al. (2007).
16. Anniversary special, "The Five Doctors" (November 23, 1983); Christmas and New Year specials, "The End of Time," pt. 1 (December 25, 2009) and pt. 2 (January 1, 2010).
17. Eysenck (1966).

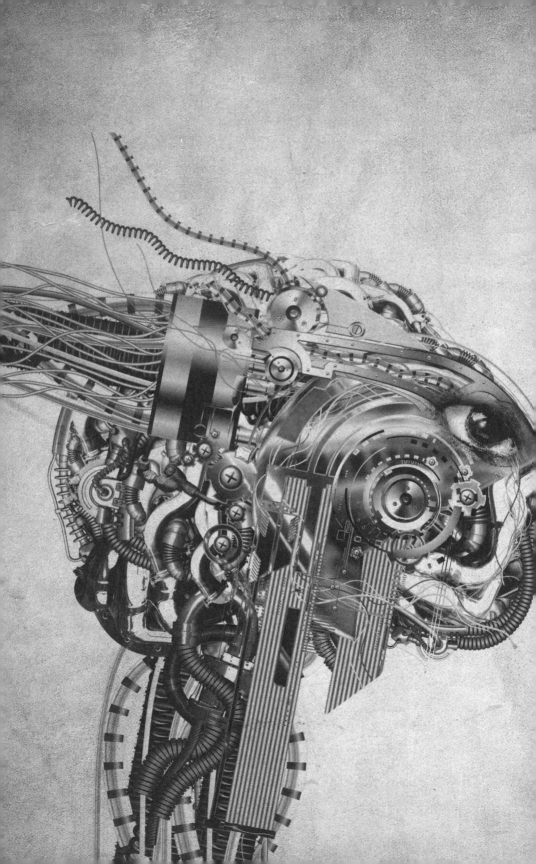

Part Two

Deep Breadth

To those who believe we hide the most powerful pieces of our minds, even from ourselves, the unconscious seems deep and vast and difficult to explore.

One of the most famous and most controversial figures in the history of psychology and psychiatry popularized the idea that each of us has a side we do not know, a vast region of our minds hidden away from our own conscious minds.

CHAPTER FOUR

The Unconscious: What, When, Where, Why, and of Course Who

WILLIAM SHARP

"How does anything get there? I have given up asking."
—Eleventh Doctor[1]

". . . analysis has accomplished its purpose
if it imparts to the novice a sincere conviction
of the existence of the unconscious. . . ."
—psychoanalyst Sigmund Freud[2]

The most significant contribution of Freud's psychoanalysis was his exploration of the unconscious. Freud sought answers to the questions of what dreams signify, what might motivate accidents, and why symptoms present in the way they do. Hard science was not concerned with the significance of a slip of the tongue or a bungled action.[3] Dreams were left to be interpreted by mystics. Freud, however, posited that these occurrences were not merely mental misfires: They had a point,

Madman and Wild Analyst

Psychoanalysis is wrongly thought to be something that blames your mother for all your woes. Freudian slips in everyday usage are "when you say one thing but mean your mother." This is more of a wild analysis. To some, this is the Doctor as madman and wild analyst. When his companion Donna Noble's mother insists that Donna is always important to her as a daughter, the Doctor drops his usual big-picture view of the world to deliver some sound but wild therapeutic advice: "Then maybe you should tell her once in a while."[4] He is blaming Donna's mother for Donna's lackadaisical attitude and fun-loving lifestyle, and he seems to be trying to say that if the mother wants Donna to be different, she herself may need to be different. Real psychoanalytic treatment proceeds much more slowly.[5]

there was a message, and that message came from the unconscious. Who or what is in the unconscious? Without examining the unconscious, we may be left to believe that forces outside of ourselves, such as luck, are to blame for our history and future.

"The laws of unconscious activity differ widely from those of the conscious," Freud said.[6] There is more in the unconscious than in the conscious. There is no linear sense of time, there is no "no," and paradoxes abound. Enter the Doctor and his blue box, where paradoxes also abound. An invitation into the world of Who can be disorienting, to say the least. The main character seems mad (or at least both brilliant and a complete fool), time and space are relative, and there is nothing he seems unable to do, and yet he talks about rules that he then proceeds to break and deals with paradoxes that create almost impossible situations. Who is this man exploring the universe?

It takes years to become an analyst and learn the language of the unconscious, but the Doctor, his companions, and his blue box illustrate some of the basic ideas. All analysts in training start the same way as do new Who fans: ordinary humans who cross over into another person's world. In exploring this, I found that the Doctor's box and my analyst couch are not that different.

Cracks in the Universe and the Unconscious

Young Amelia Pond has a crack in her bedroom wall. That crack, however, has more significance than it would if it appeared only in a single episode; it appears repetitively through several seasons. Like the Doctor's explorations of that crack, psychoanalysts try to explore the significance of the behaviors of a patient in treatment beyond the reason a behavior emerges in any one session. Like the crack in the skin of the universe, patients' struggles can be seen in much of what they do in their personal universes. The same issues can emerge in all work and play. The Doctor tries to explain the crack to Amelia, but like any interpretation it has to be given at the right time, in the right way, and with the right feeling. If it is not, the interpretation can be narcissistically wounding to the patient and useless for treatment and understanding. The artistry of when to make an intervention is part of what makes psychoanalytic treatment different from other forms of treatment. Most non-insight-oriented approaches to therapy are less concerned with the meanings and significances of problems and more focused on treating symptoms and removing behaviors. A behaviorist might try to control the behavior with rewards and punishments. A cognitive therapist might try to change the way a patient is thinking about something. Both behavioral and cognitive approaches, however, can leave the unconscious and the feeling world untouched. Exploration is the key.[7] What the patient says is unpacked in psychoanalytic technique to reveal the deeper layers of meaning. The Doctor/ psychoanalyst invites his companions to join him, and they do. Together they explore cracks and their many manifestations, eventually getting to the apparent cause.

Why don't more people choose this exploratory and insight-oriented type of psychoanalysis as a course of treatment then? Like many of the Doctor's companions, people often have an overpowering curiosity about what makes things tick in the blue box of their unconscious, but there is a cost to pay. Ignorance is bliss, and analysis is anti-ignorance. Socrates said that the unexamined life is not worth living, but it certainly doesn't lead to a happily ever after. Consider the lives of the Doctor's companions after they leave him. People don't choose psychoanalysis out of fear. The freedom from the unconscious enactments we engage in can be overwhelming and too much for many. A lot of people would prefer the quick fix of a pill to cover emotions over the slow fix of a maturational intervention on the couch to deal with them head on.

Freud looked at the common repetitive ways we act to avoid suffering and defend against that which we don't want to know. We get a hint about Amy's repetition: She is always the girl who waits and is let down by others. The Doctor encourages Amelia to look for things she is not noticing "from the corner of your eye."[8] He wants her to see what she has been ignoring, but we analysts can't rush the process just because we are in a hurry. If we do, we can get ourselves caught in a patient's repetitions. The Doctor ends up falling into the transference narrative of Amy. What does he do to let her down? He makes a promise and doesn't keep it. This happens twice at least, and he isn't aware of it either time. He tells Amy he will be back in five minutes but takes twelve years instead. He then does it again even after learning a little about the oh-so-patient Amy, leaving for another two years. A good supervisor might have helped the Doctor avoid that trap.

The Doctor as Psychoanalyst

British analyst Christopher Bollas writes, "In my view, the analyst plays both figures in the transference . . . the wise figure who sustains illusions and thereby encourages the patient to speak, and the fool who does not know what is being said to him. . . ."[9] This is a tough line to walk. How many times does the Doctor straddle those roles? He is famous for saying he has a plan even when he does not. While preventing the crack in the town called Christmas from falling into the wrong hands, he tells Clara, "I haven't got a plan, but people love it when I say that."[10] He knows his audience loves believing that when he says it. A good analyst does not necessarily know the plan at the start of treatment. Each patient is unique. In their own therapy and supervision (psychoanalysis requires each analyst be in therapy as well), analysts can keep their own neuroses in check. The structure of a treatment can contain both patient and analyst, as does the TARDIS for the Doctor and his companion. The blue box and the analyst's couch are the same in that respect.

The First Session

> "If you are a doctor, why does your box say POLICE?"
> —Amelia[11]

The first session of an analysis starts with the analyst asking some variation of "What brings you here?" In asking this, the analyst is inviting the patient to tell the story of his or her life: the past, present, future, dreams, and even day-to-day happenings. They all reveal something about the character of the person the analyst is with for that hour. Both patient and analyst, when meeting for the first time, need to get their bearings straight and establish a common language.

When we meet the young Amelia (Amy) Pond, she is praying to Santa at Easter because of a worrisome crack in her wall.[12] That scene is rich with paradoxes as are most first sessions with patients on the couch, but the analyst doesn't know all the meanings yet. The initial presenting concern is the crack (the obvious manifestation or *manifest content* of her concern as opposed to the deeper, unconscious meaning or *latent content* of the matter). The Doctor tells Amy that there can be some immediate relief, but he is going to invite her to a greater character-changing journey aboard his TARDIS/couch.

In a great example of the common ironies analysts ask patients to face at first, we learn that to close the crack, the Doctor first has to open it up. Analytic work is replete with evidence of these paradoxes. Many patients come to me and want to be less depressed or less anxious. I need to get them to open up and tell me about their depression and what is making them anxious. They resist. When patients resist, the problem persists. I have to work on their resistance until they are ready to share more. Only after we open the crack can we work on closing it, just as the Doctor does with Amy.

Closing it doesn't always solve the problem. It takes the whole course of a treatment (or multiple seasons of a show!) to find all the significances of the crack. And so the work continues.

Paradoxes: Making a Better Analyst of the Doctor
> ". . . *psychoanalysis provides a place for self-exploration*
> *for those who are in the midst of cultural shifts,*
> *conflicts, and contradictions.*"
> —psychoanalyst Neil Altman[13]

Is the Doctor an analyst or a madman? I think both. The resur-
gence in popularity with the modern episodes of the BBC series
might speak to a larger cultural trend of thinking of heroes as
a mixed bag. Villains likewise (think of the Master) have back-
stories that cause us to pity them. Things are not all black and
white. Psychoanalysis "provides a place for self-exploration for
those who are in the midst of cultural shifts, conflicts, and
contradictions."[14] I believe the Doctor's tendency to do "wild
analysis" results from his lack of personal analysis and supervision.[15] He travels without a more experienced Time Lord to
mentor him (and, in his days as a student, listens too little to
any mentor he has[16]). He has no discernible "professional" ego
of the sort that is required for this kind of work. He has issues
around keeping companions as he hates endings and avoids
them, even ripping the last pages out of books without reading
them.[17] This is why it is hard to know if he is an analyst or a
madman with a box. The Doctor uses his companions as egos
to stabilize him so that he doesn't have to develop one himself.
This causes blind spots, and the Doctor is lost in that way. But
again, there is hope.

The Eleventh Doctor says that there is one place a Time Lord
must never go: the site of his death.[18] But when he finally starts
to address his own "most feared place,"[19] he is able to trans-
form and become more than any previous incarnation of the
Doctor that we are aware of. By bravely going and facing what
is there, he becomes able to regenerate a thirteenth time even
though we have been told that Time Lords regenerate only
twelve times.[20] He is able to continue his work. In our Doctor
as analyst metaphor, now that he is not resisting a place and
feelings, he should be able to work with more of his patients'
feelings.

The Issue with Time Travel and the Unconscious

Psychoanalysis is the method we use to get a glimpse of the dynamics of the unconscious (*psychodynamics*). *Doctor Who* provides us with a great metaphor of just how uncomfortable yet tantalizing it is to delve into the unknown. It shows us that it is also dangerous work but can be life-changing and the best adventure to undertake. The companions jump in with both feet.

The unconscious is messy and uncomfortable. Psychoanalysis reveals material in the unconscious that people do not want to know about. Political theorist Joseph Schwartz uses the myth of Cassandra to make his point:

> Apollo gave Cassandra, a princess of Troy, the power of prophecy. When Cassandra spurned Apollo, he decreed she would never be believed. . . . Science gave psychoanalysis the power of prophecy. And, as it is told, psychoanalysis has spurned the discipline that gave it birth and has not been believed. . . .[21]

Studying *Doctor Who* is a great way to begin to think and play with the unconscious world as revealed in psychoanalysis. He is neither someone to write off as a madman nor is he always the consummate professional analyst. With the right support, he can do remarkable things that change the course of the universe while changing lives along the way. I am not ready to trade in my couch for a TARDIS yet, but maybe one day I will be.

References

Altman, N. (2015). *Psychoanalysis in an age of accelerated cultural change: Spiritual globalization*. New York, NY: Routledge.

Bollas, C. (1995). *Cracking up: The work of unconscious experience*. New York, NY: Psychology Press.

Freud, S. (1900/1965). *The interpretation of dreams.* New York, NY: Avon.

Freud, S. (1901/1966). The psychopathology of everyday life. *The standard edition of the complete psychological works of Sigmund Freud* (Vol. VI, pp. 8–12), Vol. VI (1901): *The psychopathology of everyday life.* London, UK: Hogarth.

Freud, S. (1912/1958). A note on the unconscious in psychoanalysis. *The standard edition of the complete psychological works of Sigmund Freud* (Vol. XII, pp. 255–266). London, UK: Hogarth Press.

Freud, S. (1937). Analysis terminable and interminable. *International Journal of Psychoanalysis, 18*(4), 373–405.

Safran, J. D. (2012). *Psychoanalysis and psychoanalytic therapies.* Washington, DC: American Psychological Association.

Schwartz, J. (1999). *Cassandra's daughter: A history of psychoanalysis.* New York, NY: Viking.

Notes

1. Modern episode 7–5, "The Angels Take Manhattan" (September 29, 2012).
2. Freud (1937), p. 401.
3. Freud (1901/1966).
4. Modern episode 4–11, "Turn Left" (June 21, 2008).
5. Safran (2012).
6. Freud (1912/1958).
7. Freud (1900).
8. Modern episode 5–1, "The Eleventh Hour" (April 3, 2010).
9. Bollas (1995), p. 20.
10. Christmas special, "The Time of the Doctor" (December 25, 2013).
11. Modern episode 5–1, "The Eleventh Hour" (April 3, 2010).
12. Modern episode 5–1, "The Eleventh Hour" (April 3, 2010).
13. Altman (2015).
14. Altman (2015), p. 5.
15. Editor's note: When the Time Lords send the Doctor on missions, they do not accompany him or maintain contact, as can be seen in classic serials 8–4, *Colony in Space* (April 10–May 15, 1971); 9–2, *The Curse of Peladon* (January 29–February 18, 1972); 10–1, *The Three Doctors* (December 30, 1972–January 20, 1973); 12–4, *Genesis of the Daleks* (March 8–April 12, 1975); 22 1, *Attack of the Cybermen* (January 5–12, 1985); and 22–4, *The Two Doctors* (February 16–March 2, 1985). The one Time Lord who assists him for a while, Romana, becomes less rigidly Gallifreyan in her ways after the completion of their original mission—classic serial 17–1, *Destiny of the Daleks* (September 1–22, 1979).
16. As Kanpo Rinpoche reported in the classic serial *Planet of the Spiders* (May 4–June 8, 1974).
17. Modern episode 7–5, "The Angels Take Manhattan" (September 29, 2012).
18. Modern episode 7–13, "The Name of the Doctor" (May 18, 2013).
19. Minisode, *The Night of the Doctor* (November 14, 2013); anniversary special, "The Day of the Doctor" November 23, 2013).
20. Christmas special, "The Time of the Doctor" (December 25, 2013).
21. Schwartz (2003), p. i.

According to the founder of the psychoan-alytic perspective, the part of personality that we consciously think of as ourselves unconsciously feels pulled between instinctive selfishness and learned morality. Is it possible to be too overwhelmed by both to know who we "really" are?

CHAPTER FIVE

Id, Superego, Egoless: Where Is the I in Who?

WILLIAM SHARP

"It won't be safe, it won't be quiet, and it won't be calm. But I'll tell you what it will be: The trip of a lifetime!"
—Ninth Doctor[1]

"The laws of unconscious activity differ widely from those of the conscious."
—psychoanalyst Sigmund Freud[2]

Psychoanalysis, the discipline Sigmund Freud created just over one hundred years ago, was a way of thinking and theorizing about the mind, studying it, and ultimately attempting to help people understand it. In addition to the obvious conscious part, Freud postulated an unconscious part to the mind that included an id, superego, and ego.[3] These Latin words translate roughly as the "it," "super-I," and "I." For Freud, *character* is the unique combination of these personality structures.

Applied to *Doctor Who*, the id can be seen in the Doctor's more impulsive, rash, and self-involved states. His superego, which fiercely identifies itself with the protection of others, balances out the id. In the ego, the psyche's mediator between those two extremes, however, the Doctor may be lacking.

What Is the Unconscious?

The unconscious is all we are unaware of, however it might influence everything in our lives. In the Freudian view, every choice or accident is tinted by each person's unique individual unconscious. Is our unconscious sending us a message to slow down if we trip while running? If we "accidentally" leave our cell phones at home one day, is the unconscious saying we need a break from people, especially those who might call us on the phone? If we forget to set the alarm at night, does the unconscious want us to sleep later?

The unconscious has two *drives* that serve as motivating forces, according to Freud. One is libidinal (a *life drive*), attempting to unify things and bring them together. It raises tension. The other is a *death drive* that strives to return us to a less tense and ultimately inert state.[4] The death drive disconnects us. The ways in which our drives take aim at objects in the external world and are fused become our character or personality. It is who we are. It is how you answer when someone asks, "Who are you?" and you answer by starting with "*I* am. . . ."

How does the unconscious work? What are its qualities and laws? And how does *Who* fit in with this? Three important elements of the unconscious are reminiscent of the Time Lord's own reality:

- It really is bigger (on the inside) than the conscious mind. Rose Tyler and so many others marvel and say the same thing about the Doctor's TARDIS when entering it for the first time.[5]

- The unconscious doesn't follow laws of time and space. Elton, the Doctor-obsessed fan whose group studies the Doctor through history, discovers that "the world is so much stranger than that. It's so much darker. And so much madder. And so much better."[6]

- There is no "no" in the unconscious. Paradoxes abound, and the way something manifests is only one level of its meaning. As the Fifth Doctor says, "There's always something to look at if you open your eyes!"[7]

Size: Greater on the Inside

Freud believed that the unconscious is infinite and thus far bigger than consciousness. The unconscious affects us far more than we are aware. He considered all the funny and embarrassing errors we make and what message from the unconscious they might contain. Its reach is greater than that of the conscious mind—like the TARDIS, larger on the inside.

Similarly, much like the Doctor's box, what happens in the vortex is affecting all of our daily lives, and most people never know this. Small choices here and there may seem inconsequential but have a ripple effect on our life events. This concept is important psychoanalytically as analysts work on helping patients see just how much of their experience of the world is created by their own choices. Certainly things happen "to us," but we have to take responsibility for the things we can control. For example, if you find you are dating a cheater and you leave that person, shame on them. If you keep dating people who turn out to be cheaters, shame on you: How are you always finding these people? If you don't ask questions about your choices, you live a life that can seem random and impulsive and without any clear connection between cause and effect. Something as simple as the direction in which the companion Donna Noble turns, either left or right, impacts the future and leads to hugely different outcomes.[8] Consider Donna before, during, and after the Doctor. Before and after adventuring with the Doctor, Donna lives a lighthearted but tumultuous life. She is impulsive. She blames family and friends when things don't go her way. She argues and seems immature for her age. During her time with the Doctor, however, she slowly begins to see what her choices have led to, and with that knowledge she decides to start doing things differently. In these ways, Donna before she meets the Doctor is like the unanalyzed patient, as is the post-Doctor Donna once she forgets it all. While she is with the Doctor, however, Donna feels and thinks in new ways, especially about herself and her importance in her world.

Nonlinear Nature
The unconscious does not operate linearly but rather outside (inside and around) time—much as the Doctor says of time itself, "from a nonlinear, non-subjective viewpoint, it's more like a big ball of wibbly wobbly, timey wimey stuff."[9] Many patients speak from my version of the TARDIS, the psychoanalytic couch where patients (like the Doctor and his companions) explore events from their past although their feelings are in the here and now. Traumas from childhood can range from being abused or neglected to being overlooked by a teacher or breaking a candy cane that Santa Claus gave you. The feelings are alive and well in the present. The affect is not locked in the past. It is like a bootstrap paradox or a self-fulfilling prophecy. Often it comes to represent some personal story arc that you are locked into, of being mistreated, neglected, alone, or sad. Like the Doctor in his TARDIS, the analyst with a couch is

propelled into a strange world often beyond time and space with its own laws and rules that have to be explored.

Layers of Meaning

Freud felt that that no "no" can exist: Everything has layers of meaning. The unconscious is always at work; that is, it is always "on." In *Doctor Who*, we are left to consider: Does the Doctor even sleep? What manifests itself to the conscious eye (*manifest content*) has deeper symbolic meanings (*latent content*). Nothing is a throwaway. This is what led Freud to conclude that dreams are the "royal road" to knowing the unconscious.[10]

Take, for instance, "the crack" in Amelia Pond's wall.[11] It is a crack but is not from the settling of a house. Rather, we find that it is crack in the skin of the universe. The Doctor admits that even if they knock down the wall, the crack will remain. This is true of images in the unconscious as well. Dreams look like something to us, but they are often far more significant than we assume and we do not take the time to explore them. If ignored, they come back in other places and in other significant ways until they are understood, exactly like Amy's crack.

British analyst Christopher Bollas writes that "unconscious thinking knows no contradictions and opposing ideas easily coexist. . . . The analyst is time-warped . . . recurrently confused, wandering in the strange county of even suspension."[12]

The Id, Ego, and Superego of Who

The id is primarily unconscious. It works on the *primary process*, which is irrational and interested in immediate gratification of impulses. It functions in accordance with what is called the *pleasure principle* (seeking immediate satisfaction of needs and desires). Think of an infant as the embodiment of the primary process and the pleasure principle: "Feed me, burp me, hold me NOW!" It could be argued that the newly regenerated

Eleventh Doctor is initially id. When Amelia Pond first meets the newly regenerated Doctor and asks who he is, he says, "I don't know yet, I am not done cooking."[13] Like an infant, he arrives and causes upheaval, not fully conscious of the needs of others until his basic needs are met. Amelia, as is true of many of the Doctor's companions, has to guide him and take care of him. She offers him every food he asks for, and he "hates" it all until he gets the fish fingers and custard. The id operates on the pleasure principle: It wants what it wants, and it wants it now.[14] At the end of that process, once his needs have been satisfied and a language between the two established, the Doctor pulls out the brilliant interpretation that if all the events that have unfolded in that first night meeting have not scared Amelia, that "must be a hell of a scary crack in your wall."[15] The Doctor is no longer id. He shows another part of himself that is more heroic, the part guided by morality.

The Doctor has a strong desire to help. He is a defender of worlds. In this light, he can be viewed as Freud's superego: the super-I. The superego is the impingement of the social world (rules, mores, our parents' attitudes, etc.) that oppose the id. It is the antithesis to the pleasure principle that guides the id. The superego is ruled by the principle of the ego ideal. The *ego ideal* is basically what has been incorporated into personality as the perfect way of behaving and living. The ideal is culturally bound and learned early in life and is full of rules and mores that most of us take for granted as the way we are supposed to behave. Very often, it is heard in the back of the mind as a critical voice saying "do this" or "don't do that." This ego ideal[16] and the superego may help explain what drives the Doctor to defend humans and why he saves the Earth over and over. It is what tortures him for his part in the supposed destruction of his own race of Time Lords. The superego is mostly in the unconscious part of the mind, but some of it is in the conscious mind.

Think of any time you hear the past words of your parents or teachers telling you how to behave in a current situation. That is the superego.

> *The good things don't always soften the bad things, but vice-versa, the bad things don't necessarily spoil the good things and make them unimportant.*
> —Eleventh Doctor[17]

> *"The group grants the leader superhuman powers. His words are given more weight and imbued with more wisdom than they possess."*
> —psychiatrist Irvin Yalom[18]

Freud's ego is a mediator that emerges to deal with the frustrating conflicts that ensue between the id and the superego. It is our "character" or "personality"—neither all good nor all bad. According to Freud's theory, we need all three: the id, ego, and superego. The various Doctors present as generally (as well as literally) all over the place. They have degrees of impulsive, attention deficit hyperactivity disorder (ADHD)-ridden behaviors that are signs of the id, alternating with self-sacrificing and morally driven behaviors indicative of the superego. There is little evidence of a functional ego working on the reality principle. There is little consistent awareness of self. In fact, the guy regenerates every now and then into someone who is considerably different! That would make Freud's head spin.

Is the Doctor egoless, then? We can find evidence for the id and superego of the Doctor but arguably not evidence for an autonomous ego, at least not within himself. For that, we need to look at his companions. It is when the Doctor and his companions are working as a group that things really click for them. The companions in this way function as the Doctor's ego. It is an externalized ego—which sounds strange, but what doesn't in the *Who* universe? Perhaps an externalized ego is the side effect of too much time in the vortex. Perhaps all the regenerations lead to difficulty forming an ego. Companions repeatedly tell the Doctor that he should not be alone because he does not do well by himself.[19] The Twelfth Doctor actually experiences some inability to recognize faces and is perplexed by his own.[20] The companions as externalized ego are what keep the Doctor from destroying himself while encouraging him to let the good times roll. Each companion balances him in some way. It is with the team—companions and Doctor—holding hands and supporting one another that there is strength and power to overcome the obstacles before them.

References

Bollas, C. (1995). *Cracking up: The work of unconscious experience.* New York, NY: Psychology Press.

Freud, S. (1900/1965). *The interpretation of dreams.* New York, NY: Avon.

Freud, S. (1901). *The psychopathology of everyday life. The standard edition of the complete psychological works of Sigmund Freud,* Vol. VI (1901): *The psychopathology of everyday life,* vii–296.

Freud, S. (1912). *A note on the unconscious in psycho-analysis. The standard edition of the complete psychological works of Sigmund Freud,* Vol. XII (1911–1913): *The case of Schreber,* Papers on Technique and Other Works, 255–266.

Freud, S. (1920). *Beyond the pleasure principle.* London, UK: Norton.

Freud, S. (1923). *The ego and the id.* London, UK: Hogarth.

Freud, S. (1933). *New introductory lectures on psychoanalysis. The standard edition of the complete psychological works of Sigmund Freud,* Vol. XXII (1932–1936): *New introductory lectures on psycho-analysis and other works,* 1–182.

Hijazi, A. M., Keith, J. A., & O'Brien, C. (2015). Predictors of posttraumatic growth in a multiwar sample of U. S. combat veterans. *Journal of Peace Psychology, 21*(3), 395–408.

McCormack, L., & McKellar, L. (2015). Adaptive growth following terrorism: Vigilance and anger as facilitators of posttraumatic growth in the aftermath of the Bali bombings. *Traumatology, 21*(2), 71–81.

Shakespeare-Finch, J., & Lurie-Beck, J. (2014). A meta-analytic clarification of the relationship between posttraumatic growth and symptoms of posttraumatic stress disorder. *Journal of Anxiety Disorders, 28*(2), 223–229.

Yalom, I. (1970). *Theory and practice of group psychotherapy.* New York, NY: Basic.

Notes

1. Modern episode 1–1, "Rose" (March 17, 2006).
2. Freud (1912).
3. Freud (1920).
4. Freud (1923).
5. Modern episode 1–1, "Rose" (March 17, 2006).
6. Modern episode 2–10, "Love and Monsters" (December 8, 2006).
7. Classic serial 19–3, *Kinda*, part 1 (February 1, 1982).
8. Modern episode 4–11, "Turn Left" (June 12, 2008).
9. Modern episode 3–10, "Blink" (June 9, 2007).
10. Freud (1900/1965), p. 608.
11. Modern episode 5–1, "The Eleventh Hour" (April 3, 2010).
12. Bollas (1995), pp. 12–13.
13. Modern episode 5–1, "The Eleventh Hour" (April 3, 2010).
14. Freud (1920).
15. Modern episode 5–1, "The Eleventh Hour" (April 3, 2010).
16. Freud (1923).
17. Modern episode 5–10, "Vincent and the Doctor" (June 5, 2010).
18. Yalom (1970), p. 198.
19. See, for example, modern episode 2–3, "School Reunion" (April 29, 2006); Christmas special, "The Runaway Bride" (December 25, 2006); modern episode 7–5, "Angels Take Manhattan" (September 29, 2012).
20. Modern episode 8–1, "Deep Breath." (August 23, 2014).

One well known, though difficult to test, theory holds that deep in the inherited portion of the unconscious dwell archetypes, universal themes that shape our stories, dreams, and expectations. Could these be part of the reason why some things scare anyone anywhere?

CHAPTER SIX

Weeping Angels, Archetypes, and the Male Gaze

MIRANDA POLLOCK AND WIND GOODFRIEND

"Don't blink. Blink and you're dead. They are fast. Faster than you can believe. Don't turn your back. Don't look away. And don't blink. Good luck."
—Tenth Doctor[1]

"Not for a moment dare we succumb to the illusion that an archetype can be finally explained and disposed of . . . The most we can do is dream the myth onwards and give it a modern dress."
—psychiatrist Carl Gustav Jung[2]

A hero is born from humble beginnings, finds guidance from a nurturing mentor, discovers special talents, falls in love, and overcomes almost insurmountable challenges to fight evil. If this story sounds familiar, it should; it's been told thousands of times in hundreds of cultures, ranging from King Arthur to Robin Hood to Katniss Everdeen. All that changes are the details—the names of the characters, the gender of the mentor, and the nature of evil. Psychologists have noted that throughout literature and legend around the world, there are basic story lines and personas that arise in pervasive and ubiquitous ways. These persistent characters fit *archetypes*, universal patterns that some psychologists argue come from a common and primordial origin of humanity that binds each of us together in a fundamental, but unconscious, manner.

Every story—including *Doctor Who*—provides examples of these archetypes in the fictional characters created for the plotlines and in the ways they interact with each other. Clearly, the Doctor is the hero or protagonist of this story, and there are seemingly endless enemies he must confront. One of the most intriguing groups of villains is the Weeping Angels. How do the Angels represent psychological concepts, including archetypes and the psychoanalytic perspective of the unconscious mind?

Angels and Archetypes

In the dark and rain, a lone woman with a camera climbs a wrought-iron fence and breaks into an abandoned, run-down house. She notices the letter "B" peeking from behind the fragments of wallpaper and eventually reveals the message, "Beware the Weeping Angels."[3] Why is this first exposure to the idea of Weeping Angels so terror inducing? Why are the Weeping Angels such an iconic enemy, from a psychological standpoint?

Angels are a common visual in contemporary culture, from decorating a holiday tree to collectibles and even in our television shows and movies. These heavenly beings often appear as caring, sympathetic, and beautiful.[4] The pervasive visual depictions of angels in art have shaped our ideas of the appearance and behavior of angels and, in turn, have shaped the portrayal of angels in popular media. Over time, angels have become a cultural symbol of the doer of good deeds, the helper, the advisor, and the personal guardian. However, the common heavenly depiction of angels is completely upended in *Doctor Who*, which moves away from the original biblical characterization and instead portrays the Weeping Angels in the series as, according to the Doctor, "the deadliest, most powerful, most malevolent life-form ever produced."[5]

The word *angel* derives from the Greek term *angelos*, meaning "messenger." In the Christian, Islamic, and Kabbalistic traditions, the *angelos* take on roles such as "messenger," "guardian," and "attendant" to God's throne.[6] In the 273 times the Christian Bible references angels, they are never mentioned as being winged, they are given male names (Gabriel, Michael, and Lucifer), and they are at least sometimes portrayed as weapon-wielding warriors. These images are a far cry from the blond and smiling guardian or the diaper-wearing cherubic archer of love. The original biblical angels are not our friends; they are God's soldiers.

The *Warrior* or *Hero* is one of the most well-known archetypes coming from the original conceptualization by Carl Jung,[7] the famous psychoanalyst and associate of Freud. Jung believed that humans all share a *collective unconscious*, a "storehouse of archaic remnants from humankind's evolutionary past."[8] This collective unconscious accounts for the common themes and characters—archetypes—that continually pop up in religious traditions and stories, in cultural legends, and in newly created fiction.

If angels fit the Warrior archetype in some of their biblical depictions,[9] how did they morph into the cute and nurturing mother or guardian figures more likely to be seen in children's toys and precious figurines? The early Christian church controlled the various facets of religious art. It was in 787 CE that the Second Council of Nicaea decided that it was lawful to depict angels in painting and sculpture. This decision allowed artists freedom to explore and alter the visual depictions of angels.[10] By the twelfth century, depictions of angels were popular in religious art and their appearance had gradually changed. Although the Bible mentions male angels, most angels now appeared androgynous, with long flowing hair and soft feminized features.

It was around the Victorian era (mid to late eighteenth century) that the images and roles of angels proliferated in popular culture, including everything from mourning angel statues in cemeteries to literary references. Angels no longer solely appeared in religious scenes; they now also represented the moral and idealistic roles of the women in the household. The "ideal" middle-class woman was compared to an angel in appearance and morality; she was referred to as the "angel in the house."[11] This modern view of an angel fits into a second Jungian archetype called the *Great Mother*. The mother character embodies nurturance, caregiving, empathy, and beauty.[12] Examples of the Great Mother archetype throughout history and various cultures include Mother Nature, the Greek goddess Gaea, the Virgin Mary, and even contemporary mother figures such as Mrs. Weasley from *Harry Potter*.

Angels have thus represented, over time, the two very distinct Jungian archetypes—the Warrior and the Great Mother. Perhaps the supernatural aspect of angels allows them to be more subjective and flexible, open to interpretation based on the modern zeitgeist of one's region and era. However, neither of these depictions applies to the terrifying Weeping Angels

Other Archetypes

Jung proposed several different archetypes he believed were pervasive in stories across cultures and time periods.[13] Some of the others he suggested include these:

- *Anima*: Our "feminine" side, even as it exists in all men, encompassing beauty, creativity, and demure sexuality. Examples of Anima through history are Helen of Troy, Juliet, and Cinderella.
- *Animus*: Masculinity, even as it exists in all women, encompassing aggression, a sense of adventure, and physical strength. Examples of Animus include Hercules, Don Juan, and Thor.
- *Trickster*: A more relatable and amusing version of an antagonist, the Trickster exemplifies intelligence and mischief. Tricksters are characters such as Loki, Brer Rabbit, clowns, and Shakespeare's Puck.
- *Child-God*: A combination of innocence, humility, and a fantastic destiny, the Child–God typically has supernatural powers but not physical strength (until possibly later in life or through magic). Examples include leprechauns, dwarves, and the Christ child.
- *Wise old man*: The embodiment of age and wisdom, the Wise Old Man is unassuming and humble, but provides essential guidance and can often predict the future. Classic representations of this archetype are seen in Teiresias (from Oedipus Rex), Merlin, and Gandalf.

that confront the Doctor time and time again. In order to truly understand the Weeping Angels, we need a third Jungian archetype: the *Shadow*. According to Jung in some of his writings, the Shadow is the worst, most terrible, darkest form of evil in all of existence. Summarized as "the devil within,"[14] "the embodiment of the unacceptable,"[15] and "the evil side of humankind,"[16] the Weeping Angels represent the most powerfully fearful beings imaginable. The Shadow is Satan; the Shadow is pure evil.

It can be argued that the Weeping Angels strike fear deep in our hearts and minds (Jung would say in our collective unconscious) for many reasons. First, we are afraid because we have gotten used to the idea of angels as guardians, as gentle feminine beings who want us to be safe. The jarring realization that the Weeping Angels are not the Great Mother, but instead are the Shadow, makes their betrayal of our implicit trust in angelic figures worse. Their entire appearance fools us; they seem to be beautiful and in mourning, which brings out human empathy—but this simply makes us lower our guard and approach them, making it easier for them to destroy us.

Finally, we are forced not to look away. This again tears at our unconscious instincts to run and hide from that which we fear. The psychological concept of staring at your enemy requires us to confront it, going against all human tendencies to seek safety and shelter. Carl Jung would be impressed with how the Weeping Angels seem specifically designed to conjure up our unconscious conceptions of evil and force us to confront the evil all around us—even, potentially, the evil in our own Shadow.

Angels and the Male Gaze

Although their appearance is somewhat ambiguous (indeed, they are alien), the Weeping Angels are female. River Song clarifies this when she is grabbed by one of them and then asks the Doctor, "Well, I need a hand back. So which is it going to be? Are you going to break my wrist or hers?"[17] The only way to survive a Weeping Angel is to stare at its female form, unblinkingly. We *must* look at it.[18]

Throughout the history of art, the female form, as depicted in paintings and sculpture, is constructed almost exclusively for the male viewer; the eye may linger on a hip, breast, or curve. As she is depicted in art, the female's eyes are typically turned away demurely. She is frozen in a vulnerable moment and unable to respond to the viewer. This act of viewing a piece of art becomes a voyeuristic activity for the viewer and is one type of *scopophilia*, a term for the sexual pleasure of looking at an object or person in an erotic fashion.[19] The idea that most visual arts are centered around a male view or perspective and that they objectify and sexualize female targets is the so-called "male gaze."[20]

The Weeping Angels are only seen in their frozen state. As we are initially introduced to them (before we realize what they are), the Angels appear as a statue—a piece of art—with their eyes covered by their hands. They do not move, they do not respond, and our gaze lingers upon them as much as it pleases us. We become voyeurs, enjoying the power of knowing they are harmless, stone, and submissive to our needs as the viewer. However, this assumption of the male gaze is another reason the Weeping Angels are terrifying: They turn the tables on their prey. We no longer receive pleasure from looking at them once we realize we *cannot* look away. They suddenly make us utterly powerless.

The Doctor explains these monsters: "They don't exist when they are being observed. The moment they are seen by any other living creature they freeze into rock . . . And you can't kill a stone. Of course, a stone can't kill you, either, but then you turn your head away. Then you blink. Then, oh yes, it can."[21] We are forced to keep our eyes upon her. We are no longer the consumers, the arrogant observers, the ones receiving pleasure by gazing upon a harmless object. We are no longer voyeurs; the Weeping Angel is the one in control. She tortures us with the realization that if we stop looking at her, we will no longer exist. We must do everything we can to try not to close our eyes.

The Weeping Angels become even more frightening when we learn that the Angels can harm us even when viewed through a television screen. River Song explains, "Whatever holds the image of an Angel, is an Angel."[22] Not only can they cause harm when we look away or blink, but any image of a Weeping Angel—whether it is a drawing, a photograph, or on a screen—can also allow that Angel access to us. The realization dawns on us that we cannot be safe, whether the Angel is in a room or even if we are watching a Weeping Angel on a screen. The lack of any ability to protect ourselves strikes fear in our deepest unconsciousness, as the root of anxiety is lack of control.[23] Cognitive psychologist George Kelly, a practicing psychotherapist, pointed this out when he theorized that we try to have *constructs* or logical frameworks to explain and predict the world, but that fear and anxiety result from failed constructs.[24] The Weeping Angels break all of our ideas about how stone things of beauty cannot hurt us; they prey on our overconfidence.

We must, however, not look *too* closely. The Doctor warns Amy Pond, "Look at the Angel, but don't look at the eyes. The eyes are not the windows of the soul. They are the doors. Beware what may enter there."[25] Amy is now caught in the agonizing trap of being forced to look at her attacker instead of fleeing from it; any voyeuristic or visually oriented pleasure is turned on its head. As the encounter progresses, we learn that in entering Amy's vision, the screen of her sight allows the Angel access to her and has allowed the Angel to enter her mind.[26] This is perhaps our deepest fear: complete loss of control and identity. Suddenly we realize that the Angels can harm us not only if we look away or blink, but also if we look into the eyes of an Angel, thus allowing it control of our minds and souls. If we look away, we will be transported to another time. If we look an Angel in the eyes, we will become an Angel. If we cannot look away and cannot look into its eyes, where is it safe for us to look? Where can we be safe? The only reasonable response is sheer panic.

To Be "Angelic"

A Weeping Angel is a frightening monster because it challenges our notions of safety and trust, removes any control, and represents a deep-seated archetype of evil. The kind and gentle angels that have graced our lives as guardians, caretakers, and mother figures are now something to be feared; the Great Mother archetype has transformed into the Warrior and the Shadow. Faced with this primordial fear from our collective unconscious, the Angels represent a foundational concept of fear in psychology. Even more terrifying, we cannot hide from the Shadow archetype, as we would from other monsters, for we must return her gaze. We cannot even look her in the eyes in a moment of brave confrontation or we will become her. The art that we so willingly consumed with voyeuristic pleasure from the "male gaze" perspective is now unsafe. There is no escape from the Weeping Angel; only the Doctor can help us.

The Weeping Angels and PTSD

Our past may seem to be locked in stone and harmless, just as the Weeping Angels[27] are quantum locked in the Who universe. Experiences with posttraumatic stress disorder (PTSD), however, show otherwise. We may close our eyes and "wish" things into the past, but when we do not keep our eyes on those things, they attack us and we end up living in the past. Intrusive memories plague us. We get mad and displace anger that might be appropriate elsewhere onto the people currently in our lives. We stop up and block certain feelings, and this leads to stunted social and emotional growth. *Doctor Who*'s Weeping Angels can be metaphors for PTSD: If we don't watch them, if we blink and stop paying attention, they can leave us trapped in the past instead of our taking the experience as a chance to grow. The flip side of PTSD is *posttraumatic growth*, in which coping with trauma causes some individuals to find purpose and improve as people.[28] The psychoanalyst's work from behind the couch is to help patients put all their thoughts and feelings into words so that they do not have to be relived and go on impacting the patients in unknown ways. Psychoanalysis teaches us to keep our eyes open, especially in the realm of the unconscious.

— William Sharp

References

Burger, J. M. (2015). *Personality* (9th ed.). Stamford, CT: Cengage.

Engler, B. (2009). *Personality theories* (8th ed.). Belmont, CA: Wadsworth.

Godwin, M. (1990). *Angels: An endangered species.* New York, NY: Simon & Schuster.

Jung, C. G. (1936/1969). The archetypes and the collective unconscious. In R. F. C. Hull (Ed.), *The collected words of C. G. Jung* (Vol. 9, pp. 87–110). Princeton, NJ: Princeton University Press.

Kelly, G. A. (1955). *The psychology of personal constructs.* New York, NY: Norton.

Lacan, J. (1981). *The four fundamental concepts of psychoanalysis.* New York, NY: Norton.

Langlinais, C. (2005). Framing the Victorian heroine: Representations of the ideal woman in art and fiction. *Interdisciplinary Humanities Journal, 22*(2), 73–87.

Longhurst, C. E. (2012, September/October). The science of angelology in the modern world: The revival of angels in contemporary culture. *The Catholic Response,* 32–36.

McAdams, D. P. (1994). *The person: An introduction to personality psychology* (2nd ed.). Fort Worth, TX: Harcourt Brace.

Mulvey, L. (1975). Visual pleasure and narrative cinema. *Screen, 16*(3), 6–18.

Rees, V. (2015). *From Gabriel to Lucifer: A cultural history of angels.* London, UK: I. B. Tauris.

Notes

1. Modern episode 3–10, "Blink" (June 9, 2007).
2. Jung (1936/1969), p. 160.
3. Modern episode 3–10, "Blink" (June 9, 2007).
4. Rees (2015).
5. Modern episode 3–10, "Blink" (June 9, 2007).
6. Longhurst (2012), p. 33.
7. Jung (1936/1969).
8. McAdams (1994), p. 103.
9. e.g., Matthew 13:49–50; Revelation 12:7.
10. Godwin (1990), p. 155
11. Langlinais (2005).
12. McAdams (1994).
13. Jung (1936/1969).
14. Engler (2009), p. 78.
15. McAdams (1994), p. 105.
16. Burger (2015), p. 102.
17. Modern episode 7–5, "The Angels Take Manhattan" (September 29, 2012).
18. Modern episode 3–10, "Blink" (June 9, 2007).
19. Lacan (1981).
20. Mulvey (1975).
21. Modern episode 3–10, "Blink" (June 9, 2007).
22. Modern episode 5–4, "The Time of Angels" (April 24, 2010).
23. Kelly (1955).
24. Kelly (1955).
25. Modern episode 5–4, "The Time of Angels" (April 24, 2010).
26. Modern episode 5–5, "Flesh and Stone" (May 1, 2010).
27. Modern episode 3–10, "Blink" (June 9, 2007).
28. Hijazi et al. (2015); McCormack & McKellar (2015); Shakespeare-Finch & Lurie-Beck (2014).

A popular yet controversial personality test offers a framework for discussing and comparing personalities along specific dimensions.

CHAPTER SEVEN

New Face, New Man:
A Personality Perspective

ERIN CURRIE

"We all change when you think about it. We're all different people all through our lives. And that's okay. . . . So long as you remember all the people that you used to be."
—Eleventh Doctor[1]

"Personality is less a finished product than a transitive process. While it has some stable features, it is at the same time continually undergoing change."
—psychologist Gordon Allport[2]

What if you could change your personality? What would you change? How would your life be different as a result? Each time the Doctor regenerates, he gets to try on a new personality and find out. *Personality* is essentially a pattern of thoughts, feelings, and actions considered typical of an individual.[3] It is more than a culmination of patterns learned through life experiences. Otherwise, the Doctor's personality would remain the same after each regeneration. This suggests that there is something essential to his personality that exists outside of his experiences.

Going a step further, what if each new personality is influenced by the needs of the Doctor? As the Doctor experiences the benefits and drawbacks of a personality style, he may, like many of us, think about what he wants to be different. One theory that emphasizes built-in tendencies that incline us to certain personality patterns while leaving space for growth is Carl Jung's theory of psychological types. He and his intellectual successors Katharine Briggs and her daughter, Isabel Briggs Myers, proposed that we have essential orientations toward the world around us that influence our thought, feeling, and behavior patterns[4] and therefore our personalities.[5] Their ideas provide a useful model for looking at the personality variations of the twelve Doctors featured as the lead characters in the *Doctor Who* TV series and how the experience of each personality could influence the next.

Controversy

Within the field of psychology, there is a history of controversy around Jung and the Myers-Briggs Type Indicator (MBTI), a personality assessment based on Jung's personality theory.[6] Jung's practice of psychoanalysis, his views on the collective unconscious, and the inclusion of spiritual elements in his writings alienated him from many in the scientific community.[7] This has overshadowed his contributions, such as the development of the concepts of introversion and extraversion, which are prevalent in modern personality research.[8]

Katharine Briggs was unwelcome in academia for creating an assessment based an extensive study of psychology literature without having a PhD.[9] Regardless, there is half a century of research on the MBTI by Briggs and her daughter, the company that purchased the rights from them, and independent academic researchers. Independent and allied research shows some evidence for the reliability and validity of the assessment, but studies also show areas in which the test needs improvement.[10] For instance, some recent research has called into question the validity of the hierarchical arrangement of Jung's factors,[11] and therefore that arrangement will not be used here to address the Doctor. In sum, there is a need for more objective, independent research and less rhetoric from both those who hate the MBTI and those who love it.

Consultants and psychologists worldwide use the MBTI as a tool in their practices because it provides a systematic way to think about differences in normal human behavior using nonstigmatizing language.[12] That is what could make it useful for examining the different psychological regenerations of the Doctor.

Personality According to Jung and His Companions

According to Jung's theory, people use two essential processes to manage their lives: decision making and processing information about the world. Two additional factors—energy focus and environment management style—fine-tune those processes according to Jung. The result is four factors, each with two orientations. Similar to handedness, people may use both orientations but one comes more naturally and is therefore used more often. People who are prevented from using their preferred orientations will supposedly have a harder time functioning.[13]

Information Processing

The two orientations for processing information are labeled Sensing and Intuition. People who prefer Sensing (indicated by the letter *S*), by definition, are those who focus on experiences from the five senses and the experiences of people they trust to figure out how the world works. A focus on the senses usually involves being close to the information, and so awareness of the immediate consequences for one's actions is common in this group. People who prefer Intuition (N) focus on relationships and patterns to understand the world or indeed the universe. This creates a big-picture view of the world and the larger impact of one's actions.[14] After he has spent centuries traveling through space and time, it could be assumed that the Doctor would automatically show an Intuitive style. That is a huge picture, after all. However, both information-processing styles are represented.

Decision Making

The orientation for decision making is based on the information a person focuses on most when deciding how to act. One type of person focuses foremost on subjective factors such as needs, values, and feelings of self and others; it's called Feeling (F). The other, Thinking (T), focuses on objective factors such as data, logic, and analysis. Each Doctor demonstrates both care for others and clever analysis, but the weights they hold for him differ.[15]

Energy

Jung suggested that there are two orientations for directing energy: Introversion (I) and Extraversion (E). Jung's ideas on these orientations overlap with but are not identical to modern ideas regarding the personality factors of Introversion and Extraversion. (For more on those see Factor File One, "The Two Factors—Extraversion and Neuroticism.") A person with a preference for Extraversion, as originally defined by Jung, gets the bulk of inspiration and energy from engaging with the environment and the beings in it. Those with a preference for Introversion, on the other hand, get the bulk of their inspiration and energy from their internal world of thoughts, feelings, and reflections.[16] Both introverted and extraverted Doctors need companions. The difference is that extraverted doctors get more energy from being around their companions.[17]

Environment Management

Briggs and Myers added a fourth factor, pointing out how they personally thought people prefer to approach the world. The orientation they labeled Perceiving (P) favors taking in information about the world and what it has to offer before drawing conclusions. Alternatively, some people prefer to use preexisting structures to navigate the world. These structures can take the form of plans, theories, and deeply held values. This preference is labeled Judging (J).[18]

The four factors interact, creating a personality system by which Briggs and Myers believed that each person manages himself or herself and the world. The resulting sixteen possible personality styles are denoted by the primary letter for each preferred orientation (e.g., Introversion, iNtuition, Feeling, and Perceiving combine as INFP).[19] Each personality style provides a different foundational framework from which each person can grow through life experience. The Doctor is no different.

It's My Party, and All of Me Is Invited

SUZANNE M. TARTAMELLA

Critics of the Myers-Briggs Type Indicator often cite its tendency to pigeonhole, to compartmentalize, to reduce complex people to one-dimensional categories. Yet, personality systems such as the Myers-Briggs offer a useful vocabulary for communicating insights about people and, in the case of *Doctor Who*, for exploring one of the most multifaceted fictional characters ever created for television. The long lineup of actors who have played the Doctor has perhaps made psychological analysis even more valuable given the stark contrast between the different versions. When used as a tool for understanding a person or character, the Myers-Briggs encourages us to consider not only reserved and outgoing behavior but also introverted and extraverted *functions*—Intuition and Sensing, Feeling and Thinking—and the degree of organization (judging vs. perceiving) a person needs to operate comfortably in his or her universe. This typing system, in other words, provides a language for exploring each person, character, or character version's unique personality quirks—examining motivations and behavioral patterns, assessing shifting attitudes toward others, and understanding the Doctor's interactions with his companions. More than that, it invites us to empathize with and even appreciate personality changes as they occur over time. Ultimately, the Myers-Briggs offers protection *against* pigeonholing—against dismissing the First or Twelfth Doctor as "grumpy" or adoring the Second or Eleventh only because he seems "wacky" and "fun-loving."

The Doctors

First Doctor: INTJ

Individuals with combined preferences for Introversion, Intuition, Thinking, and Judging come in many psychological shapes and sizes, as is true of every combination of characteristics. However, advocates of the Myers-Briggs test see a few common essential personality patterns within that diversity. One notable pattern is the tendency toward having strong internalized ideas about how the world should work that drive almost everything people do and how they do it.[20] People who follow a *judicial thinking style* (focused more on analysis than on abstract possibilities or rules) prefer activities that require evaluation, analysis, comparison, and judgment.[21] This fits several versions of the Doctor, beginning with the gruff and intellectual First Doctor. His use of objective facts to define his environment and his attempts to contain the behavior of his companions within that framework are clues to his preference for Thinking and Judging.[22] Take, for instance, his reaction when he encounters ancient Aztecs. His companion Barbara is dismayed by the impending human sacrifice, but the Doctor demands that she not interfere lest it alter human history.[23]

People with a combined preference for Introversion and Intuition may be seen as intelligent and insightful, with a far-reaching internal conceptual map they use for insight into the complex workings of the universe.[24] Combine a universe-sized big picture with a strong value placed on objective facts, and the logical result is impossibly high intellectual standards. In times of stress, the First Doctor treats those who fall short of his standards with impatience and even condescension.[25] If not guarded against, this may be a tendency among those with a combined judicial and thinking style.[26] However, toward the end of this incarnation, the Doctor shows increasing sensitivity

to the emotional needs of the people around him,[27] a change
that continues to progress into his next incarnation.

Second Doctor: ISFP

People with a combined preference for Introversion, Sensing,
Feeling, and Perceiving supposedly tend to be ready and willing to provide quiet support, often in the background, according to Myers.[28] The extent of help they provide with everyday
practical details frequently goes unrecognized until their presence is missed. A focus on details, especially as it relates to prior
experience, is a theoretical hallmark for a Sensing preference.[29]
Upon initial regeneration, the Second Doctor demonstrates the
Sensing preference as he recovers his understanding of himself
and the universe by touching mementos and reading the diary
of the experiences of his former self.[30] His use of a recorder
to play music to help him calm down and think supports an
Introverted and Sensing combination.[31]

The Second Doctor is especially sensitive to the needs of
his closest companions, experiencing great distress when he
is separated from them.[32] He is punished by the Time Lords
for meddling in the affairs of Earth on their behalf without regard for the larger structure of the time stream. This
supports a preference for Feeling and runs counter to a Judging
approach.[33] In the end, the Time Lords force him to regenerate
and exile him to Earth, leaving him stranded there by disabling
his TARDIS.[34] This could explain why the next personality
is more likely to get energy and fulfillment from interactions
with others.

Third Doctor: ENFP

One key pattern for those with preferences for Extraversion,
Intuition, Feeling, and Perceiving may be the large amount
of energy they get from and give to other people, friends

and strangers alike.[35] Myers believed that the high degree of attention sought from and directed toward many people is the hallmark of a combined preference for Extraversion and Feeling,[36] and the Third Doctor enjoys attention. He is flamboyantly yet carefully dressed, and his choice of a car is a vivid yellow Edwardian roadster. He enjoys impressing others with his intelligence and uses charm to convince others to help him save the day.[37]

Individuals with a combined preference for Extraversion, Intuition, and Perceiving appear to be known for their wit and humor. This Doctor's penchant for amusing non sequiturs is a great example.[38] It makes theoretical sense. A big picture of the world means greater awareness of the ways in which everything is related. A Perceiving preference means the Doctor is less likely to exclude information as irrelevant.[39] Add the tendency of an Extravert to think out loud, and voilà: non sequitur.

Being emotionally intertwined with people it isn't all fun and games. This incarnation of the Doctor experiences guilt for the people he cannot save, even when it's the villain.[40] It is possible that connection to these negative feelings drives him to a more objective and directive personality style.

Fourth Doctor: ENTJ

Look around a room full of executives and politicians and you might find quite a few people with a combined preference for Extraversion, Intuition, Thinking, and Judging.[41] This is not surprising considering their penchant for decisive leadership founded on a logical analysis of the bigger picture.[42] When this type of person is not in a position of power, there is a tendency to flout rules not seen as necessary, which could be common for those with a preference for Intuition, Thinking, and Judging.[43] The Fourth Doctor has little patience for ineffective people and arbitrary rules.[44]

Take-charge behavior, as well as a tendency to think out loud, indicates a preference for Extraversion.[45] The Doctor is strident, taking charge of difficult situations almost immediately whether he is invited or not.[46] Another example is his response to measured praise by a companion: "I do dislike faint praise. It was astoundingly clever, wasn't it?"[47]

Extraverted Judging brings a lot of intense, dominant energy to each situation.[48] It may be for that reason that the Doctor's next self has a personality style generally known for being a bit more detached.

Fifth Doctor: INTP
According to Jung's theory, clues to personality style come from the way a person functions both when at his or her best and when under stress.[49] Perhaps because the Fifth Doctor's tenure starts as his physical and psychological regeneration is being sabotaged by the Master,[50] much of the Fifth Doctor's personality in his first season[51] seems characteristic of what the INTP personality style may be like under major stress.[52] Myers believed that people with a combined preference for Introversion, Intuition, Thinking, and Feeling exhibit a personality style that features heightened and erratic emotionality during times of chronic or acute stress.[53] For someone with a preference for Introversion and Thinking, high levels of external stress would hinder development of his or her strongest place for psychological regeneration and decision making, that internal think tank.[54]

When at their best, people with a combined preference for Introversion, Intuition, Thinking, and Perceiving may thrive in complex situations, quickly perceiving and processing vast amounts of information. Unfortunately for the Doctor, the scope of his understanding is often too big for him to communicate effectively with others.[55] This is shown in the frequency with which his companions say things such as "Why do you always have an incomprehensible answer for everything?"[56] Maybe it's time to get back in touch with the tangible world.

Sixth Doctor: ESTP

People with a combined preference for Extraversion, Sensing, Thinking, and Perceiving may be seen by others as having an insatiable curiosity about the world and the people around them, sitting still only when required to do so by others—or so Myers believed.[57] It has been noted that social learning and cultural rules temper inborn personality traits, and so we rarely see a "pure" example of any psychological type.[58] The Sixth Doctor may be the exception. He is a caricature of the theoretical ESTP personality type. His demeanor is often highly jovial, and he assumes that others enjoy him as much as he enjoys being himself, indicating a combined preference for Extraversion and Perceiving.[59] Joviality becomes irritability when anyone slows down his pursuit of his schemes and curiosity, and this is a caricature of the Thinking and Perceiving combination.[60] A voracious joie de vivre is typical of those with combined Extroversion, Sensing, and Perceiving processes.[61] The Doctor's preference for clothing with many bright primary colors and patterns that he designs by stitching together pieces of old clothes is an expression of his personality.[62]

Toward the end, the over-the-top personality of this Doctor does start to be tempered. Maybe it starts to exhaust him. That could explain why his next personality is more somber.

Seventh Doctor: INFJ

Individuals who identify with a combined preference for Introversion, Intuition, Feeling, and Judging often report a desire for deep understanding of others and are supposedly fiercely loyal to those they care about.[63] The combined preference for

Introversion and Feeling directs interpersonal energy inward, taking time to consider situations quietly in the context of his or her values and other people's needs.[64] This preference makes the Seventh Doctor different from his predecessor in many ways. First, he is much more subdued. Second, he seems to have an intuitive sense of what motivates people, saving the day by using adversaries' desires against them.[65] This is thought to be a special skill among people with an Intuitive and Feeling orientation.[66] Even though he cares about others, the Doctor has a tendency to be gruff with people who don't live up to his standards, just like his predecessor with preferences for Introversion and Judging.[67]

Ninth Doctor: ISTP

According to type theory, people with a combined preference for Introversion, Sensing, Thinking, and Perceiving are likely to be highly creative problem solvers due to their open and imaginative approach to information that is oriented toward practical solutions. They supposedly seek new data about the physical world in response to the problems at hand.[68] You can see this in the Ninth Doctor's practical yet mischievous response to crisis.[69]

Jungian theory holds that extraverts draw energy from interacting with other people whereas introverts get energy from their internal world. When the Ninth Doctor first appears, he has been traveling without a companion.[70] Regardless, he has a grin on his face as he runs around saving the day by himself. This suggests that he doesn't lose energy in prolonged solitude, indicating a preference for Introversion.[71]

When he meets Rose, he finds someone whose drive and bravery he admires.[72] Her bravery is rooted in deep caring for others, and that puts the Doctor's Thinking and Perceiving into stark relief. In the end, the Doctor regenerates after saving Rose from the consequences of her bravery.[73] After that scene, it's no surprise that his next self takes on many of her characteristics.

Tenth Doctor: ENFJ

People with a combination of Extraversion, Intuition, Feeling, and Judging preferences are said to be attentive to the needs and feelings of others and can be fierce champions of human rights.[74] A combined preference for Intuition and Feeling is hypothesized to create a big picture of the world that is focused on the needs of others.[75] The decisions the Tenth Doctor makes center on a need to alleviate suffering.[76] His habit of rushing into a dangerous situation, taking charge, and rallying the people to save the day indicates a preference for Extraversion and Judging.[77] *Allons-y!* (Let us go!)

Despite an intense concern for the welfare of people, a key to this combined preference for big-picture Intuition and Judging becomes apparent in situations in which the person doesn't save the day. When the Doctor refuses to save the people of Pompeii from the explosion of Mount Vesuvius, he explains to his companion Donna Noble that he cannot interfere because the destruction of Pompeii is a fixed point in time, a necessary event in the time stream that is sacrosanct to Time Lords.[78] His feeling preference is still there, though, creating inner conflict that is visible in the self-hatred on his face as he leaves people to die.[79] Toward the end, the Tenth Doctor has lost many people he loves deeply for the sake of humanity. That may explain the shift to lightheartedness in his next incarnation.

Eleventh Doctor: ENTP

Individuals with a combined preference for Extraversion, Intuition, Thinking, and Perceiving seem to thrive on new challenges.[80] For this reason, they are allegedly drawn to entrepreneurship and consulting, specializing in finding new solutions to problems while leaving the drudgery of "dotting i's and crossing t's" to others. In theory, when you combine Intuition, Thinking, and Perceiving and focus it on the external world, you can get an open doorway to all the information that the world has to offer and put it together in new ways.[81] The Eleventh Doctor has a universe of information and resources at hand.[82] As a result, he is able to find nearly impossible solutions to mostly impossible situations.[83]

The extravert's need for stimulus from the world, with awareness of the countless possibilities available in a large world, can make it difficult to take day-to-day problems seriously.[84] This Doctor is goofy and lighthearted until there is a problem to solve. Dealing with a crisis in the environment brings out his ability to focus, something that seems common among individuals with a preference for Extraversion and Perceiving.[85] He also doesn't sit still for long. With all of space and time available to him to explore, a person with an ENTP preference would want to see and learn everything.[86] With all the goofiness, it can be easy to overlook the moments in which the Eleventh Doctor shows that he is haunted by past mistakes; his regrets are clearly at the front of his mind.[87]

Twelfth Doctor: INTJ

A second key pattern noted in people with preferences for Introversion, Intuition, Thinking, and Judging may be the awareness and analysis of the potential pitfalls of plans, people, and systems.[88] Myers hypothesized that a judicial approach to analyzing a very big picture requires a high level of discernment.[89] This Doctor brings us back to the INTJ personality style as he takes on a face from a man he saved in Pompeii[90] and the accent of a friend he couldn't save from Weeping Angels.[91] The INTJ personality style is well suited for scrutiny of self and others. It's all connected to the question on his mind: "Am I a good man?"[92] It seems that the Doctor finally is willing to face his past, and he chooses a personality style well suited to make that judgment.

Placing value on facts seems common in those with a combined preference for Introversion and Thinking.[93] The Twelfth Doctor tells it like it is, focusing on the objective facts of the situation without any sugarcoating.[94] He often is surprised when people react negatively to his approach. This may be something he needs to work on now that Clara isn't there to do the feeling for him.

Regeneration and Evolution

Although humans do not have the same ability to regenerate, we have the ability to learn from the consequences of our behavior and make changes. According to Jung, each of us goes through a midlife crisis in which we are faced with the limitations of the natural strengths of our personalities. We then have to choose whether to grow by incorporating the skills and strengths of other personality styles or to cling to what comes naturally and stagnate.[95] Hopefully like the Doctor, we will take the opportunity to evolve.

The Doctor has had thousands of years to learn from a range of different personality styles, including the consequences of the behaviors that stemmed from them. Every iteration has given the Doctor the opportunity to try a new approach. Each has new strengths and weaknesses and a new series of lessons to learn.

> *"My different personalities leave me in peace now."*
> —Anna Freud[96]

References

Allport, G. (1955). *Becoming: Basic considerations for a psychology of personality.* New Haven, CT: Yale University Press.

Bashtavenko, A. (2008). *Principles of typology.* Bloomington, IN: AuthorHouse.

Beckham, M. H. (2012). Building momentum: The unconventional strengths of perceiving college students. *Journal of Psychological Type, 72*(2), 27–40.

Bishop, P. (2014). *Carl Jung.* London, UK: Reaktion.

Brown, F. W., & Reilly, M. D. (2009). The Myers-Briggs Type Indicators and transformational leadership. *Journal of Management Development, 28*(10), 916–832.

Capraro, R. M., & Capraro, M. M. (2002). Myers-Briggs Type Indicator score reliability across studies: A meta-analytic reliability generalization study. *Educational & Psychological Measurement, 62*(4), 590–602.

Carey, J. C., Fleming, S. D., & Roberts, D. Y. (1989). The Myers-Briggs Type Indicator as a measure of aspects of cognitive style. *Measurement & Evaluation in Counseling & Development, 22*(2), 94–99.

Carlyn, M. (1977). An assessment of the Myers-Briggs Type Indicator. *Journal of Personality Assessment, 41*(5), 461–173.

Cohen, D., Cohen, M., & Cross, H. (1981). A construct validity study of the Myers-Briggs Type Indicator. *Educational & Psychological Measurement, 44*(3), 883–891.

Fishman, I., & Ng, R. (2013). Error-related brain activity in extraverts: Evidence for altered response monitoring in social context. *Biological Psychology, 93*(1), 225–230.

Gardner, W. I., & Martinko, M. J. (1996). Using the Myers-Briggs Type Indicator to study managers: A literature review and research agenda. *Journal of Management Theory, 22*(1), 45–83.

Harvey, R. J., Murry, W. D., & Stamoulis, D. T. (1995). Unresolved issues in the dimensionality of the Myers-Briggs Type Indicator. *Education & Psychological Measurement, 55*(4), 535–544.

Jin, B., & Austin, D. R. (2000). Personality types of therapeutic recreation students based on the MBTI. *Therapeutic Recreation Journal, 34*(1), 33–41.

Keirsey, D. (1998). *Please understand me II: Temperament, character, intelligence.* Del Mar, CA: Prometheus Nemesis.

Little, B. R. (2014). *Me, myself, and us: The science of personality and the art of wellbeing.* New York, NY: Public Affairs.

McCrae, R. R., & Costa, P. T. (1991). The NEO Personality Inventory: Using the five-factor model in counseling. *Journal of Counseling & Development, 69*(4), 367–372.

Michael, J. (2003). Using the Myers-Briggs Type Indicator as a tool for leadership development? Apply with caution. *Journal of Leadership & Organizational Studies, 10*(1), 68–81.

Myers, D. G. (2015). *Psychology* (11th ed.). New York, NY: Worth.

Myers, I. B. (1998). *Introduction to type* (6th ed.). Mountain View, CA: CPP.

Myers, I. B., & Myers, P. B. (1995). *Gifts differing: Understanding personality type.* Palo Alto, CA: Consulting Psychologists Press.

OPP (n.d.). *INTP: MBTI personality profile.* OPP: https://www.opp.com/tools/mbti/mbti-personality-types/intp.

Percival, T. Q., Smitheram, V., & Kelly, M. (1992). Myers-Briggs Type Indicator and conflict-handling intention: An interactive approach. *Journal of Psychological Type, 23*(1), 10–16.

Personality Growth (n.d.). *Here's why being in an INFJ's inner circle makes you truly blessed.* Personality Growth: http://personalitygrowth.com/heres-why-being-in-an-infjs-inner-circle-makes-you-truly-blessed/.

Pretz, J. E., & Totz, K. S (2007). Measuring individual differences in affective, heuristic, and holistic intuition. *Personality & Individual Differences, 43*(5), 1247–1257.

Reynierse, J. H., & Harker, J. B. (2008a). Preference multidimensionality and the fallacy of type dynamics: Part 1 (Studies 1–3). *Journal of Psychological Type, 68*(10), 90–112.

Reynierse, J. H., & Harker, J. B. (2008b). Preference multidimensionality and the fallacy of type dynamics: Part 2 (Studies 4–6). *Journal of Psychological Type, 68*(11), 113–138.

Saggino, A., Cooper, C., & Kline, P. (2001). A confirmatory factor analysis of the Myers-Briggs Type Indicator. *Personality & Individual Differences 30*(1), 3–9.

Sternberg, R. J. (1997). *Thinking styles.* New York, NY: Cambridge University Press.

Wacker, J., Chavanon, M., & Stemmler, G. (2006). Investigating the dopaminergic basis of extraversion in humans: A multilevel approach. *Journal of Personality & Social Psychology, 91*(1), 171–187.

Young-Bruehl, E. (2008). *Anna Freud: A biography* (2nd ed.). New Haven, CT: Yale University Press.

Notes

1. Christmas special, "The Time of the Doctor" (November 23, 2013).
2. Allport (1955).
3. Myers & Myers (1995).
4. Myers & Myers (1995).
5. Myers (2015).
6. Carey et al. (1989).
7. Bishop (2014).
8. McCrae & Costa (1991); Wacker et al. (2006).
9. Myers & Myers (1995).
10. Capraro & Capraro (2002); Carey et al. (1989); Carlyn (1977); Cohen et al. (1981); Saggino et al. (2001).
11. Reynierse & Harker (2008).
12. Myers (1998).
13. Myers (1998).
14. Myers & Myers (1995).
15. Classic serial 10–1, *The Three Doctors* (December 30, 1972–January 20, 1973); Myers & Myers (1995).
16. Myers & Myers (1995); Wacker et al. (2006).
17. Modern episode 7–5, "The Angels Take Manhattan" (September 29, 2012).
18. Myers & Myers (1995).
19. Saggino et al. (2001).
20. Reynierse & Harker (2008a; 2008b).
21. Sternberg (1997).
22. Myers (1998).
23. Classic serial 1–6, *The Aztecs,* part 1, "The Temple of Evil" (May 23, 1964).
24. Reynierse & Harker (2008a; 2008b).
25. Classic serial 10–1, *The Three Doctors,* part 1, (December 30, 1972–January 20, 1973).
26. Myers & Myers (1995); Reynierse & Harker (2008a; 2008b).
27. Classic serial 4–2, *The Tenth Planet,* part 4 (October 29, 1966).
28. Myers (1998).
29. Myers & Myers (1995).
30. Classic serial 4–3, *The Power of the Daleks,* part 1 (November 5, 1966).

31. Classic serial 4–3, *The Power of the Daleks,* part 5 (December 3, 1966); Wacker (2006).
32. Classic serial 6–2, *The Mind Robber,* part 2 (September 21, 1968).
33. Myers (1998).
34. Classic serial 6–7, *The War Games,* part 10 (June 21, 1969).
35. Jin & Austin (2000).
36. Myers (1995).
37. Classic serial 7–1, *Spearhead from Space* (January 3–24, 1970); Myers (1995).
38. Classic serial 7–1, *Spearhead from Space* (January 3–24, 1970); Reynierse & Harker (2008a; 2008b).
39. Beckham (2012).
40. Classic serial 10–1, *The Three Doctors,* part 4 (January 20, 1973).
41. Brown & Reilly (2009); Gardner & Marinko (1996); Michael (2003).
42. Myers & Myers (1995).
43. Percival et al. (1992).
44. Classic serial 17–3, *The Creature from the Pit* (October 27–November 17, 1979).
45. Fishman & Ng (2013).
46. Classic serial 12–2, *The Ark in Space,* part 2 (February 8, 1975).
47. Classic serial 16–2, *The Ribos Operation,* part 4 (September 23, 1978).
48. Reynierse & Harker (2008a; 2008b).
49. Myers & Myers (1995).
50. Classic serial 19–1, *Castrovalva* (January 4–12, 1982).
51. e.g., classic serial 19–4, *The Visitation* (February 15–23, 1982).
52. OPP (n.d.).
53. Myers & Myers (1995).
54. Myers (1998).
55. Beckham (2012); Pretz & Totz (2007).
56. Classic serial 19–4, *The Visitation,* part 1 (February 15, 1982).
57. Myers (1998).
58. Little (2014).
59. Classic episode 21–1, *The Twin Dilemma,* part 1. (March 22, 1984); Myers (1998).
60. Myers & Myers (1995).
61. Myers (1998).
62. Classic episode 21–1, *The Twin Dilemma,* part 1 (March 22, 1984); Myers (1998).
63. Personality Growth (n.d.).
64. Reynierse & Harker (2008a; 2008b); Wacker et al. (2006).
65. Classic serial 25–2, *The Happiness Patrol* (November 2–16, 1988).
66. Myers (1998).
67. Myers (1998).
68. Myers (1998).
69. Modern episode 1–3, "The Unquiet Dead" (April 9, 2005). Myers (1998).
70. Modern episode 1–1, "Rose" (March 26, 2005).
71. Myers & Myers (1995).
72. Modern episode 1–1, "Rose" (March 26, 2005).
73. Modern episode 1–13, "The Parting of the Ways" (June 18, 2005).
74. Keirsey (1998).
75. Myers & Myers (1995).
76. Modern episode 2–4, "The Girl in the Fireplace" (May 6, 2006).
77. Percival et al. (1992).
78. Modern episode 4–2, "The Fires of Pompeii" (April 12, 2008).

79. Modern episode 4–2, "The Fires of Pompeii" (April 12, 2008); Myers (1998).
80. Keirsey (1998).
81. Myers & Myers (1995).
82. Modern episode, 6–7 "A Good Man Goes to War" (June 4, 2011); Reynierse & Harker (2008a; 2008b).
83. Modern episode 5–13, "The Big Bang" (June 26, 2010).
84. Wacker et al. (2006).
85. Myers & Myers (1995).
86. Modern episode 7–4, "The Power of Three" (September 22, 2012); Reynierse & Harker (2008a; 2008b).
87. Christmas special, "The Time of the Doctor" (November 23, 2013).
88. Bashtavenko (2008).
89. Myers & Myers (1995).
90. Modern episode 4–2, "The Fires of Pompeii" (April 12, 2008).
91. Modern episode 7–5, "Angels Take Manhattan" (September 29, 2012).
92. Modern episode 8–2, "Into the Dalek" (August 30, 2014).
93. Reynierse & Harker (2008a; 2008b).
94. Modern episode 8–7, "Kill the Moon" (October 4, 2014).
95. Myers & Myers (1995).
96. Freud (1919) in a letter to her father, reprinted by Young-Bruehl (2008), p. 86.

The unconscious mind, archetypes, and a personality test based on related assumptions—do they have any place in the science of psychology? What value could a true scientist find in any of them?

CHAPTER EIGHT

Dream Lords: Would the Doctor Run with Freud, Jung, Myers and Briggs?

TRAVIS LANGLEY

"Funny thing, the unconscious. Takes all sorts of shapes."
—Tenth Doctor[1]

"Who looks outside, dreams; who looks inside, awakes."
—psychiatrist Carl Jung[2]

Before trait theorists began to define personality psychology in terms of specific characteristics and personality factors, early personality theory mainly came out of *depth psychology* (as the approaches that look *deep* into the unconscious to explain why we live as we do are collectively known). Sigmund Freud's *psychodynamic (psychoanalytic) approach* remains the best known of these areas, with Carl Gustav Jung's closely related *analytical psychology* achieving fame of its own. Their talk-based methods aimed reveal what's in the unconscious mind, include hypnosis, free association, and interpretation of dreams. Freud considered dream analysis a royal road to understanding the unconscious.[3] Other professionals would later develop psychological tests based on depth psychologists' ideas, from *projective tests* (like Rorschach's inkblot test[4]), whose developers assume people will project unconscious desires, needs, and values into ambiguous stimuli[5] to *personality tests* like the Myers–Briggs Type Indicator,[6] which sorts people into types based on how Jung viewed human nature.[7]

Controversy surrounds depth psychology. Its harshest critics call it all unscientific, unsupported, and unworthy of serious consideration.[8] So wouldn't a man of science like the Doctor, with his many centuries of experience and wisdom, reject it all outright? Maybe. Maybe not.

Freud

Many who refute Freud's theories still recognize his creativity and genius, although some go as far as personality psychologist Hans Eysenck did in asserting that Freud was "a genius, not of science but of propaganda, not of rigorous proof but of persuasion, not of the design of experiments but of literary art."[9] While the Doctor values personal qualities like genius and creativity, he also eschews dogmatic assertion of poor science. Why, then, does the Doctor say that when he and Freud met, they "got on very well"?[10]

Unconscious

The foundation of Sigmund Freud's theory and all depth psychology is the idea that the unconscious mind exerts powerful influence upon us.[11] Although the term *subconscious* litters popular culture, Freud usually spoke of it as the *unconscious*, the vast portion of the mind outside consciousness. (Chapter

Nineteen, "The Time Lord's Brain: Regeneration, Determinism, and Free Will," offers a few of the neurological explanations for mental activity often attributed to the unconscious mind.) Strax, the Sontaran nurse-warrior-butler, reports that his medical device lets him view Clara Oswald's subconscious mind, revealing "deflected narcissism, traces of passive aggressive, and lots of muscular young men doing sport,"[12] but keep in mind that Strax may be no better at describing mental phenomena than he is at identifying human organs or gender. Still, the Doctor shows himself to have a many-layered mind that fits key aspects of Freud's theory of the unconscious.

One area where Freud's views receive more favorable reception in psychology is that of the *defense mechanisms*, coping behaviors we use to protect ourselves from stress. These behaviors vary and may be healthy (e.g., altruism), unhealthy (e.g., withdrawing from others), immature (e.g., *regression*, reverting to behavior the person has outgrown), or pathological (e.g., *denial*, refusing to recognize an unnerving truth).[13] Daughter Anna Freud catalogued the defense mechanisms he had described, named most of them, and identified even more.[14] Sigmund Freud considered the most important defense mechanism to be repression,[15] and yet it remains the most controversial with the least solid evidence to support it, according to many professionals.[16]

> **Tenth Doctor (to War Doctor)**: "All those years,
>   burying you in my memory."
> **Eleventh Doctor**: "Pretending you didn't exist.
>   Keeping you a secret, even from myself."[17]

The Doctor seems to have repressed memories, most notably when he makes himself forget about his incarnation as the War Doctor so thoroughly that the so-called Eleventh Doctor on several occasions thinks he can still regenerate.[18] Only after they save Gallifrey instead of destroying it does the Eleventh Doctor come to terms with the War Doctor and know he has run out of regenerations.[19] Whether this is truly *repression* (in which the conscious mind simply cannot summon a thought that's locked away in the unconscious) or *thought suppression* (consciously blocking a thought that would be unpleasant or distracting[20]), either would fit into Freud's view that we play tricks on ourselves in order to reduce potential anxiety.

Extended lifespan will also alter the brain's potential memory capacity, making memories harder to retrieve. The longer a person lives, the more files there are in the memory cabinet. The Second Doctor can remember his family but only with effort: "I can when I want to, and that's the point, really. I have to really want to, to bring them back in front of my eyes. The rest of the time they sleep in my mind, and I forget."[21] Whereas physiological psychologists might attribute this to the brain's sheer memory capacity, Freud would more likely credit repression or suppression for the Doctor's removal of these memories from easy conscious access.

Methods

Among his earliest methods for delving into the unconscious, Freud used hypnosis. Eventually he came to distrust it, though, suspecting that suggestible, hypnotized patients were sometimes reporting dreams and fantasies as if they had really happened.[22] The Doctor uses hypnosis at times (e.g., to make his friend Dodo sleep and forget,[23] to help Sarah Jane recover information,[24] or to free various people from mind control[25]). He also shows that hypnosis can fail[26] and knows it has limits: "You can hypnotize someone to walk like a chicken or sing like Elvis; you can't hypnotize them to death. Survival instinct's too strong."[27]

Early depth psychologists often used dream analysis to seek clues as to what lurks in the unconscious. They disagreed on what specific dreams could mean and sometimes about how to study them, and yet they agreed that dreams hold great value and reveal much about the unconscious.[28] The Doctor sees significance in dreams as well: "Dreams are important, Nyssa. Never underestimate them."[29]

Science

"If Freud had been more of a scientist, he would have pressed no claims to be one. Dogmatism is anti-scientific; and there are reasons to distrust a 'truth' that forms a sect,"[30] psychologist Henry Murray wrote. Despite Freud's influence on him, Murray saw a need for empirical study. He also argued that psychology needed to develop a better understanding of human nature by studying the experiences of normal, everyday people instead of the clinical patients Freud and other therapists often emphasized. The Doctor values science and helps others appreciate it, even the savage Leela, who says she used to believe in magic, "but the Doctor has taught me about science. It is better to believe in science."[31]

The Doctor, though, looks at all of our science from a point of view millennia more advanced than our own. To some contemporary psychologists, evidence suggests that Freudian theory is wrong far more often than it is right; however, history shows that much of science has been wrong more often than it's been right. The hope is to accumulate ideas that work, weed others out, review, revise, review, revise again, and keep going even though new paradigms may turn it all on its head. To one scientist who cites Einstein, Newton, and other great minds, the Doctor says simply, "You've got a lot to unlearn."[32] He does not treat the scientist like a fool for being wrong, only for clinging to that which is wrong and failing to keep pursuing scientific truth. "A scientist's job is to ask questions," the Fourth Doctor says,[33] and Freudians ask questions aplenty.

Dogma

Existential psychologist Rollo May criticized the psychodynamic ideas spread by both Sigmund Freud and Carl Jung as being too rigid and unable to adapt to different situations.[34] Accusations that Freud and Jung began to force facts to fit their theories instead of adapting theories to fit the facts raise questions as to whether either one's views meet the scientific standard of *falsifiability*, meaning testability.[35] The Fourth Doctor observed, "You know the very powerful and the very stupid have one thing in common: They don't alter their views to fit the facts. They alter the facts to fit their views—which can be uncomfortable if you happen to be one of the facts that needs altering."[36] Even Jung criticized Freud for being too inflexible, calling him dogmatic for rigidly defending his views on how sexuality and the unconscious shape actions and personalities.[37] And yet, the Eighth Doctor later says to someone who does not believe he is a time traveler, "At least Sigmund Freud would have taken me seriously."[38]

Even if Freud's views eventually became dogmatic, psychoanalytic theory did not spring into being as doctrine. Perhaps, then, the Sigmund Freud with whom the Doctor "got on very well" is a younger Freud, exploring the unconscious and piecing together new ideas before he grew set in his ways.

Jung

Many criticisms of Freud apply to others in depth psychology as well, including Swiss psychiatrist Carl Gustav Jung, so we won't rehash those here. Jung, who by degrees bitterly broke away from Freud intellectually, made his own lasting contributions to psychiatry and psychology. Notable among them were the concepts of the collective unconscious, archetypes, and extraversion/introversion.

The Shadow

Chapter Six, "Weeping Angels, Archetypes, and the Male Gaze" describes *archetypes*, themes, and patterns that Jung believed we are unconsciously prepared for by heredity, not experience. Among them is one he called the *Shadow*, a representation of one's own hidden qualities, the dark and unrevealed side of each person's nature.[39] To grow as an individual (a process he called *individuation*), Jung believed the person should learn to understand the *Persona* (the outward mask, public face) and other archetypes to descend into the depths of the unconscious and confront the Shadow. Heroic fiction abounds with heroes facing their own dark sides or fighting enemies who are somehow mirror images of themselves. The Doctor confronts his own Shadow a bit literally when he faces the Valeyard, a mysterious Time Lord who has somehow been created as a manifestation of every dark thought or impulse the Doctor has ever had.[40] The Doctor later faces his Shadow again in the form of the Dream Lord, the part of the Doctor that taunts, ridicules, and hates himself the most.[41]

The Collective Unconscious

Beyond the conscious and unconscious mind that Freud popularized, Jung added an additional level to his model of mind: the *collective unconscious*, portions of the unconscious that all people inherit and share as members of the same species. Archetypes and instincts occupy the unconscious mind, as he saw it.[42] The Sixth Doctor has to face his Shadow in the Time Lord's sci-fi form of collective unconscious called the Matrix of Time, a computerized reservoir storing the knowledge and personalities of past Time Lords and even living Time Lords' previous incarnations. Just as Jung felt that the collective unconscious, as a deep pool of the past, could predict humanity's future path, so too can the Time Lords' Matrix predict future events.

Extraversion/Introversion

Carl Jung introduced the concepts of extraversion and introversion. Chapter Seven, "New Face, New Man: A Personality Perspective," describes these as Jung originally conceived them in terms of which situations a person draws energy from. Are you energized by being with others (extraverted) or do they make you feel drained (introverted)?[43] Factor File One, "The Two Factors—Extraversion and Neuroticism," and Chapter Nine, "Who Makes a Good Companion?" look at these terms as psychologists more commonly mean them today: personality factors, groups of traits that tend to go together.[44] The Doctor feels alone in many ways, perhaps because he is unlike everyone else, including his fellow Time Lords, and yet he repeatedly welcomes new companions. In most incarnations, he seeks the company of others while still showing that, as Jung expected of each person, he has both extraverted and introverted qualities within himself.

Myers and Briggs

The Myers-Briggs Type Indicator is both popular and controversial. Its creators' assertions that ESFPs are like this or INTJs are like that may be assertions with poor, if any, support from methodical empirical research. Dichotomizing people as Es or Is (extraverts or introverts) oversimplifies analysis and makes it harder to recognize the complexities of human behavior.

Jung said that no one is purely extraverted or introverted. Each person shows a mix of both extraverted and introverted traits, possibly mingled to the point that *ambivert* (both extravert and introvert) can a more accurate description.[45] But people who identify themselves by strings of Myers-Briggs letters leave ambiversion out. Seeing all of its problems, would the Doctor, like so many of our world's professionals, reject Myers-Briggs outright? Perhaps, but he might very well scoff at all earthly personality tests and the confidence people place in them. An ancient extraterrestrial might consider one personality test's

Modern Astrology

WIND GOODFRIEND

In spite of its corporate popularity, many psychologists find the Myers-Briggs to be the equivalent of modern astrology. The official survey's website[46] provides descriptions of each personality type for example, ENTJs pursue improvement and achievement while ESTPs are realistic but adaptable. The difficulty is that this type of vague description can apply to anyone. If your horoscope says, "Your day will be full of opportunity, but watch out for challenges," doesn't this apply to everyone?

Critics have raised many concerns, including these:[47]

- The test forces people into binary categories, ignoring subtle differences that should be measured on a continuum instead.
- People's answers to the questions may change from day to day; we all feel sometimes

Continues on following page

competitive, sometimes cooperative, sometimes optimistic, sometimes pessimistic.

- Almost no research studies have successfully linked one's theoretical "type" to any real outcomes or behaviors.

Why, then, is the test so popular? One reason may simply be that it's easy. Unfortunately, another answer may be the *Barnum effect*: When people are given vague descriptions of themselves that could apply to anyone, the descriptions are rated as highly accurate by the individuals themselves.[48] The effect's name comes from a remark about the customers for P. T. Barnum's famous sideshows of "aliens" or "mermaids," when a competitor supposedly said, "There's a sucker born every minute." Many psychologists would agree, and may even say that companies that rely solely on the Myers-Briggs are helping to prove this statement true.

Perhaps the Doctor, when told about the usage of Myers-Briggs, would be skeptical. He might even describe it as "a big ball of wibbly wobbly, psychy-wikey . . . stuff."[49]

creators as no better or worse than he would consider anybody else who created a test of something as difficult to define as personality, and might praise any who at least try. Should a crayon-wielding child be discouraged for drawing a person less realistically than a peer does? The one with more creative vision might reveal things the more realistic one might miss. There may be more art than science to how we view people in the first place.

Up from the Depths

Science is flawed—that is a fact. Whether the views of Freud and Jung are more flawed than the views of others remains the subject of ongoing debate, as does the value of the Myers-Briggs Type Indicator which grew out of Jungian ideas. We do not always know why we do the things we do—that is a fact. To many, psychoanalytic ideas about the unconscious mind feel like the right way to explain these things. Clearly, the Doctor's personal experiences reveal to him that the unconscious mind has power, such as when he wonders why he unconsciously chose to regenerate with a specific, frowny face[50] and later decides it was to send himself a message.[51]

A person thousands of years more advanced than we are might look at our science the way we look at witch doctors casting spells and ancient physicians draining sick people of blood to try to make them better. The Doctor looks at us all the same way: "We were just wondering if there were any other scientists. . . . You know, witch-wiggler, wangateur. Fortune teller?"[52] Through trial and error, the ancients learned. Superstition could impede progress, but it could also play an important role in bringing progress closer. We're all primitive from an immortal's point of view.

For all the nonsense that fills our dreams, some of the greatest stories and even some amazing scientific achievements come out of them from time to time. That doesn't mean we need to confuse sense with nonsense. It means we need to evaluate and reevaluate the things we call sense and learn sometimes from the nonsense. As the First Doctor put it, "Yes, superstition is a strange thing, my dear, but sometimes it tells the truth."[53]

References

Adler, A. (1927/1963). *Understanding human nature.* New York, NY: Premier.

Adler, G., & Jaffé, A. (Eds.) (1973). *C. G. Jung letters, Vol. 1: 1906–1950.* Princeton, NJ: Princeton University Press.

American Psychological Association (1998). Final conclusions of the American Psychological Association Working Group on the Investigation of Child Abuse. *Psychology, Public Policy, & Law, 4*(4), 933–940.

Bernstein, Z. (2015, September 3). The Valeyard and the stolen Earth. Doctor Who TV: http://www.doctorwhotv.co.uk/the-valeyard-and-the-stolen-earth-75606.htm.

Cohen, D., & Schmidt, J. P. (1979). Ambiversion: Characteristics of midrange responders on the Introversion-Extraversion continuum. *Journal of Personality Assessment, 43*(5), 514–516.

Dickson, D. H., & Kelly, I. W. (1985). The 'Barnum effect' in personality assessment: A review of the literature. *Psychological Reports, 57*(1), 367–382.

Eveleth, R. (2013, March 26). The Myers-Briggs personality test is pretty much meaningless. Smithsonian: http://www.smithsonianmag.com/smart-news/the-myers-briggs-personality-test-is-pretty-much-meaningless-9359770/?no-ist.

Eysenck, H. J. (1947). *Dimensions of personality.* London, UK: Trubner.

Eysenck, H. J. (1985). *Decline and fall of the Freudian empire.* New York, NY: Viking.

Frankel, V. E. (2016). *Doctor Who and the Hero's Journey: The Doctor and companions as chosen ones.* North Charleston, SC.

Freud, A. (1936). *The ego and defense mechanisms.* London, UK: Imago.

Freud, S. (1900/1965). *The interpretation of dreams.* New York, NY: Avon.

Freud, S. (1915/1963). Repression. In P. Rieff (Ed.), *General psychological theory* (pp. 104–115). New York, NY: Collier.

Freud, S. (1917/1963). Introductory lectures on psycho-analysis: Part III. General theory of the neurosis. In J. Strachey (Ed. and Trans.), *The standard edition of the complete works of Sigmund Freud* (Vol. 16, pp. 241–477). London, UK: Hogarth.

Freud, S. (1940). An outline of psychoanalysis. In *The standard edition of the complete works of Sigmund Freud* (Vol. 23, pp. 141–207). London, UK: Hogarth.

Hayne, H., Garry, M., & Loftus, E. F. (2006). On the continuing lack of evidence for repression. *Behavioral & Brain Sciences, 29*(5), 521–522.

Horney, K. (1939). *New ways in psychoanalysis.* New York, NY: Norton.

Jung, C. G. (1907/1909). *The psychology of dementia praecox.* New York, NY: Journal of Nervous and Mental Disease Publishing.

Jung, C. G. (1917). On the psychology of the unconscious. In R. F. C. Hull (Trans.), *Collected works* (Vol. 7). London, UK: Routledge & Kegan Paul.

Jung, C. G. (1921/1976). *Psychological types.* Princeton, NJ: Princeton University Press.

Jung, C. G. (1963). *Memories, dreams, reflections.* New York, NY: Pantheon.

Jung, C. (1966). *Two essays on analytical psychology* (3rd ed.). Princeton, NJ: Princeton University Press.

Kramer, P. D. (2006). *Freud: Inventor of the modern mind.* New York, NY: Harper Perennial.

Krauss Whitbourne, S. (2010, August 10). When it comes to personality tests, a dose of skepticism is a good thing. Psychology Today: https://www.psychologytoday.com/blog/fulfillment-any-age/201008/when-it-comes-personality-tests-dose-skepticism-is-good-thing.

Langley, T. (2013, December 27). *Doctor Who: The man who regrets and the man who forgets.* Psychology Today: https://www.psychologytoday.com/blog/beyond-heroes-and-villains/201312/doctor-who-the-man-who-regrets-and-the-man-who-forgets.

Langley, T. (2015, March 7). *Would "Doctor Who" call Freud, Jung, Myers & Briggs stupid?* Psychology Today: https://www.psychologytoday.com/blog/beyond-heroes-and -villains/201603/would-doctor-who-call-freud-jung-myers-briggs-stupid.

May, R. (1983). *The discovery of being: Writings in existential psychology.* New York, NY: Norton.

McCrae, R. R., & Costa, P. T., Jr. (1987). Validation of the five-factor model of personality across instruments and observers. *Journal of Personality & Social Psychology, 52*(1), 81–90.

McGowan, D. (1994). *What is wrong with Jung?* Buffalo, NY: Prometheus.

McNally, R. J. (2005). Debunking myths about trauma and memory. *Canadian Journal of Psychiatry, 50*(13), 817–822.

Murray, H. A. (1940). Sigmund Freud: 1856–1939. *American Journal of Psychology, 53*(1), 134–138.

Myers & Briggs Foundation (n.d.). *MBTI basics.* Myers & Briggs Foundation: http://www.myersbriggs.org/my-mbti-personality-type/mbti-basics/.

Myers, I. B., & Myers, P. B. (1995). *Gifts differing: Understanding personality type.* Palo Alto, CA: Consulting Psychologists Press.

North, A. (2014, July 18). Why Myers-Briggs is totally useless—but wildly popular. New York Times: http://op-talk.blogs.nytimes.com/2014/07/18/why-myers-briggs -is-totally-useless-but-wildly-popular/.

Popper, K. R. (1963). *Conjectures and refutations: The growth of scientific knowledge.* London, UK: Routledge & Kegan Paul.

Rorschach, H. (1921). *Psychodiagnostics.* New York, NY: Grune & Stratton.

Stromberg, J., & Caswell, E. (2015, October 8). *Why the Myers-Briggs test is totally meaningless.* Vox: http://www.vox.com/2014/7/15/5881947/myers-briggs-personality-test -meaningless.

Vaillant, G. E. (1977). *Adaptation to life.* Boston, MA: Little, Brown.

Webster, R. (1995). *Why Freud was wrong: Sin, science, and psychoanalysis.* Halesworth, Suffolk, UK: Orwell.

Wegner, D. M. (1989). *White bears and other unwanted thoughts: Suppression, obsession, and the psychology of mental control.* London, UK: Guilford.

Woodworth, R. S. (1917). Some criticisms of the Freudian psychology. *Journal of Abnormal Psychology, 12*(3), 174–194.

Notes

1. Modern episode 4–3, "Planet of the Ood" (April 29, 2008).
2. In Adler & Jaffé (1973), p. 33.
3. Freud (1900/1965), p. 608.
4. Rorschach (1921).
5. A. Freud (1936).
6. Myers & Myers (1980).
7. Jung (1921/1976).
8. e.g., Kramer (2006); McGowan (1994); North (2014); Popper (1963); Stromberg & Caswell (2015); Webster (1995); Woodworth (1917).
9. Eysenck (1985), p. 208.
10. *Doctor Who* (1996 TV movie).
11. S. Freud (1940).
12. Modern episode 8–1, "Deep Breath" (August 23, 2014).
13. Vaillant (1977).

14. A. Freud (1936).
15. S. Freud (1915/1963).
16. American Psychological Association (1998); Hayne et al. (2006); McNally (2005).
17. Anniversary special, "The Day of the Doctor" (November 23, 2013).
18. Most notably in modern episode 6–8, "Let's Kill Hitler" (August 27, 2011).
19. Christmas special, "The Time of the Doctor" (December 25, 2013); for more elaborate analysis, see Langley (2013).
20. Wegner (1989).
21. Classic serial 5–1, *The Tomb of the Cybermen*, pt. 3 (September 16, 1967).
22. S. Freud (1915/1963; 1917/1963).
23. Classic serial 3–9, *The War Machines* (June 25—July 16, 1966).
24. Classic serial 14–2, *The Hand of Fear* (October 2–23, 1976).
25. Classic serial 8–1, *Terror of the Autons* (January 2–23, 1971).
26. Classic serial 22–6, *Revelation of the Daleks* (March 23–30, 1985).
27. Christmas special, "The Christmas Invasion" (December 25, 2005).
28. Adler (1927/1963); Freud (1900/1965); Horney (1939); Jung (1963).
29. Classic serial 20–2, *Snakedance*, pt. 1 (January 18, 2013).
30. Murray (1940), p. 138.
31. Classic serial 1–15, *The Horror of Fang Rock*, pt. 4 (September 24, 1977).
32. Classic serial, *Shada*, unfinished due to a technicians' strike (scheduled for January–February, 1980); eventually produced as Eighth Doctor audio play (December 10, 2005).
33. Classic serial 17–2, *City of Death*, pt. 2 (October 6, 1979).
34. May (1983).
35. Langley (2015).
36. Classic serial 14–4, *The Face of Evil*, pt. 4 (January 22, 1977).
37. Jung (1907/1909).
38. *Doctor Who* (1996 TV movie).
39. Jung (1966).
40. Classic serial 23–4, *The Trial of a Time Lord: The Ultimate Foe* (November 29–December 6, 1986); Bernstein (2015).
41. Modern episode 5–7, "Amy's Choice" (May 15, 2010); Frankel (2016).
42. Jung (1917).
43. Jung (1921/1976).
44. Eysenck (1985); McCrae & Costa (1987).
45. Cohen & Schmidt (1979).
46. Myers & Briggs Foundation (n.d.).
47. Eveleth (2013).
48. Dickson & Kelly (1985); Krauss Whitbourne (2010).
49. "People assume that time is a strict progression of cause to effect, but actually from a non-linear, non-subjective viewpoint, it's more like a big ball of wibbly-wobbly, timey-wimey stuff."—Tenth Doctor in modern episode 3–10, "Blink" (June 9, 2007).
50. Modern episode 8–1, "Deep Breath" (August 23, 2014).
51. Modern episode 9–5, "The Girl Who Died" (October 17, 2015).
52. Classic serial 18–4, *State of Decay*, pt. 1 (November 22, 1980).
53. Classic serial 4–1, *The Smugglers*, pt. 4 (October 1, 1966).

Factor File Two

The Three Factors—
Add Psychoticism or Openness?

TRAVIS LANGLEY

Stars do not float through the galaxy independently of one another. Gravity tugs stars into groups and galaxies into clusters, forming relationships we barely see because we cannot watch them through all of time and space. From our sliver of time and our viewpoint bound to one planet's location, we gaze. Detecting relationships among such large numbers of anything—whether interstellar bodies or personality traits— can take a long time, and understanding the relationships we observe even longer.

Renewal

When psychologist Hans Eysenck's two-factor theory fell short of describing personality thoroughly enough, person- ality psychologists persisted in trying to identify which constellations of traits would best sum us up. Eysenck's own view underwent renewal and became his *three-factor theory.*[1] Simply identifying that some traits go together does not reveal what ties them together, and therefore different researchers will look at the same personality factors, interpreting them differently and giving them different names. Compare it to people creating a club: They already share something that brought them together, and they can disagree on the meaning of whatever ties them together and what name the club should have. How long does it take the handful of people investigating the mysterious Doctor to name their group the London Investigation 'N' Detective Agency, a.k.a. LINDA?[2] Scrutinizing the third collection of traits he detected through factor analysis, Eysenck came to interpret it as a set that suggested proneness to developing a *psychosis*, severe detachment from reality, and so he named the cluster *psychoticism.* Other researchers who looked at the same findings, though, would view them in other ways.

Psychoticism
Once he expanded his views to make room for another major personality factor, Eysenck equated the third factor with psychotic potential because the factor included a number of traits involving creativity and he believed creativity and madness went hand in hand. "Creativity has from the earliest times been thought to be related to psychosis or 'madness,'" he noted.[3] The Doctor and Amy see the artist Vincent van Gogh suffer from his inner demons,[4] and the real Vincent's multiple maladies remain the subject of diagnostic debate to this day.[5] The Doctor's own creative, divergent way of thinking and his tendency to question the status quo likely figure into why some Time Lords call him "a madman."[6]

Examples of Psychoticism Traits[7]
  Aggressiveness
  Antisociality
  Creativity
  Egocentrism
  Impersonal Nature
  Impulsivity
  Lack of Empathy
  Tough-mindedness

Openness

Other three-factor theories emerged as different researchers ran their own factor analyses and inferred different meanings from what they found. Among the best known was the *NEO* model proposed by personality researchers Robert McCrae and Paul Costa: neuroticism, extraversion, openness. *Openness* (also called *openness to experience*) involves curiosity, ingenuity, analysis, intellectual pursuit, appreciation of things others deem impractical, and readiness for new and unusual experiences.[8] Few fictional characters are more up for new experience than the Doctor, who leaves Gallifrey and rarely slows down as he rushes from one adventure to the next.

Examples of Openness Traits
  Abstract Thinking
  Active Imagination
  Appreciation of Culture and Intelligence
  Challenging Norms
  Curiosity
  Independent Thinking
  Intellectual Flexibility
  Interest in Adventure

Originality
Preference for Variety
Unconventional Beliefs

Counting Constellations

Though the Doctor wears many faces and behaves in many different ways, common features connect all of his incarnations and distinguish who he is from who everyone else he can ever encounter. Despite the differences between different theorists' personality factor models, some common features connect them and distinguish them from other theories of who we are. One way or another, each view describes personality in terms of traits, each combines traits into broad dimensions, and the extraversion/introversion dimension runs through them all.

So Eysenck had his three factors while McCrae and Costa had theirs. Should psychoticism or openness be added to the list? Psychoticism included numerous traits that openness omitted. After conducting an extensive review of all personality factor research, looking at the many personality disorder lists identified by different researchers,[9] McCrae and Costa added two plus two and got five.[10] Factor File Three, "The Five Factors— Adventures in the OCEAN," shares how.

References

Chowdhury, A. N. (2008). Vincent van Gogh and mental illness. *British Journal of Psychiatry, 193*(2), 167–168.

Eysenck, H. J. (1966). Personality and experimental psychology. *Bulletin of the British Psychological Society, 19*(1), 1–28.

Eysenck, H. J. (1993). Creativity and personality: Suggestions for a theory. *Psychological Inquiry, 4*(3), 147–178.

Eysenck, H. J., & Eysenck, M. W. (1985). *Personality and individual differences: A natural science approach.* New York, NY: Plenum.

Goldberg, L. R. (1982). From Ace to Zombie: Some explorations in the language of personality. In C. D. Spielberger & J. N. Butcher (Eds.), *Advances in personality assessment* (Vol. 1, pp. 203–234). Hillsdale, NJ: Erlbaum.

McCrae, R. R., & Costa, P. T., Jr. (1985). Openness to experience. In R. Hogan & W. H. Jones (Eds.), *Perspectives in personality* (Vol. 1, pp. 145–172).

McCrae, R. R., & Costa, P. T., Jr. (1987). Validation of the five-factor model of personality across instruments and observers. *Journal of Personality & Social Psychology, 52*(1), 81–90.

Ter Borg, M., & Trenité, D. K. (2012). The cultural context of diagnosis: The case of Vincent van Gogh. *Epilepsy & Behavior, 25*(3), 431–439.

Tupes, E. C., & Christal, R. E. (1961). Recurrent personality factors based on trait ratings. *USAF ASD Technical Report* (No. 61–97). Lackland Air Force Base, TX: U. S. Air Force.

Voskuil, P. (2013). Diagnosing Vincent van Gogh, an expedition from the sources to the present "mer à boire." *Epilepsy & Behavior, 28*(2), 177–180.

Notes

1. Eysenck (1966).
2. Episode 2–10, "Love & Monsters" (June 17, 2006).
3. Eysenck (1993), p. 155.
4. Episode 5–10, "Vincent and the Doctor" (June 5, 2010).
5. Chowdhury (2008); Ter Borg & Trenité (2012); Viskuil (2013).
6. e.g., anniversary special, "The Day of the Doctor" (November 23, 2013).
7. Eysenck & Eysenck (1985).
8. McCrae & Costa (1985).
9. e.g., Tupes & Christal (1961).
10. McCrae & Costa (1987).

Social animals that we are, we often identify ourselves by the company we keep.

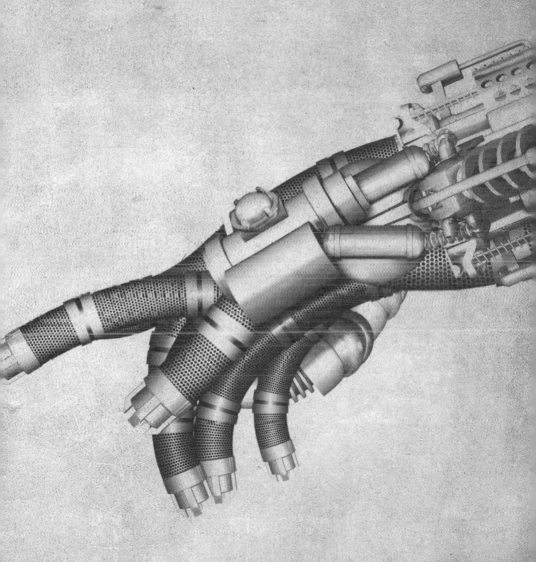

Part Three

Hands to Hold

Physical qualities and personality can both be attractive. Circumstances can also heighten a person's appeal. Danger excites us and can make other feelings more exciting as well.

CHAPTER NINE

Who Makes a Good Companion?

SARITA J. ROBINSON

*"There's a lot of things you need to get across this universe.
Warp drive, wormhole refractors. You know the thing you
need most of all? You need a hand to hold."*
—Tenth Doctor[1]

"Through others we become ourselves."
—psychologist Lev S. Vygotsky[2]

Psychologists, especially occupational psychologists, have
often wondered whether it would be possible to identify
if a person would be a good fit for a job role. For example,
is it possible from an interview or an observation to identify someone who has the resilience to be a teacher or the
compassion to be a nurse? Identifying selection criterion for
different occupational roles is big business because choosing
the wrong person can be costly and in some cases dangerous. The Doctor, from his granddaughter Susan Foreman

and her teachers Barbara Wright and Ian Chesterton through many dozens of others who follow, has shown the need for companionship. However, it is clear that selecting a companion is a difficult task as a good companion will need to have a certain psychological makeup to enjoy traveling with the Doctor.

We know that the Doctor has had many companions. Some have been aliens (such as Romana from Gallifrey, Adric from Alzarian in E-Space, Nyssa from Tracken, and Vislor Turlough from Trion). Other companions have been robotic (such as K-9, the shape-changing robot Kamelion, and the Cyberman head called Handles). However, the Doctor often chooses an Earthling, although not all of them make the grade. For example, both Captain Jack Harkness and Ashildr (also known as "Me") are rejected by the Doctor because they are immortal. The Doctor tells Ashildr that his companions have to be like "mayflies" to remind him of what is important in life.[3] So how does the Doctor select his companions, and what other characteristics is he looking for?

Who Makes a Good Traveling Companion?

Sometimes companions are thrust upon the Doctor. Romana (or Romanadvoratrelundar, to give her full name) is sent by the Time Lords to help the Fourth Doctor fulfill the White Guardian's mission to find the Key to Time.[4] Some companions, such as Dodo Chaplet and Tegan Jovanka, appear to stumble into the TARDIS, believing it to be a genuine police box.[5] Others, such as Amy Pond, wait patiently for the Doctor to take them traveling. No matter how a potential companion gets on board the TARDIS, the Doctor has the ultimate power to decide if he or she is worthy of a TARDIS key.

Although modern selection processes for adventurers can have a psychological basis, historically selection has been a little more hit and miss. Ernest Shackleton, the famous polar explorer, recruited men for his 1914 Nimrod Expedition. The story goes that he placed an advertisement in a London newspaper asking for volunteers for a hazardous journey: "Low wages, bitter cold, long hours of complete darkness. Safe return doubtful. Honour and recognition in event of success." Shackleton received five thousand applications, which he divided into three piles labeled *Mad, Hopeless,* and *Possible.*[6] Shackleton's selection criteria for fellow adventurers appeared to include optimism, patience, physical endurance, idealism, and courage. These qualities are also seen in many of the Doctor's companions, and so it is possible that the Doctor takes some advice from Shackleton.

Today, the selection criteria for adventurers are thought to be more robust, but it is only recently that detailed psychological screening has been included in astronaut selection procedures.[7] Before psychological screening was commonplace, it was assumed that one could spot who had the "right stuff." People with the right stuff were thought to be easy to spot as they would be independent, expressive, and driven to work hard, whereas people with the "wrong stuff" tended to be competitive, impatient, and irritable. Selectors also wanted to screen out people with "no stuff," people who are unassertive with low levels of motivation.[8] It is clear that the Doctor does not want to select people with the wrong stuff or no stuff.

The Doctor's Selection Process

The Doctor does, on the majority of occasions, select companions who have the right stuff. All of his companions tend to be independent and expressive with a strong work ethic. However, the Doctor's selection process is quite messy. What other factors does he take into account?

The Doctor often selects companions who have either medical or academic qualifications. For example, both Martha Jones (who is a medical student when she first meets the Doctor) and Harry Sullivan (a lieutenant surgeon in the Royal Navy) are medically trained. In fact, one of the Doctor's companions, Dr. Grace Holloway, is an accomplished cardiologist who actually triggers the Doctor's regeneration after subjecting him to an ill-judged heart operation.[9]

Perhaps the Doctor is selecting companions on the basis of their intelligence quotient (IQ). IQ is determined by a set of tests that are designed to measure human intelligence. High IQ levels are thought to be associated with occupations such as medicine and academic jobs. It is likely that if River Song (a.k.a. Melody Pond) with her doctorate in archaeology, Zoe Heriot the astrophysicist, and Dr. Elizabeth Shaw the UNIT science officer recruited from Cambridge University took an IQ test, they would score highly. However, psychologists are starting to think that IQ alone is not the best predictor of success in occupations such as medicine. Recent research suggests that traits of self-discipline and motivation are also important.[10] In fact, not all of the Doctor's companions would have scored well on traditional IQ tests. Jo Grant, for example, who is hired by UNIT to be the Doctor's lab assistant, says she actually failed her science exams.[11] Many of the Doctor's companions have not had high-powered jobs, with Ace working as a waitress, Rose Tyler working in a department store, and Donna Noble working as a temp. Indeed, when Romana boasts to the Doctor that she graduated from the Time Lord Academy on Gallifrey with top honors, the Doctor is not impressed.[12] He points out that she lacks experience. Therefore, it is clear that the Doctor, like occupational psychologists, knows that academic smarts do not automatically mean that someone is the right fit for a job role.

Intelligence

In fact, some psychologists today suggest that the traditional IQ view of intelligence is limited and that there is more than one way in which to be clever. The multiple intelligences model that was introduced by developmental psychologist Howard Gardner suggests that people can be smart in different ways:[13]

- *Linguistic intelligence*—good oral communication skills, including the ability to express yourself and your point of view. Investigative journalist Sarah Jane Smith would perform well on tests of linguistic intelligence.
- *Logical-mathematical intelligence*—having the ability to think logically, see patterns, and deduce solutions from the evidence presented. Adric, the mathematics genius from the planet Alzarius in E-Space, is likely to score highly on tests that measure this.
- *Musical intelligence*—having the ability to make music. There is very limited evidence of musical intelligence in the Doctor's companions; maybe this is a trait the Doctor does not value in them.
- *Bodily-kinesthetic intelligence*—the ability to control your body carefully in the physical world. Leela demonstrates this quality as a warrior of the Sevateem.
- *Spatial intelligence*—the ability to recognize and use the space around you. Harry Sullivan, who works

with the Doctor at UNIT, is likely to score quite
low on this trait as he is well known for being
clumsy.

- *Intrapersonal intelligence*—the ability to understand
your own thoughts and feelings and the ways
they affect your behavior. Many of the Doctor's
companions have high levels of this type of intelligence. Clara Oswald has helped the Doctor understand how his behavior affects others.

- *Interpersonal intelligence*—the ability to understand
other people's needs and motivations. All the Doctor's companions show high levels of this. The
Doctor may feel he needs them because he may not
always understand the life-forms he meets while
they are likely to grasp the essence of any crisis and
make the personal connection quickly.

Gardner's *interpersonal intelligence* is similar to another concept:
emotional intelligence. *Emotional intelligence (EI)*[14] refers to a set
of skills that allow people to do the following:

- Understand and express their own emotions as well
as the emotions of others.
- Regulate their own emotions and the emotions of
others.
- Use their abilities to motivate, plan, and achieve
their goals.

Only a few of the Doctor's associates appear to be low in EI.
The Brigadier and maybe his daughter Kate Stewart would
do well to improve their EI abilities. For example, Kate does
not want to negotiate with the Zygons and feels that bombing
them would be a better approach.[15] In most cases, the Doctor's

companions care passionately about all the life-forms they meet while they journey through time and space. Many companions even put themselves in harm's way to help life-forms they have just met. Rose, for example, takes pity on the Dalek who has been tortured by Henry van Statten, and she pleads with the Doctor for the Dalek's life.[16] Donna Noble insists that the Doctor save Lucius Caecilius and his family from the volcanic eruption in Pompeii.[17] (Helping others despite risk to oneself is a defining aspect of *altruism*.[18])

However, although intelligence testing (whether IQ, multiple intelligences, or EI) can tell us about some of the characteristics of a person, they cannot tell us everything we need to know in order to tell if someone would be good in a certain role, such as being a good traveling companion. In addition to intelligence tests, psychologists can use personality measures to see if a person is a good fit for a certain job role. For example, having a high IQ might make you good at mathematics, but you might not be a good mathematics teacher if you do not like people.

Personality

Psychologists have identified five main personality factors (the Big Five) that are universally present in both Western and non-Western cultures.[19] From what we have seen, these characteristics seem to be present throughout our world. It is thought that most people fall between two extreme points on a scale for each of the five factors (as opposed to being completely at one end or the other).

The Dark Triad: Psychopathy, Machiavellianism, and Narcissism

The Doctor rarely gets his choice of companions wrong, but one exception is Adam Mitchell. As well as suffering from time sickness, Adam has some of the personality characteristics that fall within the *dark triad*.[20] The term refers to three personality types that appear to be typical of people who are manipulative and exploitative:

- *Narcissism:* Narcissists lack empathy and have a high level of entitlement. People with narcissistic personalities do not make good companions; they are not team players and are out only for themselves.[21] Adam displays some narcissistic characteristics, as he seems interested only in how he can profit from his travels. For example, he tries to download advances in technology with no consideration for the impact of his actions.
- *Machiavellianism:* People with Machiavellian personality traits tend to be manipulative and are willing to exploit others.[22] People with this may lack a moral code and have a high level of self-interest and deception. We can see that Adam is self-interested when he does not actively help the residents of Satellite 5.
- *Psychopathy:* People with psychopathic traits display low levels of empathy and are reckless, showing little remorse for their behavior.[23] Again, Adam shows some of these traits. He is reckless, going for major brain surgery so that he can download information about technological advances. When he is caught, he does not appear guilty or apologetic; he just tries to justify his actions.

Openness to Experience

People range from being very curious to being very cautious. It is a fair assumption that all the Doctor's companions are very curious. Ace, for example, with her homemade science lab, has managed to find her way to the planet Svartos before joining the Doctor on his travels. Then there is Clara Oswald, who replies to the Doctor's questions about where she would like to go with "somewhere awesome."[24] A companion expelled from the TARDIS by the Doctor, Adam Mitchell, shows a low level of openness. In fact, he does not cope well with his travels, fainting the first time he sees the Earth from space and being reluctant to try the beef-flavored slushy that Rose offers him.[25]

Conscientiousness

People range from being organized and effective to being disorganized and spontaneous. The Doctor's companions tend to have a high level of conscientiousness. Clara Oswald organizes her work as a teacher around her travels with the Doctor.[26]

Extraversion

People range from being very outgoing to being reserved and preferring their own company. The Doctor's companions tend to be very outgoing and so have a high degree of extraversion. Ace in particular stands out as a companion who has a very extraverted nature. She is always quick to make friends and with her boom box really is the "life and soul" of the party.

Agreeableness

The Doctor's companions tend to have a high degree of agreeableness, being caring, cooperative, and considerate. People who are less agreeable have low levels of empathy and little concern for the health and well-being of others. One of the key characteristics of all the Doctor's companions is their caring nature. After the Daleks murder Victoria's father, Jamie becomes very protective of her as they travel with the Second Doctor.[27]

Neuroticism

People range from being very nervous to being confident. Generally, the Doctor's companions display low levels of nervousness and have the ability to deal with even the most stressful situations. Tegan, for example, refuses to stay safe in the TARDIS with the Watcher but instead goes to help the Doctor even though the planet is falling apart.[28] In most adventures the Doctor's companions show a remarkable ability to stay calm, cool, and collected. Psychological research into the ways in which individuals react to emergency situations suggests that only 10 to 25 percent of people have the ability to stay mentally alert and carry out prompt and well thought out responses.[29] The vast majority of the population do not respond well to life-threatening events and can suffer from *cognitive paralysis* in which they fail to undertake any actions at all. Obviously, this would not be very helpful for the Doctor's companions, who need to be able to work well under pressure. In fact, most of the Doctor's companions excel under pressure. Martha Jones, for example, independently travels around, spreading the word of the Doctor in a world controlled by the villainous Master and the Toclafane.[30]

What Are the Benefits for the Doctor of a Traveling Companion?

There are many psychological advantages to having a good social support network. Without a friend or family member to turn to, humans can feel lost and alone. When the Doctor picks up Rose, we know that he has been traveling without a companion for some time.[31] However, the Doctor (through most of his history outside the Time War) rarely has traveled on his own. Having a companion has many advantages for the Doctor:

- *Help with moral decisions.* The Doctor draws on the experiences of his companions and uses them as his moral compass. When weighing whether he has the right to destroy the entire Dalek race, the Fourth Doctor asks Sarah Jane.[32] By calling on the help of companions such as Sarah Jane, he is able to get a new perspective on his decisions.
- *Emotional support.* Psychologists know that friendships and emotional support are extremely important for remaining mentally healthy.[33] The Doctor seems to have strong emotional ties to his companions and appears to be devastated when they leave. Missy (the Master), however, suggests that the Doctor's relationship with his companions is not equal and that he sees them as faithful pets.[34] Even if this is the case, psychologists have found that having a pet also can be beneficial to one's mental well-being.[35]
- *Physical benefits.* The Doctor's companions can help him remain physically healthy. Mel Bush puts the Doctor on a regimen of carrot juice and exercise. Some researchers suggest that people who feel lonely can have health problems and that exercise is much easier if one has a friend to help one out.[36]

After the Doctor?

Traveling with the Doctor has a profound effect on many of his companions. Some companions are forced to leave the TARDIS, but some decide for themselves that it is time for them to stop their travels and move on with their lives. Ian Chesterton tells the First Doctor that he misses sitting in a pub and drinking a pint of beer as he chooses to return home,[37] and Martha Jones decides to stop traveling with the Tenth Doctor after she decides that their relationship is not healthy for her.[38] However, it is clear that the Doctor is emotionally attached to his traveling companions and does want the best outcome for them. For example, even though the Tenth Doctor wipes Donna's memory of their travels together, he returns on her wedding day and gives her a winning lottery ticket as a wedding gift.[39] Even when the Doctor cannot save his companions, he tries to do his best for them. After River Song dies in the Library, saving the people trapped by its computer, the Doctor is able to upload her to the Library's mainframe so that a version of her can continue to live on.[40]

On a positive note, most of the companions seem to grow from the traumas they have witnessed on their adventures. Nyssa, for example, chooses to leave the Fifth Doctor and remain on the hospital ship *Terminus* to help formulate a cure for a disease shortly after witnessing fellow companion Adric's death.[41] Amy and Rory lead a happy life after being catapulted back to 1938 and then adopting a son (as they report in messages they leave for the Doctor and Rory's father).[42] Psychologists refer to these positive outcomes after trauma as *posttraumatic growth*.[43]

The Key to Companions

It is clear that selecting anyone for a job role is difficult. Occupational psychologists have researched for many years to see how different traits can fit with different occupations. It is clear that although the Doctor does not subject his companions to psychometric testing, he does appear to know who will make a good traveling companion. The Doctor selects those who are moral, motivated, academically and emotionally intelligent, extraverted, agreeable, and conscientious and above all are able to deal with a stressful situation. Only occasionally does he give someone undeserving the TARDIS key.

> *"We need each other, and the sooner we learn*
> *that, the better it is for us all."*
> —developmental psychologist Erik Erikson[44]

References

Bar-Tal, D. (1985–1986). Altruistic motivation to help: Definition, utility, and operationalization. *Humboldt Journal of Social Relations, 13*(1–2), 3–14.

Buckels, E. E., Jones, D. N., & Paulhus, D. L. (2013). Behavior confirmation of everyday sadism. *Psychological Science, 20*(1), 1–9.

Cacioppo, J. T., & Cacioppo, S. (2014). Social relationships and health: The toxic effects of perceived social isolation. *Social & Personality Psychology Compass, 8*(2), 58–72.

Calhoun, L. G., & Tedeschi, R. G. (Eds.). (2014). *Handbook of posttraumatic growth: Research and practice.* London, UK: Routledge.

Chabrol, H., Van Leeuwen, N., Rodgers, R., & Sejourne, N. (2009). Contributions of psychopathic, narcissistic, Machiavellian, and sadistic personality traits to juvenile delinquency. *Personality & Individual Differences, 47*(7), 734–739.

Chidester, T. R., Helmreich, R. L., Gregorich, S. E., & Geis, C. E. (1991). Pilot personality and crew coordination: Implications for training and selection. *International Journal of Aviation Psychology, 1*(1), 25–44.

Cleckley, H. (1941). *The mask of sanity.* St. Louis, MO: Mosby.

Duckworth, A. L., & Seligman, M. E. (2005). Self-discipline outdoes IQ in predicting academic performance of adolescents. *Psychological Science, 16*(12), 939–944.

Gardner, H., & Hatch, T. (1989). Educational implications of the theory of multiple intelligences. *Educational Researcher, 18*(8), 4–10.

Goleman, D. (1988, June 14). *Erikson, in his own old age, expands his view of life.* New York Times: https://www.nytimes.com/books/99/08/22/specials/erikson-old.html.

Fromm, E. (1964). *The heart of man.* New York, NY: Harper & Row.

Hare, R. D. (1991). *The Hare psychopathy checklist-revised.* North Tonawanda, NY: Multi-Health Systems.

Hare, R. D., & Neumann, C. N. (2006). The PCL-R assessment of psychopathy: Development, structural properties, and new directions. In C. Patrick (Ed.), *Handbook of psychopathy* (pp. 58-88). New York: Guilford.

Harpur, T. J., Hare, R. D., & Hakstian, A. R. (1989). Two-factor conceptualization of psychopathy: Construct validity and assessment implications. *Psychological Assessment,* 1(1), 6-17.

Jakobwitz, S., & Egan, V. (2006). The "dark triad" and normal personality traits. *Personality & Individual Differences,* 40(3), 331–339.

Leach, J. (1994*). Survival psychology.* London, UK: Macmillan.

McCrae, R. R., & Terracciano, A. (2005). Universal features of personality traits from the observer's perspective: Data from 50 cultures. *Journal of Personality & Social Psychology, 88*(3), 547.

Paulhus, D. L., & Williams, K. M. (2002). The Dark Triad of personality: Narcissism, Machiavellianism, and psychopathy. *Journal of Research in Personality,* 36, 556–63.

Reich, J. W. (1982). *Experimenting in society.* Glenview, IL: Scott Foresman.

Salovey, P., & Mayer, J. D. (1990). Emotional intelligence. *Imagination, Cognition and Personality, 9*(3), 185–211.

Santy, P. A. (1994). *Choosing the right stuff: The psychological selection of astronauts and cosmonauts.* Westport, CT: Praeger.

Skeem, J. L., Polaschek, D. L. L., Patrick, C. J., & Lilienfeld, S. O. (2011). Psychopathic personality: Bridging the gap between scientific evidence and public policy. *Psychological Science in the Public Interest,* 12(2), 95–162.

Smith, M. (2007). *Polar crusader: A life of Sir James Wordie.* Edinburgh, Scotland: Birlinn.

Van der Horst, M., & Coffé, H. (2012). How friendship network characteristics influence subjective well-being. *Social Indicators Research, 107*(3), 509–529.

Vygotsky (1931/1997). The collected works of L. S. Vygotsky, Vol. 4: *The history of the development of higher mental functions.* New York, NY: Plenum.

Wells, D. L. (2009). The effects of animals on human health and well-being. *Journal of Social Issues, 65*(3), 523–543.

Wing, R. R., & Jeffery, R. W. (1999). Benefits of recruiting participants with friends and increasing social support for weight loss and maintenance. *Journal of Consulting & Clinical Psychology, 67*(1), 132.

Notes

1. Modern episode 2–11, "Fear Her" (December 15, 2006).
2. Vygotsky (1931/1997), p. 96.
3. Modern episode 9–6, "The Woman Who Lived" (October 24, 2015).
4. Classic serial 16–1, *The Ribos Operation,* part 1 (September 2, 1978).
5. Classic serials 3–5, *The Massacre of St. Bartholomew's Eve,* part 4 (February 5, 1966); 18–7, *Logopolis,* part 1 (February 28, 1981).
6. Smith (2007).
7. Santy (1994).
8. Chidester et al. (1991).
9. *Doctor Who* (1996 TV movie).
10. Duckworth & Seligman (2005).
11. Classic serial 8–1, *Terror of the Autons,* part 1 (January 2, 1971).
12. Classic serial 16–1, *The Ribos Operation,* part 1 (September 2, 1978).
13. Gardner & Hatch (1989).
14. Salovey & Mayer (1990).

15. Modern episode 9–7, "Zygon Invasion" (October 15, 2015).
16. Modern episode 1–6, "Dalek" (April 30, 2015).
17. Modern episode 4–2, "Fires of Pompeii" (April 12, 2008).
18. Bar-Tal (1985–1986); Reich (1982).
19. McCrae & Terracciano (2005).
20. Book et al. (2016); Jakobwitz & Egan (2006); Paulhus & Williams (2002). For information on the dark tetrad, which also includes sadism, see also Buckels et al. (2013); Chabrol et al. (2009).
21. American Psychiatric Association (2013).
22. Christie & Geis (1970).
23. Cleckley (1941); Hare (1991); Hare & Neumann (2006); Harpur et al. (1989); Skeen et al. (2011).
24. Modern episode 7–7, "The Rings of Akhaten" (April 6, 2013).
25. Modern episode 1–7, "The Long Game" (May 7, 2005).
26. Beginning in the anniversary special, *The Day of the Doctor* (November 23, 2013).
27. Classic serial 4–9, *The Evil of the Daleks*, part 7 (July 1, 1967).
28. Classic serial 18–7, *Logopolis* (February 28–March 21, 1981).
29. Leach (1994).
30. Modern episode 3–12, "The Sound of Drums" (June 23, 2007).
31. Modern episode 1–1, "Rose" (March 26, 2005).
32. Classic serial 12–4, *Genesis of the Daleks* (March 8–April 12, 1975).
33. Cacioppo & Cacioppo (2014).
34. Van der Horst & Coffé (2012).
35. Modern episode 8–12, "Death in Heaven" (November 8, 2014).
36. Wing & Jeffery (1999).
37. Classic serial 8–2, *The Chase* (June 26, 1965).
38. Modern episode 3–13, *Last of the Time Lords* (June 30, 2007).
39. Christmas special, "The End of Time" (January 1, 2010).
40. Modern episode 4–8, "Silence in the Library" (May 31, 2008).
41. Classic serial 20–4, *Terminus*, part 4 (February 15, 1983).
42. Modern episode 7–5, *The Angels Take Manhattan* (September 29, 2012); video, *P.S.* https://www.youtube.com/watch?v=XWU6XL9xI4k (October 12, 2012).
43. Calhoun et al. (2014).
44. Quoted by Goleman (1988).

Do "opposites attract" or do "birds flock together"—or are both expressions no more than trite platitudes? How do differences and similarities shape relationships between two people, and what role might they play when we have choices to make between one relationship and others?

CHAPTER TEN

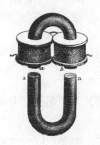

By Any Other Name: Evolution, Excitation, and Expansion

WIND GOODFRIEND

"Nice to meet you, Rose. Run for your life."
—Ninth Doctor[1]

> *"That which we call a rose*
> *By any other name would smell as sweet."*
> —playwright William Shakespeare[2]

Over the course of a lifetime, we meet thousands and thousands of people. Some of us believe that in the entire world there is one person we are each destined to find who will fulfill our folktale concept of enduring true love. Psychologists, however, tend to believe that we are attracted to some people and not to others because of a variety of factors in the individuals involved and their specific circumstances. Countless articles, books, and book chapters have explored attempts to study this phenomenon scientifically.[3] Among the thousands of people you have met in your life, what made some individuals stand out? What attracted you to them? What made you fall in love? Why might one rose draw someone's interest unlike any other flower?

Evolutionary Perspective on Love

When Darwin published *On the Origin of Species* in 1859,[4] more than just biology was revolutionized. Although the field of psychology was barely in its infancy at that time, the idea of human evolution affecting behavior is now pervasive in psychology textbooks. In short, the *evolutionary perspective on love* includes the belief that attraction and sexual behaviors are the products of generations of natural selection and competition for desirable mates. Importantly, the evolutionary perspective offers the idea that we are attracted to certain characteristics that are universally appealing regardless of culture, media exposure, or individual factors such as religion and education level because those characteristics have been helpful to the survival and passage of genetic patterns. What are those traits, and does Rose Tyler have them? She is the first companion of the twenty-first century,[5] the one through whom modern viewers first discover *Doctor Who*,[6] and the one for whom many viewers in our universe and perhaps the Doctor in his keep pining.[7]

Facial Features
The first feature that the evolutionary perspective on psychology predicts will be universally attractive in females is referred to as the *babyface bias*, or the idea that men think that women are pretty if their faces have stereotypically childish facial features. These features include smooth and unblemished skin, large eyes, a wide mouth, full lips, and a small nose. Altogether, this

package of features is called *facial neoteny*. Women who have a combination of facial neoteny and a fully adult and feminine body are considered the most beautiful around the world.[8] The actress who portrayed Rose and the characteristics chosen for the character certainly show this combination. Her wide eyes and broad, toothy smile are mesmerizing, and her fair skin and blond hair provide a youthful appearance that is appealing to many admirers, including the Ninth and Tenth Doctors.[9]

Youth

Rose's youth is also appealing according to the evolutionary perspective. At the time she meets the Doctor, she is nineteen years old.[10] The evolutionary perspective from psychology argues that youth in women matters to men because it provides a clue about a woman's reproductive health. Importantly, a woman's ability to bear a healthy child declines rapidly after she reaches age twenty.[11] Even as men age, their preference for significantly younger women remains stable; psychological studies have shown that men in their thirties tend to prefer women who are about five years younger but men in their fifties prefer women who are about fifteen years younger.[12] Although research is lacking on the preferences of aliens who are about a thousand years old, if we extrapolate this trend, Rose's youthful face and age will be very appealing because she is of prime age for reproductive capacity.

Body Type

Another trait possessed by Rose is likely to be very appealing to any other male admirers who cross her path: her body type. Although different cultures have preferences for heavier versus thinner women in general and in their media representations, such as models, the evolutionary perspective in psychology predicts that Rose's body type will be the most universally appealing.[13] This comes from research on what is called the *waist-to-hips ratio*. If you measured the circumference of your waist and compared it with the circumference of your hips, what would the ratio be? According to dozens of research studies done in a wide variety of cultures, men universally tend to find a waist-to-hips ratio right around .70 to be the most sexually appealing,[14] meaning a woman's waist should be 70 percent of the circumference of her hips. This classic "hourglass" shape emphasizes full hips (capable of healthy reproduction) and a small waist (indicative of aerobic fitness), both of which are clues to genetic health. If one estimate is correct,[15] Rose Tyler's measurements are 25 inches (waist) and 35 inches (hips), giving her a waist-to-hips ratio of .714, the perfect body according to this perspective.

Surely, though, the Doctor is a complex and intelligent man and it takes more than looks to win his love.

Excitation Transfer

Beauty matters, but for years psychologists have known that attraction is also affected by the circumstances in which two people meet. One of the best-known phenomena that can result in "love at first sight" is called *excitation transfer theory*.[16] Excitation transfer starts with the idea that when you are highly attracted to someone or in love, you will have a *physiological* response to that person. Your heart will beat faster; your breathing will increase; you may feel a bit dizzy and light-headed. We also know that some environmental circumstances will cause physiological arousal, such as when you're scared. If you are put into a frightening situation, you may experience the exact same bodily reactions: increased heartbeat and breathing, dizziness, and so on. The crux of excitation transfer theory is the prediction that sometimes we'll be physiologically aroused by environmental factors but that we can misunderstand those feelings and believe they're really caused by something else, including attraction to another person. Sometimes this effect is called *misattribution of arousal* because humans are fairly poor at understanding their own reactions and can translate fear into attraction.

A Shaky Bridge

A classic psychological study that tested excitation transfer is called the *shaky bridge study*.[17] Here, researchers went to a canyon and spent time next to two different bridges, one of which was higher, longer, and much shakier than the other. Next to each bridge, a female experimenter waited for middle-aged men who were alone to cross the bridge. Immediately after crossing, she asked them a few questions, thanked them for participating in the study, and offered them her phone number in a flirtatious manner. The real test of excitation transfer would come when experimenters saw which of the men called the woman to ask her out.

Fully half (50 percent) of the men who had just crossed the shaky, scary bridge called the woman later, whereas a mere 13 percent of the men from the sturdy bridge called her. It was the exact same woman in both conditions; the only difference was the circumstances. When our bodies are aroused by something in our environment, it's easy to feel the blood rushing through our veins and to feel that something important is happening. It is also easy to think that these feelings are due to attraction to someone nearby instead of attributing the arousal to its true source.

Excitation for Rose

Excitation transfer may be another factor in why the Doctor is especially attracted to Rose Tyler. Their first meeting occurs when both are being attacked by killer mannequins, an adventure that culminates with Rose swinging across a room to save the day and landing in the Doctor's arms while they both are sweaty and full of adrenaline.[18] Physical excitement in such circumstances could be translated into emotional excitement and attraction to each other.

A beautiful woman with all the right proportions and an exhilarating situation should not be enough. The Doctor meets beautiful women (and men and trees) all the time and is constantly fighting for his life. Although these factors are present in Rose, they are also true of most of his companions, and therefore these superficial variables do not fully explain why Rose Tyler seems so special.

Self-Expansion Theory

The final theory that we need to understand Rose's place in the Doctor's hearts is *self-expansion theory.*[19] The foundation for self-expansion theory in psychology is that "in a close relationship each person includes in the self, to some extent, the other's resources, perspectives, and identities."[20] Essentially, this theory argues that once you are in a committed relationship with someone, your separate identity or "self" is no longer independent. Instead, the two members of the couple have *interdependent identities*: One's cognitive and emotional concept of "self" includes the other person.

The Doctor's Ideal Self

This self-expansion to include another person is one reason why we're attracted to people. Because we strive to be the best "selves" we can be, we therefore search for partners who can help us attain that goal. Self-expansion theory may explain why the Doctor's companions often fall in love with him. Many of the companions live relatively banal, boring lives, worried about paying bills and satisfying demanding mothers. When the Doctor appears, he presents an unparalleled opportunity for adventure. Flying around in a time machine, visiting fantastic worlds, and having unlimited resources provides a better opportunity for self-expansion than most people could ever imagine. He explicitly points this out to Rose after their first adventure when he invites her to become his companion: "You could stay here, fill your life with work and food and sleep, or you could go anywhere."[21]

To Expand toward Rose

But is it possible for the Doctor to experience self-expansion? Could a mere human, a young woman with no resources and barely any tangible things to offer, be appealing to a Time Lord? This question is exactly what makes Rose Tyler special, because the answer, for her, is yes. It seems that the Doctor falls in love with Rose because *she offers him the opportunity to grow.* Knowing Rose seems to allow the Doctor to change his self-concept in ways that are extremely rare, and this is what self-expansion theory states is the reason why we fall in love.[22] We see changes in the Doctor's sense of self most clearly when he and Rose encounter what the Doctor most hates and fears: Daleks. Instead of hatred and fear, Rose feels empathy and compassion toward this single, lonely, and fearful being and attempts to be nurturing to the Dalek. A *model* (someone demonstrating behavior) can inspire us to mimic the behavior we observe, potentially making us more helpful, caring people.[23] Because Rose's example leads the Doctor to see this one Dalek as an individual being, the Doctor actually apologizes to it and realizes that his current self is not the self he wants to be.

Rose's ability to challenge the Doctor, to confront his weaknesses and make him stronger, kinder, and wiser, is what makes her special. This may be why the Doctor feels a love for Rose beyond his love for his other companions: She pushes him to expand his cognitive and emotional self in ways he never encountered before. She gets him to see the humanity in a variety of situations during their time together, but she also allows him to be personal and sweet. A poignant example of her ability to reach him is seen when they are trapped in a typically dangerous situation. Instead of panicking and clinging to the Doctor in fear, Rose gets him to dance with her, to do something simple and human.[24]

Self-expansion theory is relevant as the Doctor can truly see Rose as his equal instead of as an inferior being, and this equality allows them both to change and grow through their interdependent selves. The Doctor's respect and admiration for Rose being on his intellectual and courageous level is seen when he believes he's about to die (again) and his final words express his faith in her: "I've seen fake gods and bad gods and demi-gods and would-be-gods. If I believe in one thing—just one thing—I believe in her."[25]

The Uniqueness of Rose

Rose Tyler is special because she challenges the Doctor to expand his hearts, his mind, and his sense of self in ways that are truly, deeply meaningful. She has a pretty face and a curvy body, and their circumstances are exciting, but that isn't

Predictors of Attraction

What are some of the other variables that psychology has identified as predicting interpersonal or romantic attraction? The list is long, but these are a few of the most important variables:

- *Similarity:* Many studies have shown that similarity brings people together and that couples are more likely to experience happiness and longevity if the members have a similar age, socioeconomic status, religion, values, and sense of humor.[26]
- *Physical proximity:* Simply being around someone for more interactions provides an opportunity to get to know each other and potentially fall in love. A well-established phenomenon in psychology is the *mere exposure effect*, or the fact that just becoming more familiar with an object or person typically leads us to prefer that object or person.[27]
- *Reciprocal liking:* It also matters if our love or attraction is requited. We are more attracted to people we know are attracted to us—this return of our interest is both flattering and comforting. We are more likely to risk falling in love if we believe the risk may be worthwhile because the other person loves us in return.[28]

enough for real love. Rose *matters*. She is the Doctor's equal in bravery and his superior in empathy and selflessness. He values her because she makes him a different person. She makes him better, and that is why he loves her.

References

Aron, A., & Aron, E. N. (1986). *Love and the experience of self: Understanding attraction and satisfaction.* New York, NY: Hemisphere.

Aron, A., & Aron, E. N. (1996). Self and self expansion in relationships. In G. J. O. Fletcher & J. Fitness (Eds.), *Knowledge structures in close relationships: A social psychological approach* (pp. 325–344). Mahwah, NJ: Erlbaum.

Aron, A. P., Mashek, D. J., & Aron, E. N. (2004). Closeness as inclusion of the other in the self. In D. J. Mashek & A. Aron (Eds.), *Handbook of closeness and intimacy* (pp. 27–42). Mahwah, NJ: Lawrence Erlbaum.

Back, M. D., Schmukle, S. C., & Egloff, B. (2008). Becoming friends by chance. *Psychological Science, 19*(5), 439–440.

Bate, E. (2015, September 22). *18 reasons Rose Tyler was undeniably the best companion on "Doctor Who."* Buzz Feed: https://www.buzzfeed.com/eleanorbate/bad-wolf?utm_term=.uoEB9W4M4x#.bpzBjVd5de.

Body Measurements (n.d.). *Billie Piper.* Body Measurements: http://www.bodymeasurements.org/billie-piper-bra-size/.

Bryant, J., & Miron, D. (2003). Excitation-transfer theory. In J. Bryant, D. Roskos-Ewoldsen, & J. Cantor (Eds.), *Communication and emotion: Essays in honor of Dolf Zillmann* (pp. 31–59). Mahwah, NJ: Erlbaum.

Buss, D. M. (1994). *The evolution of desire.* New York, NY: Basic.

Caspi, A., & Herbener, E. S. (1990). Continuity and change: Assortative marriage and the consistency of personality in adulthood. *Journal of Personality & Social Psychology, 58*(2), 250–258.

Darwin, C. (1859). *On the origin of species by means of natural selection.* London, UK: John Murray.

Dutton, D. G., & Aron, A. P. (1974). Some evidence for heightened sexual attraction under conditions of high anxiety. *Journal of Personality & Social Psychology, 30*(4), 510–517.

Jones, D. (1995). Sexual selection, physical attractiveness, and facial neoteny: Cross-cultural evidence and implications. *Current Anthropology, 36*(5), 723–748.

Kenrick, D. T., & Keefe, R. C. (1992). Age preferences in mates reflect sex differences in reproductive strategies. *Behavioral and Brain Sciences, 15*(1), 75–133.

Lazarus, S., & Walker-Arnott (2013, August 22). *Steven Moffat: Doctor Who was "amazing" Billie Piper's show . . . she brought it back.* Radio Times: http://www.radiotimes.com/news/2013-08-22/steven-moffat-doctor-who-was-amazing-billie-pipers-show-she-brought-it-back.

Lefebvre, V. A. (2004). On sharing a pie: Modeling costly prosocial behavior. *Behavioral and Brain Sciences, 27*(4), 565–566.

Lowe, C. A., & Goldstein, J. W. (1970). Reciprocal liking and attributions of ability: Mediating effects of perceived intent and personal involvement. *Journal of Personality & Social Psychology, 16*(2), 291–297.

Mackinnon, S. P., Jordan, C. H., & Wilson, A. E. (2011). Birds of a feather sit together: Physical similarity predicts seating choice. *Personality & Social Psychology Bulletin, 37*(9), 79–8922.

Roach, M. (2008). *Bonk: The curious coupling of science and sex.* New York, NY: Norton.

Shakespeare, W. (1600). *Romeo and Juliet* (Act II, Scene 2).

Singh, D. (1993a). Adaptive significance of physical attractiveness: Role of waist-to-hip ratio. *Journal of Personality & Social Psychology, 65*(2), 293–307.

Singh, D. (1993b). Body shape and women's attractiveness: The critical role of waist-to-hip ratio. *Human Nature, 4*(3), 297–321.

Zillmann, D. (1983). Transfer of excitation in emotional behavior. In J. T. Cacioppo & R. E. Petty (Eds.), *Social psychophysiology: A sourcebook* (pp. 215–240). New York, NY: Guilford.

Notes

1. Modern episode 1–1, "Rose" (March 26, 2005).
2. Shakespeare (1600).
3. PsycINFO database search conducted May, 2016.
4. Darwin (1959).
5. Modern episode 1–1, "Rose" (March 26, 2005).
6. Lazarus & Walker-Arnott (2013).
7. Bate (2015).
8. Jones (1995).
9. Modern episode 1–1, "Rose" (March 26, 2005).
10. Modern episode 1–1, "Rose" (March 26, 2005).
11. Buss (1994).
12. Kenrick & Keefe (1992).
13. Roach (2008).
14. See, for example, Singh (1993a, 1993b).
15. Body Measurements (n.d.).
16. Bryant & Miron (2003); Zillmann (1983).
17. Dutton & Aron (1974).
18. Modern episode 1–1, "Rose" (March 26, 2005).
19. Aron & Aron (1996).
20. Aron et al. (2004).
21. Modern episode 1–1, "Rose" (March 26, 2005).
22. Aron & Aron (1986).
23. Lefebvre (2004).
24. Modern episode 1–10, "The Doctor Dances" (May 28, 2005)
25. Modern episode 2–9, "The Satan Pit" (June 10, 2006).
26. e.g., Caspi & Herbener (1990); Mackinnon et al. (2011).
27. Back et al. (2008).
28. Lowe & Goldstein (1970).

When someone wants a relationship with someone who's smart with a great personality, what does that mean? Psychology shows that both intelligence and personality are more complex and varied than such a simple description can convey.

CHAPTER ELEVEN

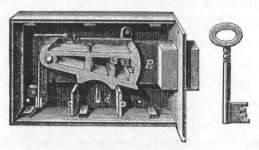

A Companion's Choice: Do Opposites Attract?

ERIN CURRIE

"Oh, Amy. You have to sort your men out. Choose, even."
—Dream Lord[1]

> *"The meeting of two personalities is like the contact of two chemical substances: If there is any reaction, both are transformed."*
> —psychiatrist Carl Jung[2]

In psychology, we attempt to answer the great questions of human behavior. Poets, politicians, and scientists of many stripes have called relationships the most difficult enigma of all. The *Who* universe is no different, with much fan discussion given to the Doctor's choice of companions.[3] After all, each companion has his or her (usually her) own unique impact on the Doctor and his adventures. The personalities of each Doctor and each companion combine to create new opportunities for humorous, challenging, heartwarming, and nerve-racking interplay, as can be the case when any two people embark on a relationship of any nature. Several of the classic Doctors have an entourage of companions, and one modern Doctor, the Eleventh, travels with a married couple. There, in addition to personality interplay between companion and Doctor, you have personality dynamics playing out among pairs, trios, or more.

The dynamic between companions Amelia "Amy" Pond and Rory Williams is different from most companion entourage arrangements in that the significance of their relationship rivals their individual relationships with the Doctor. Although the Doctor chooses to bring both Amy and Rory along with him, clearly it is Amy's choice of companion that matters most. How is a person to choose? Both personality psychology and interpersonal psychology address compatibility and attraction, helping us understand how people choose companionship and what leads to relationship satisfaction. Will Amy choose the adventurous, dashing hero or her quiet, unfailing friend? Her choice will be examined through the lenses of these two fields of study.

Individual Personalities

Personality traits are one focus of research on relationship choice. It makes intuitive sense that the repeating pattern of behaviors, thoughts, and feelings that form a person's essential character would have an impact on that person's perceived attractiveness.[4] The research corroborates this intuitive stance by showing that there are a few personality traits that are generally favored, including emotional stability and conscientiousness.[5] However, the majority of attraction research focuses not on the personality traits of an individual, but on the perception and interaction between the players' personalities. Some of the most heavily researched *personality factors*, groups of traits that tend to go together (covered in the Factor Files at the end of each section in this book), interact to influence relationship success.

Case 1: The Girl Who Waited

Amy shows high levels of emotional stability. When the Doctor first meets young Amy, she has a crack in her wall from which weird voices emanate. While other children would panic and hide under the covers, she calmly and concisely prays to Santa to send help.[6] The hallmark of this emotional stability is the capacity to deal with the task at hand without being waylaid by one's emotional reactions.[7] When the Doctor barges into her house ten years later, it is clear from her questions that she is angry. Instead, of being overwhelmed by her anger about his abandonment, however, she deals with the intruder and tries to figure out what happened to her all those years ago.[8]

Amy shows high levels of *dominance*, which is the assertion of control, in that she tends to take matters into her own hands, diving in and directly dealing with whatever situation comes her way.[9] People high in dominance prefer to make the decisions, or at least be able to influence the decision maker. Amy also shows high levels of *openness to experience*, a trait that includes seeking out new and different experiences and creativity in problem solving.[10] In the midst of danger she scans her environment and makes the best out of what is available. Openness to new ideas and experiences means that a person is better able to adapt to the reality of his or her surroundings instead of getting bogged down by preconceived notions of how things should be. One great example of these two traits in combination occurs when Amy, upon being locked below decks, grabs a cutlass and a pirate outfit and charges the pirates without regard for her lack of sword-fighting skills.[11] Any preconceptions about lack of sword-fighting skills clearly didn't stop her charge.

Extraversion is an orientation toward active engagement with, and stimulus-seeking from, the world outside oneself.[12] Amy's high level of extraversion is evident in her tendency to walk boldly into exciting experiences with less thought of risk, a facet of extraversion that researchers have labeled *surgency*.[13] People high in extraversion have less sensitivity toward risk cues and greater need for excitement than people low in extraversion, also known as *introverts*.[14] Combine that with a fair dose of stubbornness, which Big Five personality factor researchers would call low *agreeableness*, which is being more confrontational than cooperative,[15] and you have a force to be reckoned with.[16]

Case 2: The Boy Who Waited

Rory shows low openness to experience in combination with a low level of extraversion, especially with regard to the facet of *surgency*[17] (highly positive emotional reactivity). This is portrayed in Rory's ultimate goal at the beginning of the series: to build a calm, quiet life as a small-town doctor and start a family with Amy.[18] He isn't worried about saving the world, just the woman he loves and his patients. Low extraversion is also referred to as *introversion*. Research links regions of the brain involved in risk aversion to higher levels of introversion.[19] This is demonstrated by Rory's quiet demeanor. He doesn't tend to say much until something is very important to him.[20]

At the outset of Rory's adventures, he is the picture of submissiveness as he is led around by Amy.[21] He lets an impatient hospital doctor rudely dismiss his concern about a client, even in light of solid evidence supporting his concern: a picture of a client who is comatose in a hospital, but also, inexplicably, simultaneously walking his dog in the park.[22] Dear Rory is also highly conscientious, a trait generally defined as reliable, careful, and well-organized.[23] It doesn't get more reliable and devoted than a man sitting alone in a cave for two thousand years, protecting the woman he loves.[24] Rory is a combination of introversion, a low level of openness to new experiences, extreme submissiveness, and conscientiousness. Because of these traits, he is less likely to be led astray from his goals by the many wonders of the universe, unlike the Doctor, whom Rory perceives as competition for Amy.[25]

Case 3: He Who Makes Them Wait

Openness to new experiences and high levels of extraversion are this Doctor's personality calling card. He has all time and space to explore and a seemingly insatiable need for new experiences.[26] Unfortunately, this pairs with a low level of conscientiousness. He gets caught up in the excitement of the moment and forgets to keep track of things like the everyday needs of others, such as changing lightbulbs and staying in contact with people who care about you.[27] Low conscientiousness and openness to new experiences come together in the Doctor and result in a lack of planning. Although he frequently tells his companions that he has a plan, in reality his plan is more of a goal, an armful of tools, a next step, and his reliance on his ability to improvise.[28] Most folks with a high level of conscientiousness would not consider this a plan.[29]

His high level of extraversion is most notable in how much he enjoys showing off how clever he is. One element of extraversion is seeking and thriving off social reinforcement.[30] At one point he goes as far as to shout at his companions, "I'm being extremely clever up here and there's no one to stand around looking impressed. What's the point of having you all?"[31] The Eleventh Doctor is also high in social dominance. He is always directing the flow of energy of people around him, whether he is telling them what to do or influencing them without them realizing it.[32] The way his extraversion and dominance combine with a lower level of emotional stability makes traveling with him quite the exciting, action-packed ride.

Relationships

Do opposites really attract or is similarity better? Some research promotes the idea that similarities attract. A lot of the research on attraction in dating and early relationships shows that people report a preference for partners with similar personality traits, supporting the old adage that "birds of a feather flock together."[33] Other research promotes complementarity of personality as being highly attractive. This is a take on the idea that "opposites attract." These studies suggest that people seek out others who fill in the gaps of their skills, strengths, and interpersonal approaches.[34] For instance, psychologists studying dominance have found that people who consider themselves dominant respond more positively during cooperative tasks when paired with people who behave in a submissive manner and vice versa, compared to working with similar individuals.[35] Both of these matchmaking strategy "camps" get to have their say in Amy's choice.

Pair 1: Amy and the Doctor

The people in the similarities camp would find Amy's attraction to the Eleventh Doctor unsurprising because they are very much alike. They are both ready to run in and explore each new situation.[36] This behavior reflects shared high levels of openness to new experiences and extraversion.[37] Their shared trust in their ability to talk or flirt their way out of trouble reflects combined high levels of extraversion and dominance.[38] About the only significant difference between the two of them is in emotional stability. Amy takes a more practical approach, even when faced with gut-wrenching decisions.[39] Being low in emotional stability, this Doctor tends to be excitable, able to find joy in many things but also prone to immense anger and despair.[40] Add a cool blue box that can carry her to exciting new adventures through all time and space and it's no surprise that Amy considers choosing the Doctor over Rory after he saves her from the Weeping Angels.[41]

Pair 2: Amy and Rory

People in the complementarity camp would likely be cheering for Rory. He and Amy are different when it comes to almost every personality trait, and his strengths complement Amy's. First, Amy is dominant to Rory's submissive. This area of complementarity is one of the most supported by the research on relationship satisfaction.[42] Amy charges into danger and Rory faithfully follows, supports, and saves as needed.[43] This is not to say that Rory is cowardly, compared to Amy. There are just different paths to bravery. As the Last Centurion, Rory stands guard over Amy for thousands of years,[44] and he takes on numerous foes, such as the Cybermen, the Silence, and the Headless Monks to rescue Amy and their baby.[45] Their different approaches to risk-taking are due, in part, to differences in levels of extraversion.[46] When Rory takes a look at his environment, he is more likely to notice what could be dangerous.[47] Further, he is less likely to seek out risk because it isn't accompanied by a feeling of happy excitement from a new experience.[48]

Luckily for Amy and the Doctor, Rory is loyal and dependable. His high levels of conscientiousness and agreeableness mean they can count on him to get them out of whatever mess they talk him into. They can also depend on him to care for the needs of the people they encounter while they are busy trying to solve the mystery.[49]

Unfortunately, quiet, supportive strength like Rory's is often overlooked in favor of more dashing figures like the Doctor.

People often fail to appreciate approaches different from theirs. Research finds that people actually *feel* more satisfaction from a partner who is complementary to them, even though they *say* they prefer similarity. This indicates that people may not always be aware of what they really want in a partnership.[50] For Amy, it takes thinking that she has lost Rory when facing the Dream Lord for her to fully appreciate what Rory means to her.[51]

Pair 3: Amy's Boys

It isn't just Amy and the Doctor, and Amy and Rory. Rory and the Doctor have an interesting relationship as well. The complementarity folks would applaud their dynamic. The Doctor is attention-seeking and flamboyant, where Rory is quiet. The Doctor shows higher extraversion and dominance in that he rushes toward adventure and danger and takes everyone along for the ride.[52] Rory is more submissive, especially at the beginning. He prefers to consider possible dangers before rushing in.[53] Like many highly conscientious people, he would prefer to have a plan in place before taking action.[54] The Doctor's focus is on the new opportunities waiting around every corner of time and space.[55] Meanwhile, Rory's focus is on what he cares about most: the well-being of Amy and the individuals he meets on their adventures.[56] Over time, though, as predicted by the complementarity research, they come to respect and rely on each other's strengths to solve problems, most notably when Amy is in danger.[57]

The Power of Three

Happily, Amy gets to choose both and everyone wins! She chooses faithful Rory as her husband.[58] The complementarity camp is supported. Amy chooses the dashing Doctor as

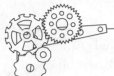

Relationship Stages

The Eleventh Doctor is the exception in the modern series by having more than one companion on an on-going basis. However, each classic Doctor up through the Fifth has an entourage for at least part of his journey. Group dynamics come into play when you go beyond the dyad.[59] Group dynamics theorist Bruce Tuckman developed a theory of how groups develop and evolve.[60]

Stage One: Forming	People in the group start to get to know each other. Although Amy knows both Rory and the Doctor, they all learn more about each other in the context of the group.[61]
Stage Two: Storming	Tension arises as people vie for roles in the group. Although the Doctor is accustomed to being in charge, he cedes that role to Amy while Rory struggles to figure out where he fits.[62]
Stage Three: Norming	Everyone settles into their roles in the group. Amy is the leader who unites them, Rory is the caretaker, and the Doctor is the brains.[63]
Stage Four: Performing	People are comfortable in their relation-ships and group roles, so they start trying new growth behaviors. The Doctor slows down and becomes more relational while Rory becomes more fierce and confi-dent. Amy, meanwhile, learns to rely on others.[64]
Stage Five: Adjourning	The group disbands, preferably when the members have grown as individuals. Amy and Rory start to talk about fully partic-ipating in their life on Earth.[65] Although they experience grief when they're finally separated from the Doctor, they move on to have separate adventures.[66]

her best friend.[67] The similarity camp is supported. Additionally, the Doctor and Rory develop a friendship based on deep mutual respect, trust, and shared interests and experiences, also supporting the complementarity premise.[68]

The complementarity research indicates that people become especially effective utilizing each other's strengths when they have a common goal.[69] Even though their methods differ, Amy, Rory, and the Doctor all want to save the day and use differing strengths to compensate for each other's various weaknesses.[70] They work together to show how powerful a complementary team can be.[71] Amy helps the doctor focus his vast knowledge of space and time, which Rory connects to the experiences of individuals caught in the crossfire. In the end it's the loss of the power of the relationship of this trio that makes it so heartbreaking when the Weeping Angels force Amy to choose after all.[72]

References

Banta, T. J., & Hetherington, M. (1963). Relations between needs of friends and fiancés. *Journal of Abnormal Psychology, 66*(4), 401–404.

Bohns, V. K., Lucas, G. M., Molden, D. C., Finkel, E. J., Coolsen, M. K., Kumashiro, M., Rusbult, C. E., & Higgins, E. T. (2013). Opposites fit: Regulatory focus complementarity and relationship well-being. *Social Cognition, 31*(1), 1–14.

Botwin, M. D., Buss, D. M., & Shackelford, T. K. (1997). Personality and mate preferences: Five factors in mate selection and marital satisfaction. *Journal of Personality, 65*(1), 107–136.

Cundiff, J. M., Smith, T. W., Butner, J., Critchfield, K. L., & Nealey-Moore, J. (2015). Affiliation and control in marital interaction: Interpersonal complementarity is present but is not associated with affect or relationship quality. *Personality & Social Psychology Bulletin, 41*(1), 35–51.

Dryer, D. C., & Horowitz, L. M. (1997). When do opposites attract? Interpersonal complementarity versus similarity. *Journal of Personality & Social Psychology, 72*(3), 592–603.

Fishman, I., & Ng, R. (2013). Error-related brain activity in extraverts: Evidence for altered response monitoring in social context. *Biological Psychology, 93*(1), 225–230.

Furler, K., Gomez, V., & Grob, A. (2014). Personality perceptions and relationship satisfaction in couples. *Journal of Research in Personality, 50*, 33–41.

Johnson, D. L., Wiebe, J. S., Gold, S. M., Andreassen, N. C., Hichwa, R. D., Watkins, G. L., & Boles Ponto, L. L. (1999). Cerebral blood flow and personality: A Positron Emission Tomography study. *American Journal of Psychiatry, 156*(2), 252–257.

Jung, C. G. (1933/1995). *Modern man in search of a soul* (5th ed.). Orlando, FL: Harcourt.

Little, B. R. (2014). *Me, myself, and us: The science of personality and the art of well-being.* New York, NY: Public Affairs.

Markey, P. M., & Kurtz, J. E. (2006). Increasing acquaintances and complementarity of behavioral styles and personality traits among college roommates. *Personality & Social Psychology Bulletin, 32*(7), 907–916.

Markey, P. M., & Markey, C. N. (2007). Romantic ideals, romantic obtainment, and relationship experiences: The complementarity of interpersonal traits among romantic partners. *Journal of Social and Personal Relationships, 24*(4), 517–533.

McCrae, R. R. (1994). Openness to experience: Expanding the boundaries of Factor V. *European Journal of Personality, 8*(4), 251–272.

McGlynn, R. P., Harding, D. J., & Cottle, J. L. (2009). Individual-group discontinuity in group-individual interactions: Does size matter? *Group Processes & Intergroup Relations, 12*(1), 129–143.

Patrick, S. (2013, November 19). Best of 'Doctor Who' 50th anniversary poll: Ten favorite companions. BBC America: http://www.bbcamerica.com/anglophenia/2013/11/best-doctor-50th-anniversary-poll-10-favorite-companions.

Schmitt, D. P. (2002). Personality, attachment and sexuality related to dating relationship outcomes: Contrasting three perspectives on personal attribute interaction. *British Journal of Social Psychology, 41*(4), 589–610.

Tuckman, B. W., & Jensen, M. A. (1977). Stages of small-group development revisited. *Group & Organization Studies, 2*(4), 419–427.

Wacker, J., Chavanon, M., & Stemmler, G. (2006). Investigating the dopaminergic basis of extraversion in humans: A multilevel approach. *Journal of Personality & Social Psychology, 91*(1), 171–187.

Notes

1. Modern episode 5–7, "Amy's Choice" (May 15, 2010).
2. Jung (1933/1995), p. 49.
3. Patrick (2013).
4. Schmitt (2002).
5. Furler et al. (2014).
6. Modern episode 5–1, "The Eleventh Hour" (April 3, 2010).
7. Botwin et al. (1997).
8. Modern episode 5–1, "The Eleventh Hour" (April 3, 2010).
9. Dryer & Horowitz (1997).
10. McCrae (1994).
11. Modern episode 6–3, "The Curse of the Black Spot" (May 7, 2011).
12. Little (2014).
13. Wacker et al. (2006); Botwin et al. (1997).
14. Fishman & Ng (2013); Wacker et al. (2006).
15. Botwin et al. (1997).
16. Modern episode 6–10, "The Girl Who Waited" (September 10, 2011).
17. Botwin et al. (1997).
18. Modern episode 5–7, "Amy's Choice" (May 15, 2010).
19. Johnson et al. (1999).
20. Modern episode 5–6, "Vampires of Venice" (May 8, 2010).
21. Modern episode 6–8, "Let's Kill Hitler" (August 27, 2011).
22. Modern episode 5–1, "The Eleventh Hour" (April 3, 2010).
23. Botwin et al. (1997).
24. Modern episode 5–13, "The Big Bang" (June 26, 2010).
25. Wacker et al. (2006).

26. Modern episode 7–4, "The Power of Three" (September 22, 2012).
27. Modern episode 7–2, "Dinosaurs on a Spaceship" (September 8, 2012).
28. Modern episode 5–13, "The Big Bang" (June 26, 2010).
29. Botwin et al. (1997).
30. Fishman & Ng (2013).
31. Modern episode 6–1, "The Impossible Astronaut" (April 23, 2011).
32. Modern episode 6–6, "The Almost People" (May 28, 2011).
33. Botwin et al. (1997); Markey & Markey (2007).
34. Bohns et al. (2013).
35. Dryer & Horowitz (1997).
36. Modern episode 5–2, "The Beast Below" (April 10, 2010).
37. Botwin et al. (1997); Wacker et al. (2006).
38. Fishman & Ng (2013).
39. Modern episode 5–7, "Amy's Choice" (May 15, 2010).
40. Modern episode 7–5, "The Angels Take Manhattan" (September 29, 2012).
41. Modern episode 5–5, "Flesh and Stone" (May 1, 2010).
42. Markey & Markey (2007).
43. Modern episode 6–5, "The Rebel Flesh" (May 21, 2011).
44. Modern episode 5–13, "The Big Bang" (June 26, 2010).
45. Modern episode 6–7, "A Good Man Goes to War" (June 4, 2011).
46. Wacker et al. (2006).
47. Johnson et al. (1999).
48. Wacker et al. (2006).
49. Modern episode 6–5, "The Rebel Flesh" (May 21, 2011).
50. Dryer & Horowitz (1997).
51. Modern episode 5–7, "Amy's Choice" (May 15, 2010).
52. Wacker et al. (2006).
53. Modern episode 6–5, "The Rebel Flesh" (May 21, 2011).
54. Botwin et al. (1997).
55. Modern episode 7–4, "The Power of Three" (September 22, 2012).
56. Modern episode 5–9, "Cold Blood" (May 29, 2010).
57. Bohns et al. (2013).
58. Modern episode 5–7, "Amy's Choice" (May 15, 2010).
59. McGlynn et al. (2009).
60. Tuckman & Jensen (1977).
61. Modern episode 5–1, "The Eleventh Hour" (April 3, 2010).
62. Modern episode 5–6, "Vampires of Venice (May 8, 2010).
63. Modern episode 5–13, "The Big Bang" (June 26, 2010).
64. Modern episode 6–7, "A Good Man Goes to War" (June 4, 2011).
65. Modern episode 7–4, "The Power of Three" (September 22, 2012).
66. Modern episode 7–5, "The Angels Take Manhattan" (September 29, 2 012).
67. Modern episode 6–13, "The Wedding of River Song" (October, 1 2011).
68. Modern episode 6–7, "A Good Man Goes to War" (June 4, 2011).
69. Bohns et al. (2013).
70. Bohns et al. (2013).
71. Modern episode 7–4, "The Power of Three" (September 22, 2012).
72. Modern episode 7–5, "The Angels Take Manhattan" (September 29, 2012).

Factor File Three

The Five Factors—
Adventures in the OCEAN

TRAVIS LANGLEY

Researchers keep assigning different names to our personality factors, our clusters of traits that tend to go together, based on how the researchers each interpret the mix of traits they see. Different people, focusing on different details and patterns in how the Doctor acts, refer to the Doctor as Professor, Spaceman, Old One, Skipper, Oncoming Storm, Destroyer of Worlds, Fancy Pants, Grandad, or Pops,[1] and they may all be right. A single version of the Doctor can be Caretaker, Proconsul, Predator, Mad Monk, and Raggedy Man all in one,[2] and a single individual can relate to the Doctor as both her sweetie and her damsel in distress.[3] Each epithet is based on a relatively small number of characteristics and experiences.

Finding a single word that perfectly encompasses every single trait in a specific person or within one personality factor might not be possible. Even when researchers agree on how many global factors exist, they refer to the overall list of factors by an assortment of names: OCEAN, CANOE, Pentagon, five-factor model (FFM), and most commonly "the Big Five."[4]

The Power of Five

Over the course of many studies to determine how many factors best sum up individual personality, the number that turned up most often was five.[5] In an extensive review of the published research, personality researchers R. R. McCrae and P. T. Costa concluded that this number best fit all the available evidence.[6] They gave their version of the *five-factor model* the acronym *OCEAN* for the names they assigned the factors: openness, conscientiousness, extraversion, agreeableness, neuroticism. Analyzing the constellation of traits that H. J. Eysenck had called psychoticism,[7] McCrae and Costa saw not a single factor but instead identified two separate factors within it, conscientiousness and agreeableness.[8]

Conscientiousness
Information bombards us. Our brains filter much of it out, and then whatever reaches our awareness, we sort in different ways. So much information assaults the Doctor's senses that he feels it might drive him mad.[9]

At one extreme is the person who obsesses over every detail and strives to be orderly, organized, and efficient in dealing with every item, even if attention to detail might mean missing the big picture. At the other extreme is the reckless, disorganized person who takes shortcuts and hopes for the best. The

Eleventh Doctor, in particular, prefers to "talk very fast, hope something good happens, take the credit—that's usually how it works."[10]

The cognitive abilities to receive and store information (*crystallized intelligence*) or make use of it (*fluid intelligence*) are not the same thing as personality traits. Despite his attention to some details, the Doctor is oblivious to many others. "The Doctor has no idea of time," says the First Doctor's companion, Dodo Chaplet. This strikes her as paradoxical and "rather funny" for such an experienced time traveler;[11] fellow Time Lord Romana similarly tells the Fourth Doctor that he's always getting the time wrong;[12] and Tegan calls the Fifth Doctor less accurate than a broken clock.[13] Spontaneity, haste, inattention, annoyance with perfectionism, unreliability in a number of areas, and lack of thoroughness or long-term goals suggest someone low in conscientiousness.

Regardless of his many signs of carelessness, though, he certainly can persevere. Persistence and determination are aspects of conscientiousness. Even though a disheartened Eighth Doctor loses sight of his promise to "never give up, never give in"[14] when he chooses to regenerate as a warrior and be the "Doctor no more,"[15] giving up is an exception in his personality, not his typical characteristic. *Personality* refers to behaviors typical of us, rather than the aberrations. In time the Doctor rediscovers hope[16] and then shows greater commitment and persistence than ever before when he stays on Trenzalore for nearly a millennium, rather than giving in.[17] Throughout most of his regenerations, despite his lack of conscientiousness in many other ways, his resolve remains one of his most enduring features.

Examples of Conscientiousness Traits
   Achievement Motivation
   Adherence to Schedules
   Attention to Detail
   Competitiveness
   Controlling Nature
   Dutifulness
   Lack of Spontaneity
   Orderliness
   Organization
   Perfectionism
   Perseverance
   Precision
   Preparation
   Reliability
   Self-Control
   Thoroughness
   Time Awareness

Agreeableness

A person may be outgoing, assertive, talkative, and lively without being nice at all. The First, Sixth, and Twelfth Doctors strike many people they encounter as being most disagreeable, and every Doctor may rub people the wrong way. Agreeable individuals want to help others and feel great compassion and concern for them, qualities that often drive the Doctor, but he also tends to be argumentative, sarcastic, insulting, and indifferent to how many people feel about him. The most extremely agreeable person wants peace at any price and prioritizes getting along with others above all else. The Doctor stays ready to ruffle feathers.

Examples of Agreeableness Traits
Compliance
Concern for Others
Cooperation
Encouragment
Modesty
Need to Be Liked
Need to Get Along
Optimism about People
Softheartedness
Sympathy
Time for Others
Trust

Wherein Lie Right and Wrong?

The five-factor model of personality has become one of the best-known tenets of personality psychology. The Big Five carry big clout. Even so, researchers continue to examine our constellations of traits to try to account for all the mind's dark matter, the parts of us that the five-factor map of known mental space may have left out. Some say that it overlooked one of the most important dimensions of human behavior and history—good and evil.[18] For example, a highly agreeable person might do many good things to earn someone's approval, but then again, so might an evil minion.

Factor File Four: "The Six Factors—A Good Man?" takes a look at how we might define the best and worst in us all.

References

Book et al. (2016); Lee & Ashton (2005); Lee & Ashton (2012); Međedović, J., & Petrović, (2015).

Costa, P. T., & McCrae, R. R., Jr. (1992). Four ways five factors are basic. *Personality & Individual Differences, 13*(6), 667–673.

Eysenck, H. J. (1992). Four ways five factors are *not* basic. *Personality & Individual Differences, 13*(6), 653–665.

Fiske, D. W. (1949). Consistency of the factorial structures of personality rating from different sources. *Journal of Abnormal Psychology*, 44(3), 329-344.

Funder, D. (2001). Personality. *Annual Review of Psychology*, 52, 197-221.

Goldberg, L. R. (1982). From Ace to Zombie: Some explorations in the language of personality. In C. D. Spielberger & J. N. Butchers (Eds.), *Advances in personality assessment* (Vol. 1, pp. 203–234). Hillsdale, NJ: Erlbaum.

McCrae, R. R., & Costa, P. T., Jr. (1987). Validation of the five-factor model of personality across instruments and observers. *Journal of Personality & Social Psychology, 52*(1), 81–90.

Tupes, E. C., & Christal, R. E. (1961). Recurrent personality factors based on trait ratings. *USAF ASD Technical Report* (No. 61–97). Lackland Air Force Base, TX: U.S. Air Force.

Notes

1. Classic serial 24–4, *Dragonfire* (November 3–December 7, 1987); modern episode 4–2, "Fires of Pompeii" (April 12, 2008); classic serial *The Mysterious Planet* (September 6–27, 1986); audio play *Terror Firma* (August, 2005); modern episode 1–13, "The Parting of the Ways" (June 18, 2005); modern episode 4–14, "Journey's End" (July 5, 2008); classic anniversary special, *The Five Doctors* (November 25, 1983); anniversary special, "The Day of the Doctor" (November 23, 2013); classic serial 4–2, *The Tenth Planet* (October 8–29, 1966).
2. Christmas special, "The Doctor, the Widow, and the Wardrobe" (December 25, 2011); modern episodes 5–1, "The Eleventh Hour" (April 3, 2010); 7–1, "Asylum of the Daleks" (September 1, 2012); 7–6 "The Bells of St. John" (March 30, 2013); 7–12, "Nightmare in Silver" (May 11, 2013).
3. Modern episode 4–8, "Silence in the Library" (May 31, 2008); Christmas special, "The Husbands of River Song" (December 25, 2015).
4. Goldberg (1982).
5. Fiske (1949); Funder (2001); Goldberg (1982); Tupes & Christal (1961).
6. McCrae & Costa (1987).
7. Eysenck (1992).
8. Costa & McCrae (1992).
9. Modern episode 1–13, "The Parting of the Ways" (June 18, 2005).
10. Christmas special, "The Time of the Doctor" (December 25, 2013).
11. Classic serial, *The Savages*, pt. 1 (May 28, 1966).
12. Classic serial, *Shada*, unfinished due to technicians' strike (scheduled for January–February, 1980); eventually produced as Eighth Doctor audio play (December 10, 2005).
13. Classic serial, *The Visitation*, pt. 1 (February 15, 1982).

14. Anniversary special, "The Day of the Doctor" (November 23, 2013).

15. Minisode, *The Night of the Doctor* (November 14, 2015).

16. Anniversary special, "The Day of the Doctor" (November 23, 2013).

17. Christmas special, "The Time of the Doctor" (December 25, 2013).

18. Book et al. (2016); Lee & Ashton (2005, 2012); Međedović, J., & Petrović (2015).

Anything we have can potentially become part of how we see ourselves and how others see us, too. So can all the things we have lost.

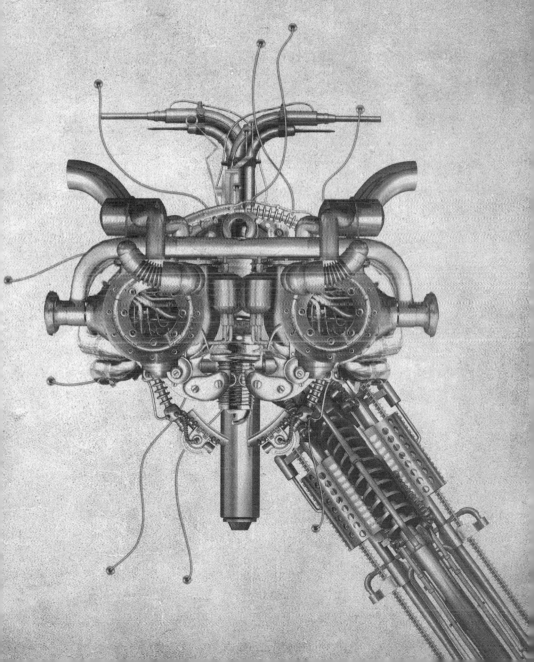

Part Four

Lost Things

How we face death is inherently part of how we face life. We are mortals who can imagine immortality, dread our own demise, and fear for the loss of others. We all outlive some who matter to us. Which is healthier—running from mortality or coming to terms with it?

CHAPTER TWELVE

Death and the Doctor: Interview on How Immortals Face Mortality

JANINA SCARLET
AND AARON SAGERS

"I have lost things you will never understand."
—Eleventh Doctor[1]

"The more unlived your life, the greater your death anxiety. The more you fail to experience your life fully, the more you will fear death."
—psychologist Irvin Yalom[2]

Death is inevitable. Fear of death is universal, usually beginning at an early age when children first observe the impermanence of living things. When they question their parents about death, they may receive little guidance and are often asked simply not to think about death.[3] Death can be a taboo topic about which some people may be afraid to speak out loud or at all.[4] Although the Doctor is able to regenerate, which may prolong his life, he fears for his own life at times and seems uncomfortable with the subject of his companions' mortality.[5] Is this fear of death natural and healthy, and if so, what are some ways in which a person may be able to reduce his or her mortality fears?

Fear of Death

Fear of death can manifest in different ways, from feeling overwhelming anxiety to taking extreme risks. For some people, trying to overcome the fear of death may involve watching scary movies or playing violent video games. For others, it may involve engaging in potentially life-threatening sports such as skydiving.[6] After experiencing the death of a loved one, an individual may no longer wish to risk getting into situations that may lead to witnessing the death of another being. This may result in the individual's avoidance of people or animals who are nearing death or avoidance of talking about death. Each of these forms of avoidance, though seemingly helpful in the short term, may lead to added emotional suffering in the long term.[7] For the Doctor, who has both experienced death in the form of regeneration and lost many people in his life to death, this is an especially painful topic.

We asked actors who played the Doctor and River, two characters who are able to regenerate and outlive those around them, how those characters face mortality.

> **Aaron Sagers:** How does the Doctor view death?
> **David Tennant (Tenth Doctor):** He's running away from the mortality of the people he spends time with. I don't think he likes it when he has to face up to it. I thought that was really well done in

Toby Whithouse's script with the school reunion story.[8] I thought it was a really clever thing to do, to have a companion who had got a bit older—and for Rose to see that. The interview between those two characters where she's looking [at Sarah Jane] and goes, "Oh, I see what happens; I get dumped because you can't face up to the fact that we get old and you don't." It is a great thing to play as a character note.

The types of therapeutic interventions that are best suited to help people overcome the fear of death include existential therapy and humanistic therapy. Whereas *existential therapy* seeks to resolve the conflict many humans have about their mortality and the meaning of their lives, *humanistic therapy* focuses on acceptance of unchangeable struggles in order to foster personal growth.[9] Psychologist Irvin Yalom, known for his work in both existential psychology and humanistic psychology, suggests that for most people it is not easy to live with a constant awareness of death. He adds that as an individual goes through each stage of life, he or she may experience a new surge of death anxiety.[10] As the average human life span grows longer and the species gets closer to perpetuating its members through cybernetics or replication via artificial intelligence, perspectives on death may change and each period as human, cyborg, or artificial intelligence (AI) may be seen as a different stage in life; however, every transition or form of renewal may be as dreaded as death by some because the previous version will still die. By this account, regenerations may be thought of as different stages of the character's life, with each one possibly affecting his or her struggle with death. How will these characters change?

Matt Smith (Eleventh Doctor): When one person dies and another person comes along, you're not changing. It is just the same bloke getting a new face. So I don't know. I always compare it to Hamlet, weirdly enough. I think the actor basically brings all his own makeup. All his own foibles, all his own humors, all his own silliness, really.

Sagers: How did River change over time and through her own regeneration?

Alex Kingston (River Song/Melody Pond): I don't know if she did change over time. She has shown different facets of her personality over the years. You certainly got to see a bad side of her, and then you see a vulnerable side. I don't think she necessarily changed, it's just that the audience has gotten more opportunity to learn more about her.

When asked about the saddest Doctor regeneration, Matt Smith voiced an opinion similar to that of many viewers:[11] "Definitely David's."

Grief

Perhaps even more than his own death, the Doctor fears the deaths of those closest to him. In particular, the Doctor fears losing his friends and companions.[12] In fact, when one or more of his friends leave him, the Doctor may go through years of isolation and grief, as the Eleventh Doctor did when he lost his longtime companions Amy and Rory.[13] Such prolonged grief, if untreated, may lead to an individual's withdrawal from his or her support groups; this isolation often exacerbates the effects of grief. In addition, failure to process a loss one has experienced

A Model of Grief

In 1969 Swiss psychiatrist Dr. Elisabeth Kübler-Ross published a book, *On Death and Dying,* based on her work with patients with terminal illnesses. In that book Kübler-Ross identified the five stages of grief that she observed:

1. **Denial**—refusing to believe that an individual or a loved one is going to die or has passed away. Often people believe that someone has made some kind of a mistake and that the situation will resolve itself. For example, after River's death, the Doctor ignores her virtual presence because he seems to be in denial about the fact that she is dead.[14]

2. **Anger**—blaming someone for the loss. After Clara dies, the Twelfth Doctor is furious and begins to make threats to other Time Lords.[15]

3. **Bargaining**—making an offer to reduce the likelihood of the tragic outcome, such as when the Tenth Doctor downloads the deceased River into a computer[16] or the Twelfth Doctor tries to trick the universe into letting Clara continue her life.[17]

4. **Depression**—feeling tremendous loss or sadness after the realization that the death cannot be prevented. The Doctor sulks for a time in nineteenth-century London after losing Amy and Rory.[18]

5. **Acceptance**—making peace with the inevitable loss, such as when the Doctor finally tells River good-bye.[19]

may lead to a number of mental and physical problems, such as depression, chronic pain, sleep disorders, and other illnesses.[20]

People's grief reactions can often be predicted by their functioning before they experience loss. For example, mothers who reported fearing for their own deaths and the premature deaths of others were more likely to experience prolonged or complicated grief (grief lasting more than six months that causes significant impairment in a person's functioning and does not naturally lessen over time).[21] In addition, preloss dependency on the individual is more likely to lead to prolonged grief as opposed to acceptance of death, which may lead to death resilience.[22] Finally, guilt over the deaths of others and avoidance of processing that guilt may prolong an individual's grief.[23]

> **Matt Smith:** I think that's very interesting. I think there is so much about that. One of the things I really gravitated toward, actually, was the blood on his hands and the guilt he carries. That is sort of why, for me anyway, there was always the sense of joviality—of him being upward and spritely. Because he is sort of fighting this undercurrent of darkness constantly.

Acceptance and Meaning

Some research studies suggest that the age at death and the specific circumstances surrounding it are most responsible for the way one will cope with loss.[24] On the other hand, other studies suggest that acceptance of death and finding meaning in the tragedy are most predictive of resilience.[25] In fact, *terror management theory* explains how a person may overcome inner conflict when faced with the fear of death, suggesting that close friendships may serve as a buffer against death terror.[26] Specifically, scientists suggest that humans' fear of their own mortality may encourage them to maintain close friendships, which may make an individual feel less anxious about his or her death.[27] Other studies find that close friendships, such as those the Doctor maintains with his companions, may actually reduce the risk of stress-related deaths, possibly because of the physical and emotional benefits of social connection.[28] It is possible that the Doctor may be trying to manage his own death-related fears by maintaining close friendships. However, he tends to avoid remaining in relationships in which his friends are nearing death.[29]

> **Sagers:** Does [the Doctor] view human life as
> precious?
> **Smith:** Yeah, but he is always sort of leaving people
> behind. Think of all the clerics and all those
> random characters that sort of get locked behind.
> With David's Doctor, when he lost Rose, it was
> a complete nightmare for Martha. Rose felt, as a
> viewer, like such a sort linchpin for Number 10.
> And it is weird why he admires humanity so much:
> Because people do spend all of their lives together,
> and he never really gets to do that with anyone.

The Doctor seemingly struggles with establishing close connections with his companions, and this may be the reason for his struggle with death acceptance. In fact, death acceptance and death fears appear to be related in that both depend on one's perceived life meaning.[30] Whereas some people may have uncompleted life missions or the perception of an unfulfilled life, people who believe that they have lived a meaningful life are more likely to accept their death.[31] This was the case for the

Face of Boe. The Face of Boe appears to be an older version of
Captain Jack Harkness, who can't die except from old age. In
his last moments the Doctor is devastated to witness his friend's
death, but the Face of Boe greets his fate with acceptance.[32]

Scientists have identified different types of death acceptance,
including neutral, approach, and escape.[33] The *neutral* acceptance of death appears to be the healthiest approach and entails
not fearing death but instead allowing it to happen as and when
it should, as does the Face of Boe.[34] The *approach* acceptance is
one in which an individual is happy to die/regenerate, often
as a result of a belief in an afterlife. This seems to be how
the War Doctor greets his own regeneration when he says that
he is "wearing a bit thin" and allows the regeneration to take
place.[35] With *escape* acceptance, an individual wishes to die to
escape the pain and suffering he or she is enduring. For example, Vincent van Gogh wishes to die and takes his own life to
escape the deep emotional suffering he experiences.[36] Overall,
death acceptance, especially neutral and approach acceptance
types, appears to be related to better coping with death. In
contrast, the fear of death is more closely related to depression
and poorer coping with mortality.[37]

> **Kingston:** [The Doctor] loves humankind. He
>   doesn't know exactly why he has this affinity with
>   human beings, but he does. He wants to save them,
>   and that's very powerful.
> **Smith:** And any central character that is essentially
>   the kind of superhero of the piece that fixes the
>   world with a toaster and a ball of string. . . . That's
>   how he saves the day: through being mad. That's
>   sort of brilliant.
> **Kingston:** He does it with his smarts, not with guns.
> **Smith:** He is a pacifist, really.

Conquering the Fear of Death

The interviews, the episodes, and the research studies all seem to suggest the same message: Making meaning of one's life is most important in reducing one's fear of one's own death as well as allowing the individual to cope with the deaths of others.[38] When someone, such as the Doctor, avoids getting close to people for fear of losing them, he or she is more likely to experience prolonged grief and depression after a loss.[39] In contrast, acceptance of one's mortality and the mortality of others, as is demonstrated by the War Doctor,[40] is more likely to allow a person to cope better with a loss.[41]

References

Barr, P., & Cacciatore, J. (2008). Personal fear of death and grief in bereaved mothers. *Death Studies, 32*(5), 445–460.

Bonanno, G. A., Wortman, C. B., Lehman, . . . & Nesse, R. M. (2002). Resilience to loss and chronic grief: A prospective study from preloss to 18-months postloss. *Journal of Personality & Social Psychology, 83*(5), 1150.

Center for Substance Abuse Treatment. (1999). Brief interventions and brief therapies for substance abuse. In *Treatment improvement protocol series* (no. 34, pp. 105–119). Rockville, MD: Substance Abuse and Mental Health Services Administration.

Doctor Who Amino (2015, June 20). *Regeneration.* Doctor Who Amino. http://www .aminoapps.com/page/doctor-who/4815354/regeneration.

Doctor Who Answers (2012). *Saddest regeneration.* Doctor Who Answers. http://doctorwho .answers.wikia.com/wiki/Forum:Saddest_Regeneration.

Karekla, M., & Constantinou, M. (2010). Religious coping and cancer: Proposing an acceptance and commitment therapy approach. *Cognitive & Behavioral Practice, 17*(4), 371–381.

Kastenbaum, R. (Ed.). (2000). *The psychology of death.* New York, NY: Springer.

Keesee, N. J., Currier, J. M., & Neimeyer, R. A. (2008). Predictors of grief following the death of one's child: The contribution of finding meaning. *Journal of Clinical Psychology, 64*(10), 1145–1163.

Kübler-Ross E. (1969). *On death and dying.* London, UK: Routledge.

Mikulincer, M., Florian, V., & Hirschberger, G. (2004). The terror of death and the quest for love: An existential perspective on close relationships. In J. Greenberg, S. L. Koole, T. Pyszczynski, J. Greenberg, S. L. Koole, & T. Pyszczynski (Eds.), *Handbook of experimental existential psychology* (pp. 287–304). New York, NY: Guilford.

Miles, M. S., & Demi, A. S. (1992). A comparison of guilt in bereaved parents whose children died by suicide, accident, or chronic disease. *Omega: Journal of Death & Dying, 24*(3), 203–215.

Plumb, J. C., Orsillo, S. M., & Luterek, J. A. (2004). A preliminary test of the role of experiential avoidance in post-event functioning. *Journal of Behavior Therapy & Experimental Psychiatry, 35*(3), 245–257.

Poulin, M. J., Brown, S. L., Dillard, A. J., & Smith, D. M. (2013). Giving to others and the association between stress and mortality. *American Journal of Public Health, 103*(9), 1649–1655.

Shatan, C. F. (1973). The grief of soldiers: Vietnam combat veterans' self-help movement. *American Journal of Orthopsychiatry, 43*(4), 640–653.

Toblin, R. L., Riviere, L. A., Thomas, J. L., Adler, A. B., Kok, B. C., & Hoge, C. W. (2012). Grief and physical health outcomes in U.S. soldiers returning from combat. *Journal of Affective Disorders, 136*(3), 469–475.

Ware, B. (2012). *The top five regrets of the dying: A life transformed by the dearly departing.* Carlsbad, CA: Hay House.

Wong, P. T., Reker, G. T., & Gesser, G. (1994). Death Attitude Profile—Revised: A multidimensional measure of attitudes toward death (pp. 121–128). In R. A. Niemeyer (Ed.), *Death anxiety handbook: Research, instrumentation, and application.* Washington, DC: Taylor & Francis.

Yalom, I. (2008). *From staring at the sun: Overcoming the terror of death.* San Francisco, CA: Jossey-Bass.

Notes

1. Modern episode 7–7, "The Rings of Akhaten" (April 6, 2013).
2. Yalom (2008), p. 49.
3. Yalom (2008).
4. Kastenbaum (2000).
5. e.g., modern episode 2–3, "School Reunion" (April 29, 2006).
6. Yalom (2008).
7. Plumb et al. (2004); Yalom (2008).
8. Modern episode 2–3, "School Reunion" (April 26, 2006).
9. Center for Substance Abuse Treatment (1999).
10. Yalom (2008).
11. e.g., Doctor Who Amino (2015); Doctor Who Answers (2012).
12. e.g., modern episode 2–3, "School Reunion" (April 29, 2006).
13. e.g., Christmas special, "The Snowmen" (December 25, 2012).
14. Modern episode 7–13, "The Name of the Doctor" (May 18, 2013).
15. Modern episode 9–11, "Heaven Sent" (November 28, 2015).
16. Modern episode 4–9, "Forest of the Dead" (June 7, 2008).
17. Modern episode 9–12, "Hell Bent" (December 5, 2015).
18. Christmas special, "The Snowmen" (December 25, 2012).
19. Modern episode 7–13, "The Name of the Doctor" (May 18, 2013).
20. Shatan (1973); Toblin et al. (2012).
21. Barr & Cacciatore (2008).
22. Bonanno et al. (2002).
23. Miles & Demi (1992).
24. Keesee et al. (2008).
25. Keesee et al. (2008); Mikulincer et al. (2004).
26. Mikulincer et al. (2004).
27. Mikulincer et al. (2004).
28. Poulin et al. (2013).

29. e.g., modern episodes 2–3, "School Reunion" (April 29, 2006); 7–5, "The Angels
    Take Manhattan" (September 29, 2012).
30. Wong et al. (1994).
31. Ware (2012).
32. Modern episode 3–3, "Gridlock" (April 14, 2007).
33. Wong et al. (1994).
34. Modern episode 3–3, "Gridlock" (April 14, 2007).
35. Anniversary special, "The Day of the Doctor" (November 23, 2013).
36. Modern episode 5–10, "Vincent and the Doctor" (June 5, 2010).
37. Wong et al. (1994).
38. Mikulincer et al. (2004); Poulin et al. (2013); Wong at el. (1994).
39. Bonanno et al. (2002).
40. Anniversary special, "The Day of the Doctor" (November 23, 2013).
41. Wong et al. (1994); Yalom (2008).

Posttraumatic stress disorder differs a bit from common conceptions of it. Not every trauma produces posttraumatic stress, and not everyone who suffers it suffers the same way. When does a person who has experienced many traumas hurt the most? Which is the straw that breaks?

CHAPTER THIRTEEN

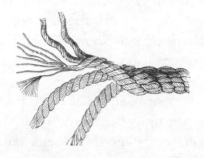

Post-Time War Stress Disorder

KRISTIN ERICKSON AND MATT MUNSON, WITH STEPHEN PRESCOTT AND TRAVIS LANGLEY

"We lost. Everyone lost. They're all gone now. My family. My friends."
—Tenth Doctor[1]

"Guilt is perhaps the most painful companion of death."
—psychiatrist Elisabeth Kübler-Ross[2]

A person can experience trauma without developing post-traumatic stress disorder (PTSD). In fact, soldiers, first responders, and people living in war zones can experience many traumatic events without developing it, although their odds certainly increase.[3] When the television program *Doctor Who* returned after a long period of cancellation, the Doctor returns as a man suffering a deep psychological wound after a great trauma. The mere suggestion of the Time War nearly brings the Ninth Doctor to tears.[4] Avoiding or getting upset by a topic or a stimulus can indicate many different difficulties with or without PTSD.[5] Actual diagnosis requires much more information. Details emerge over time, but it is not until the War Doctor, the incarnation of the Doctor who participates in the Time War, appears that viewers learn how he decided he would have to destroy all Daleks and Time Lords to end the war and save the universe,[6] and it is this cataclysmic event that ultimately shapes the modern Doctor into the person he becomes from the Ninth Doctor onward.

Diagnostic Criteria: Who Suffers from PTSD?

Myths and misconceptions about PTSD abound. Despite the volume of available information, many people misunderstand what posttraumatic stress disorder is, along with the when, where, why, who, and how of it.[7] For one thing, the majority of people exposed to events that qualify as severe trauma do not develop it, and not all traumas affect people equally. Tragedy of human design (e.g., murder, rape, war) leads to PTSD more often than do other traumatic events (e.g., accidents, natural disasters).[8] *Survivor guilt* (feeling guilt for surviving when others did not) and other forms of trauma-related guilt make PTSD more likely and complicate its treatment,[9] although guilt can help some individuals experience *posttraumatic growth* in that they find purpose, grow as people, and accomplish good things.[10] Impressed by how well the Tenth and Eleventh Doctors handle a UNIT/Zygon conflict, the War Doctor speculates that guilt may make the Doctor a better man and save many lives.[11]

The American Psychiatric Association's *Diagnostic and Statistical Manual of Mental Disorders* (a.k.a. the *DSM-5* for its fifth edition[12]) lists a specific set of criteria that must be met for a person to qualify as having PTSD. The event that ends the Time War is clearly traumatic (meeting criterion A), but so are many other events in the Doctor's millennia-long life. Whether he then has PTSD therefore depends on his personal reactions in terms of how often, how severely, and how many of the other criteria (listed as B through H in the DSM-5) he meets:

A. The patient has experienced or witnessed or was confronted with an unusually traumatic event.

B. The patient repeatedly relives the event.

C. The patient repeatedly avoids trauma-related stimuli and has a numbing of general responsiveness.

D. Negative alterations in cognitions and mood are associated with the traumatic event.

E. The patient has symptoms of hyperarousal that were not present before the traumatic event.

F. The duration of the symptoms is longer than one month.

G. The symptoms cause clinically important distress or impair functioning in occupational, social, or personal aspects of life.

H. The disturbance is not attributable to the physiological effects of a substance or any other medical condition.

Many of these symptoms have a number of qualifiers (the applicable ones are discussed below) that can limit when a professional would consider them symptomatic in the Doctor or anyone else.

A. Trauma

The DSM-5 lists qualifiers for this criterion: The event involves actual or threatened death or serious physical injury to the patient or to others, and the patient felt intense fear, horror, or helplessness. War is undisputedly traumatic. Combat, carnage, and potential catastrophe for the entire cosmos[13] ultimately push the War Doctor to make a decision that brings an end to the war and seems to result in both sides of the conflict being wiped from existence.[14]

B. Reliving the Trauma

For a PTSD diagnosis to apply, the DSM–5 requires that the patient relive the event repeatedly in at least one of a set of specific ways. The Doctor experiences at least two of them: flashbacks and intrusive, distressing recollections. A *flashback* consists of mentally reliving trauma, however briefly, so vividly that the individual feels as though the traumatic event is recurring.[15] According to Clara Oswald, the Eleventh Doctor talks about the Time War "all the time,"[16] indicating that the version of the Doctor who tries hardest to forget actually has frequent recollections. Deliberately trying to avoid thinking about something can at times paradoxically make an individual think about aspects of it even more while keeping that person from finding a healthy way to process distress.[17] These do not appear to happen to him as often as other intrusive recollections, which are also distressing.

Combined, the Doctor's occasional flashbacks[18] and having recollections about the Time War "all the time" meet this criterion for PTSD.

C. Avoiding Reminders

Avoiding trauma-related stimuli is practically a core competency for the Doctor. When a representative of the Forest of Cheem expresses her sorrow over the Ninth Doctor's distress because she knows that he is the last of his people, he shows only a flash of sadness before he snaps back to the task at hand of saving the station.[19] This Doctor, more than any other, tries to live in the moment. Present-focused people experience less depression than do those who ruminate over the past and less anxiety than do those who fret about the future.[20] For some people who are trying to avoid depression and anxiety without distorting reality, focusing on the present can be a coping strategy[21] Focusing on the present while refusing to think about a prior trauma may provide some short-term relief, but it can worsen symptoms in the long term when an individual has avoided facing stressful facts and feelings—as is seen in too many combat veterans.[22]

The Ninth Doctor's first line of dialogue on screen is telling: "Run!"[23] Running from the past and from things that bother him has been a consistent part of the Doctor's behavior to the point that it is a *central trait*, a defining quality that affects much of an individual's behavior.[24] In childhood, he runs from secrets he learns in the Time Lords' Matrix[25] and from "the raw power of time and space" he beholds in the Untempered Schism at age eight. "I never stopped."[26] The theme of running via the physical action of running or the Doctor's request to run can be interpreted as an indication of his ongoing desire to avoid trauma-related stimuli. While a preexisting avoidant trait would not be a posttraumatic symptom, avoidance could cause the person to experience a severe stress reaction to specific trauma.

Avoidance can take numerous forms and can even involve lying to avoid an uncomfortable truth. When the Tenth Doctor explains to Martha some of the nature of the war and its effects on him, he acknowledges that he has been lying about his people so that he "could pretend, just for a bit. I could imagine they were still alive underneath the burnt orange sky." The Tenth Doctor has not been *delusional* about them because he does not convince himself of a falsehood that is grossly inconsistent with his reality, nor is he experiencing a psychotic degree of *denial*[27]

Us vs. Them

JEREMY J. MANCINI

"We're not the same! I'm not the— No, wait, maybe we are."
—Ninth Doctor to Dalek[28]

"By positing a 'me-us-them' distinction, we live with the
illusion of moral superiority. . . ."
—psychologist Philip Zimbardo[29]

Falsely believing that "I am not that kind of person" comes from the human inclination to separate one's identity from those whose behavior runs contrary to what is "right."[30] Psychologist Philip Zimbardo, having spent his career investigating how circumstances bring out the worst[31] or best[32] in people, argues that we are all born with "mental templates" to become good or evil. When faced with reminders of the recent Time War, the Ninth Doctor shouts at a Dalek (then believed to be the last one), saying it should kill itself, to which it responds, "You would make a good Dalek."[33] The hero's unheroic behavior arises from his hatred of Daleks, desire to separate himself from them and possibly from the version of himself that warred against them, and need to believe he could never be like them. A false sense of identity prevents a person from seeing his or her similarities to the enemy, the "other." Zimbardo explains that we have the ability to adapt to the situation in order to survive even if to survive means to destroy. The Doctor shows this not only when he tries to exterminate this Dalek but also when he finally sees its better qualities. Both Doctor and Dalek change.

because he admits the truth to himself and knows when he is pretending.[34]

D. Negative Changes in Thought and Mood

The DSM-5 provides a list of items related to negative alterations in cognitions and mood associated with the traumatic event, two of which must be present to satisfy this criterion. The Doctor easily satisfies at least that many.

Detachment or isolation. Perhaps the most prevalent of the seven possible conditions, this pertains to feeing distant and disconnected from other people, one of the most frequently reported symptoms among combat veterans with PTSD.[35] The Doctor makes a choice at times to stay detached and isolated in an attempt at self-preservation. The Tenth, Eleventh, and Twelfth Doctors all spend long periods traveling by themselves, more so than any pre–Time War Doctors.

Negative self-evaluation. PTSD sufferers may hold persistent, exaggerated beliefs or expectations about themselves. Before he enters the Time War, "the good man" and "the Doctor" are the same thing in the Eighth Doctor's mind.[36] Later, though, the Eleventh Doctor hates himself[37] and believes he is not a good man.[38] When negative self-evaluation becomes ingrained in a person's self-concept, it does not easily subside. Even after rectifying the things he did as the War Doctor,[39] the Twelfth Doctor doubts that he is good, but he still tries.[40]

E. Elevated Arousal

The criterion of *hyperarousal* (excessive arousal inappropriate for current circumstances, markedly increased from pre-trauma levels) can be satisfied with two of the six specifiers listed in the DSM-5. Of those six, the Doctor meets several. Whether he shows posttraumatic changes, demonstrating them to a degree not present before the trauma, may be open for debate.

- *Irritable behavior and angry outbursts.* Anger intensification has become one of the most widely recognized adjustment problems for many war veterans.[41] The Doctor has some angry outbursts or episodes of irritability, such as when the Ninth Doctor succumbs to the weight of his Time War experiences and yells, "The Daleks have failed. Why don't you finish the job and make the Daleks extinct. Rid the universe of your filth! Why don't you just die!"[42] Earlier incarnations of the Doctor, even the crankier ones, did not explode as readily into upset, shouting rants. Arguably, though, these examples might not meet this qualifier because provocation is apparent in every instance.
- *Reckless or self-destructive behavior.* People who have suffered trauma may engage in risky or harmful behavior,[43] particularly if they feel self-loathing or guilt for having survived when others did not (*survivor guilt*).[44] Exhibiting reckless or self-destructive behavior is almost the hallmark of any Doctor adventure. Typically, his regeneration is prefaced by a choice to sacrifice himself by entering willingly into a deadly situation. *Before the Time War, the Doctor regenerates eight times over the course of many centuries, but in a mere six years after the war,[45] he burns through what should be his final four regenerations (War Doctor to Ninth, Ninth to Tenth, Tenth's Meta-Crisis, Tenth to Eleventh[46]).*
- *Hypervigilance.* Extreme alertness to danger can be appropriate for people in dangerous professions. Nearly one-third of Vietnam War veterans eventually experienced PTSD, and many felt an ongoing sense of threat.[47] The Doctor is alert to the possibility of danger but does not tend to show excessive vigilance given his lifestyle and therefore does not

satisfy the requirements for this qualifier. In fact, he
often needs to show greater vigilance.

• *Problems with concentration.* Posttraumatic difficulties with concentration and attention are visible
not only in combat participants but also in people
living in warn-torn environments.[48] War can make
it hard for people to think straight. Although poor
concentration seems to be another constant with
the Doctor, it grows worse after the Time War.
During his building of a makeshift TARDIS, the
Eleventh Doctor exhibits acute poor concentration
as he argues with Idris (the personification of his
own TARDIS) while work needs to be done with
no time to spare.[49]

• *Sleep disturbance. Insomnia* (a pattern of frequent and
extreme difficulty falling or staying asleep) or restless sleep is common among PTSD sufferers. When
his companions sleep, the Eleventh Doctor goes
off on extra adventures.[50] This may be because his
species simply requires less sleep, and so the greater
issue is whether his sleep is notably poorer after the
Time War than before. For each of these qualifiers
and criteria, there must be alterations from previous behavior. To be posttraumatic they must differ
dramatically after the trauma. Long before the War
Doctor ends the Time War, the Fourth Doctor says,
"Sleep is for tortoises."[51]

Comparing pretrauma functioning with posttrauma functioning is essential. In the Doctor's case, not every arousal disturbance is new to him after the trauma. Showing at least two of
the criteria in ways clearly different from before the trauma,
though, is sufficient for a diagnostic assessment of this qualifier.

F. Duration

Symptoms must persist for more than one month to qualify as PTSD. The duration of the symptoms is difficult to quantify, as many of the Doctor's adventures happen off screen, his age is reported inconsistently, and the post–Time War Doctor never indicates which world's years he means when he refers to his age. Nevertheless, more than a month goes by.

G. Impaired Functioning

With PTSD, the disturbance causes impairment in social, occupational, or other areas that are important to the individual.[52] The Doctor's lack of social grace and awareness worsens in the Twelfth Doctor, whose social deficiency is so pronounced that he takes to using apology cue cards with prewritten phrases and expressions to help him navigate the murky waters of social interaction. When he uses a card that reads, "I'm very sorry for your loss. I'll do all I can to solve the death of your friend/family member/pet,"[53] he is effectively using the kind of *social cue card* that has helped some children with autism spectrum disorders improve and maintain their social skills.[54] This becomes necessary as a method of compensating for his impairments.

H. Disturbance Not Attributable to Substance Abuse or Other Medical Condition

Victims of PTSD suffer a high rates of substance abuse.[55] For so many, alcoholism and other substance disorders are consequences, not the cause, of their PTSD symptoms. Substance abuse has never been the Doctor's forte, though, meaning we cannot attribute his PTSD symptoms to an external agent. The Tenth Doctor takes credit for inventing the banana daiquiri[56] but we have no evidence of him consuming one; the Eleventh drinks a sip of wine but promptly spits it out, uncertain whether he has ever tasted wine before;[57] and while the Twelfth pours a drink for himself and a cyborg,[58] nothing indicates that he drinks much. The Doctor may consume alcohol more after the Time War than before, but because these occurrences appear rare and never to excess, any posttraumatic symptoms he experiences not due to substance use.

Specifiers

To reach a full diagnosis, we must consider specifiers as set forth in the DSM-5. Does the individual show any *dissociative symptoms*, signs of splitting portions of mental contents away from conscious awareness? Examples include feeling a sense of unreality of self or body, of time moving slowly, or as though one were in a dream. Whether or not he sometimes shows the forms of dissociation specified in the DSM-5's description of PTSD (depersonalization or derealization) not attributable to his circumstances, the Eleventh Doctor does split portions of mental contents away from conscious awareness when he lies to himself about the War Doctor (addressed in Chapter 8, "Dream Lords: Would the Doctor Run with Freud, Jung, Myers, and Briggs?")—a clear example of dissociation.

Final Diagnosis

On the basis of these considerations and the various criteria exhibited by the Doctor, we can conclude that he suffers from chronic posttraumatic stress disorder with dissociative symptoms. We diagnose his PTSD as *chronic* because he has suffered from it for a long time. The kind of avoidance, thought and mood changes, and social impairment that some people may use to evade their suffering in the short term can prolong it in the long term by keeping them from developing other ways of coping and managing distress. The Doctor has never been one to share his past pains easily, rarely even discussing his own loved ones, and so when trauma affects him, he does not know how to express his pain. Soldiers and others who experience so much trauma may suffer silently, keeping their painful stories locked inside.

References

Allport, G. W. (1937). *Personality: A psychological interpretation.* New York, NY: Holt.

American Psychiatric Association (2013). *Diagnostic and statistical manual of mental disorders* (5th ed.). Washington, DC: American Psychiatric Association.

Berger, D. M. (1977). The survivor syndrome: A problem of nosology and treatment. *American Journal of Psychotherapy, 31*(2), 238–151.

Boyd-Wilson, B. M., Walkey, F. H., & McClure, J. (2002). Present and correct: We kid ourselves unless we live in the moment. *Personality & Individual Differences, 33*(5), 691–702.

Caballero, A., & Connell, J. E. (2010). Evaluation of the social cue cards for preschool age children with autism spectrum disorders. *Journal of Behavior Assessment & Intervention in Children, 1*(1), 25–42.

Caplan, R. D., Tripathi, R. C., & Naidu, R. K. (1985). Subjective past, present, and future fit: Effects on anxiety, depression, and other indicators of well-being. *Journal of Personality & Social Psychology, 48*(1), 180–197.

Cassell, W. A., Charles, T., Dubey, B. L., & Janssen, H. (2014). SIS incites long term PTSD combat memories and survivor guilt. *Journal of Projective Psychology & Mental Health, 21*(2), 68–80.

Charlop-Christy, M. H., & Kelso, S. (2003). Teaching children with autism conversational speech using a cue card written script program. *Education & Treatment of Children, 26*(2), 108–127.

Dekel, S., Mamon, D., Solomon, Z., Lanman, O., & Dishy, G. (2016). Can guilt lead to psychological growth following trauma exposure? *Psychiatry Research, 236,* 196–198.

Dixon-Gordon, K. L., Tull, M. T., & Gratz, K. L. (2014). Self-injurious behaviors in posttraumatic stress disorder: An examination of potential moderators. *Journal of Affective Disorders, 166,* 359–367.

Eysenck, M. W., Payne S., & Santos, R. (2006). Anxiety and depression: Past, present, and future events. *Cognition & Emotion, 20*(2), 274–294.

Fortunato, V. J., & Furey, J. T. (2011). The theory of MindTime: The relationships between future, past, and present thinking and psychological well-being and distress. *Personality & Individual Differences, 50*(1), 20–24.

Freud, A. (1936). *The ego and defense mechanisms.* London, UK: Imago.

Gonzalez, O. I., Novaco, R. W., Eger, M. A., & Gahm, G. A. (2016). Anger intensification with combat-related PTSD and depression comorbidity. *Psychological Trauma: Theory, Research, Practice, & Policy, 8*(1), 9–16.

Gros, D., Szafranski, D. D., Brady, K. T., & Back, S. E. (2015). Relations between pain, PTSD symptoms, and substance use in veterans. *Psychiatry: Interpersonal & Biological Processes, 78*(3), 277–287.

Hahn, A. M., Tirabassi, C. K., Simons, R. M., & Simons, J. S. (2015). Military sexual trauma, combat exposure, and negative urgency as independent predictors of PTSD and subsequent alcohol problems among OEF/OIF veterans. *Psychological Services, 12*(4), 378–383.

Handley, R. V., Salkovskis, P. M., Scragg, P., & Ehlers, A. (2009). Clinically significant avoidance of public transport following the London bombings: Travel phobia or subthreshold posttraumatic stress disorder? *Journal of Anxiety Disorders, 23*(8), 1170–1176.

Held, P., Owens, G. P., & Anderson, S. E. (2015). The interrelationships among trauma-related guilt and shame, disengagement coping, and PTSD in a sample of treatment-seeking substance users. *Traumatology, 21*(4), 285–292.

Held, P., Owens, G. P., Schumm, J. A., Chard, K. M., & Hansel, J. E. (2011). Disengagement coping as a mediator between trauma-related guilt and PTSD severity. *Journal of Traumatic Stress, 24*(6), 708–715.

Hoge, C. W., & Warner, C. H. (2014). Estimating PTSD prevalence in US veterans: Considering combat exposure, PTSD checklist cutpoints, and PTSD. *Journal of Clinical Psychiatry, 75*(12), e1439–e1441.

Holowka, D. W., Marx, B. P., Kaloupek, D. G., & Keane, T. M. (2012). PTSD symptoms among male Vietnam veterans: Prevalence and associations with diagnostic status. *Psychological Trauma: Theory, Research, Practice, & Policy, 4*(2), 285–292.

Holtz, P. (2015, February 3). *8 common myths about PTSD debunked*. Task and Purpose: http://taskandpurpose.com/8-common-myths-ptsd-debunked/.

Husain, S. A., Allwood, M. A., & Bell, D. J. (2008). The relationship between PTSD symptoms and attention problems in children exposed to Bosnian war. *Journal of Emotional & Behavioral Disorders, 16*(1), 52–62.

Jacobsen, L. K., Southwick, S. M., & Kosten, T. R. (2001). Substance use disorders in patients with posttraumatic stress disorder: A review of the literature. *American Journal of Psychiatry, 158*(8), 1184–1190.

Krebs, G., Hirsch, C. R., & Mathews, A. (2010). The effect of attention modification with explicit vs. minimal instructions on worry *Behavioural Research & Therapy, 48*(3), 251–256.

Kübler-Ross, E. (1969). *On death and dying*. New York, NY: Macmillan.

Litz, B. T., Weathers, F. W., Monaco, V., Herman, D. S., Wulfsohn, M., Marx, B., & Krane, T. M. (1996). Attention, arousal, and memory in posttraumatic stress disorder. *Journal of Traumatic Stress, 9*(3), 497–518.

Pigeon, W. R., Campbell, C. E., Possemato, K., & Ouimette, P. (2013). Longitudinal relationships of insomnia, nightmares, and PTSD severity in recent combat veterans. *Journal of Psychosomatic Research, 75*(6), 546–550.

Price, J. L. (n.d.). *Findings from the National Vietnam Veterans' Readjustment Study*. U.S. Department of Veterans Affairs: http://www.ptsd.va.gov/professional/research-bio/research/vietnam-vets-study.asp.

Pugh, L. R., Taylor, P. J., & Berry, K. (2015). The role of guilt in the development of post-traumatic stress disorder: A systematic review. *Journal of Affective Disorders, 182*, 138–150.

PTSD Alliance (n.d.). *Posttraumatic stress disorder myths*. PTSD Alliance: http://www.ptsdalliance.org/common-myths/.

Roemer, L., Litz, B. T., Orsillo, S. M., Ehlich, P. J., & Friedman, M. J. (1998). Increases in retrospective accounts of war-zone exposure over time: The role of PTSD symptom severity. *Journal of Traumatic Stress, 11*(3), 597–605.

Santiago, P. N., Ursano, R. J., Gray, C. L., Rynoos, R. S., Spiegel, D., Lewis-Fernandez, R., Friedman, M. J., & Fullerton, C. S. (2013, April 11). *A system review of PTSD prevalence and trajectories in DSM-5 defined trauma exposed populations: Intentional and non-intentional traumatic events*. PLOS ONE: http://journals.plos.org/plosone/article?id=10.1371/journal.pone.0059236.

Sidran Institute (n.d.). *Myths and facts about PTSD.* Sidran Institute: http://www.sidran. org/resources/for-survivors-and-loved-ones/myths-and-facts-about-ptsd/.

Sender, H. (2014, August 22). *Doctor Who season 8: How old is the Doctor? Recap of the Doctor's real age leading up to Peter Capaldi (timeline).* International Business Times: http://www.ibtimes.com/doctor-who-season-8-how-old-doctor-recap-doctors -real-age-leading-peter-capaldi-timeline-1667064.

Staggs, S. (n.d.). *Myths & facts about PTSD.* Psych Central: http://psychcentral.com/lib/ myths-and-facts-about-ptsd/.

Stanley, I. H., Hom, M. A., & Joiner, T. E. (2016). A systematic review of suicidal thoughts and behaviors among police officers, firefighters, EMTs, and paramedics. *Clinical Psychology Review, 44*(1), 25–44.

Tanielian, T., & Jaycox, L. (2008). *Invisible wounds of war.* Santa Monica, CA: RAND.

Wilson, L. C. (2015). A systematic review of probable posttraumatic stress disorder in first responders following man-made mass violence. *Psychiatry Research, 229*(1–2), 21–26.

Wegner, D. M., Schneider, D. J., Carter, S. R., & White, T. L. (1987). Paradoxical effects of thought suppression. *Journal of Personality & Social Psychology, 53*(1), 5–13.

Zimbardo, P. G. (1969). The human choice: Individuation, reason, and order versus deindividuation, impulse, and chaos. In W. J. Arnold & D. Levine (Eds.), *Nebraska Symposium on Motivation* (Vol. 17). Lincoln: University of Nebraska Press.

Zimbardo, P. G. (1971, October 25). *The psychological power and pathology of imprisonment.* A statement prepared for the U.S. House of Representatives Committee on the Judiciary, Subcommittee No. 3: Hearings on Prison Reform, San Francisco, CA.

Zimbardo, P. G. (2004/2006). A situationist perspective on the psychology of evil: Understanding how good people are transformed into perpetrators. In R. Falk, I. Gendzier, & R. Lifton, *Crimes of war: Iraq* (pp. 366–369). New York, NY: Nation.

Zimbardo, P. G. (2006). Power turns good soldiers into "bad apples." In R. Falk, I. Gendzier, & R. Lifton, *Crimes of war: Iraq* (p. 370). New York, NY: Nation.

Zimbardo, P. G. (2007). *The Lucifer effect: Understanding how good people turn evil.* New York, NY: Random House.

Zimbardo, P. G. (n.d.). Understanding heroism. The Heroic Imagination Project: http://b.3cdn.net/raproject/ed834126c9c0786b1e_93m6i2aqj.pdf.

Notes

1. Modern episode 3–3, "Gridlock" (April 14, 2007).
2. Kübler-Ross (1969), p. 169.
3. Hahn et al. (2015); Hoge & Warner (2014); Pigeon et al. (2013); Roemer et al. (1998); Stanley et al. (2016); Wilson (2015).
4. Modern episode 1–2, "The End of the World" (April 2, 2005).
5. Handley et al. (2009).
6. Modern episode 7–13, "The Name of the Doctor" (May 18, 2013); anniversary special, "The Day of the Doctor" (November 23, 2013).
7. Holtz (2015); PTSD Alliance (n.d.); Sidran Institute (n.d.); Staggs (n.d.).
8. Santiago et al. (2013).
9. Held et al. (2011; 2015); Pugh et al. (2015).
10. Dekel et al. (2016).
11. Anniversary special, "The Day of the Doctor" (November 23, 2013).
12. American Psychiatric Association (2013).
13. Christmas and New Year specials, "The End of Time," part 1 (December 25,

2009) and part 2 (January 1, 2010); anniversary special, "The Day of the Doctor" (November 23, 2015).
14. Anniversary special, "The Day of the Doctor" (November 23, 2013).
15. American Psychiatric Association (2013).
16. Anniversary special, "The Day of the Doctor" (November 23, 2013).
17. Krebs et al. (2010); Litz et al. (1997); Wegner et al. (1987); Wisco et al. (2013).
18. e.g., New Year's special, "The End of Time," part 2 (January 1, 2010).
19. Modern episode 1-2, "The End of the World" (April 2, 2005)
20. Caplan et al. (1985); Eysenck et al. (2006); Fortunato & Furey (2011).
21. Boyd-Wilson et al. (2002).
22. Tanielian & Jaycox (2008).
23. Allport (1937).
24. Modern episode 9-12, "Hell Bent" (December 5, 2015).
25. Modern episode 1-1, "Rose," (March 26, 2005).
26. Modern episode 3-12, "The Sound of Drums" (June 23, 2007).
27. Freud (1936).
28. Modern episode 1-6, "Dalek" (April 30, 2005).
29. Zimbardo (2004/2006), p. 367.
30. Zimbardo (2004/2006; 2006).
31. Zimbardo (1969; 1971; 2007).
32. Zimbardo (n.d.).
33. Modern episode 1-6, "Dalek" (April 30, 2005).
34. Modern episode 3-3, "Gridlock" (April 14, 2007).
35. Holowka et al. (2012).
36. Minisode, *The Night of the Doctor* (November 13, 2013).
37. Modern episode 5-7, "Amy's Choice" (May 15, 2010).
38. Modern episode 6-7, "A Good Man Goes to War" (June 4, 2011).
39. Anniversary special, "The Day of the Doctor" (November 23, 2015).
40. Modern episode 8-2, "Into the Dalek" (August 30, 2014).
41. Gonzalez et al. (2016).
42. Modern episode 1-6, "Dalek" (April 30, 2005).
43. Dixon-Gordon et al. (2014)
44. Berger (1977); Cassell et al. (2014).
45. Sender (2014).
46. Anniversary special, "The Day of the Doctor" (November 23, 2015); modern episode 1-13, "The Parting of the Ways" (June 18, 2005); 4-13, "Journey's End" (July 5, 2008); New Year's special, "The End of Time," part 2 (January 1, 2010).
47. Price (n.d.).
48. Husain et al. (2008).
49. Modern episode 6-4, "The Doctor's Wife" (May 14, 2011).
50. Minisode, *Good Night* (November 22, 2011).
51. Classic serial 14-6, *The Talons of Weng-Chiang*, part 3 (March 12, 1977).
52. American Psychiatric Association (2013).
53. Modern episode 9-3, "Under the Lake" (October 3, 2015).
54. Caballero & Connell (2010).
55. Gros et al. (2015); Jacobsen et al. (2001).
56. Modern episode 2-4, "The Girl in the Fireplace" (May 6, 2006).
57. Modern episode 6-1, "The Impossible Astronaut" (April 23, 2011).
58. Modern episode 8-1, "Deep Breath" (August 23, 2014).

Enduring one loss after another can wear a person down. Some people may avoid potentially satisfying experiences as one way to avoid loss at the end. Experiencing the best things in life means taking risks and making ourselves vulnerable.

CHAPTER FOURTEEN

Behind Two Hearts:
Grief and Vulnerability

JENNA BUSCH
AND JANINA SCARLET

"He was different once, a long time ago. Kind, yes. A hero, even. A saver of worlds. But he suffered losses which hurt him. Now he prefers isolation to the possibility of pain's return."

Madame Vastra[1]

"Vulnerability sounds like truth and feels like courage. Truth and courage aren't always comfortable, but they're never weakness."

—social work researcher Brené Brown[2]

It is a sad fact that most people experience numerous losses throughout their lives.[3] After experiencing losses, some people shut down and avoid interacting with others,[4] while others might thrive and demonstrate extreme resilience.[5] Since the Doctor has lived for over two thousand years, he has arguably experienced more losses than most, his hearts undoubtedly broken by the many deaths he had endured. Between the deaths of his many companions and the people and aliens whose lives he has touched in some way, he's had more than his share of grief and guilt. After devastating losses, such as those the Doctor endures, some people cope by committing to their work, others by communicating with others, and still others by trying to avoid feeling anything at all.[6] What, then, is the most effective way of coping with loss and past heartache?

Grief

Grief is the typical reaction one may experience after a painful loss due to death, a breakup, a job change, or a change in one's health status.[7] In turn, grief that results from a sudden traumatic loss, called *traumatic grief*, can negatively affect the person's psychological and physiological health. For example, after Clara's death, the Doctor spends two billion years in a energy loop, dealing with his grief.[8]

When a group of researchers interviewed people whose spouses were diagnosed with terminal illness, they found that even the impending eventuality of such a traumatic loss had significant health effects on the partners. Specifically, spouses of people diagnosed with life-threatening illnesses were more likely to develop high blood pressure and heart problems, demonstrate poorer eating habits, consider committing suicide, and eventually develop cancer, compared to people whose spouses did not have life-threatening illnesses.[9] After learning the Brigadier died,[10] losing Amy and Rory,[11] and saying goodbye to River Song,[12] the Doctor's personality changes and he becomes more withdrawn.

Experiential Avoidance

One of the common ways people try to deal with grief is to suppress any painful thoughts or emotions that arise after the loss.[13] Avoiding or suppressing painful experiences is called *experiential avoidance*.[14] Experiential avoidance may sometimes provide brief relief because the individual is temporarily able to escape his or her painful emotions. However, in the long run, experiential avoidance may lead to worsening symptoms.[15]

The consequences of experiential avoidance vary. Overall, experiential avoidance after a traumatic loss is likely to result in prolonged grief, depression, and painful catastrophic thoughts about the loss. The Doctor often throws himself into his travels to distract himself from his sadness at the loss of his companions. For instance, after the Eleventh Doctor loses Donna,[16] he doesn't take on a regular companion until he regenerates into the Twelfth Doctor.

Social Isolation
In addition to worsening psychological symptoms, experiential avoidance can bring on potentially serious health conditions. Specifically, avoidance in the form of social isolation can lead to inflammation, which in turn can trigger a number of physiological and psychological conditions, including chronic pain and depression.[17] Chronic social isolation can also cause neurological changes, such as a reduction in the brain's *white matter*. White matter consists of specific structures responsible for sending and delivering messages between the different structures of the brain and the rest of the nervous system. If the white matter is reduced, then the brain and the body might not function properly.[18] For example, multiple sclerosis (MS) is a disease caused by inflammation that destroys white matter and affects the person's ability to regulate his or her functions.[19]

Sometimes people might blame themselves for a traumatic loss, even when they had nothing to do with the tragedy. When the Doctor loses Amy and Rory, he is devastated. He retreats to the Paternoster Gang and retires for a long time.[20] Though his friends, the Paternoster Gang (Madam Vastra, Jenny Flint, and Strax), try to entice him with mysteries to solve, he avoids participating.[21]

Shame and Guilt

When people blame themselves for a tragic loss, they might experience guilt or shame. Guilt is regret for a specific action, whereas shame refers to feeling bad about oneself as a whole. Overall, people who experience shame are more likely to struggle with grief than individuals who experience guilt, and men are more likely to be affected by shame than women.[22] Thoughts that might arise from shame or guilt after losing a loved one are likely to prompt people to struggle with prolonged grief and depression.[23]

There are numerous instances where the Doctor expresses regret, guilt, and shame about having been the only survivor of the Time War, which destroyed his entire race as well as a large proportion of the Daleks.[24] It affects him throughout his Ninth, Tenth, and Eleventh incarnations. Only after he realizes that Gallifrey still exists in a pocket universe can he begin to let go of his guilt.[25]

Vulnerability

The opposite of experiential avoidance is *vulnerability*. Vulnerability refers to the willingness to face uncertainty, risk, and emotional exposure. Instead of avoiding situations that might result in heartache, vulnerability refers to taking chances even

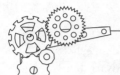

The Wholehearted Way

Vulnerability researcher Brené Brown has found that people who reported living the most fulfilling lives were ones who were open to vulnerability. She refers to these individuals as *wholehearted*. Wholehearted individuals embrace vulnerability by being open to both success and failure, love and heartbreak, as well as creativity, play, and laughter.[26] Wholehearted individuals seem to possess qualities like these:

- *Authenticity*—being true to oneself, rather than responding to other people's expectations. After living for so many years, the Doctor does not do what others think he *should* do. He follows his own directions, his own rules, and his own moral values.
- *Self-compassion*—letting go of perfectionism and practicing self-acceptance and self-support.
- *Resilience*—letting go of numbing through connection: Connecting to others helps him avoid growing numb to experience and emotions. Even though he knows that he might lose them, the Doctor continues to bring new companions in to travel with him.
- *Practicing gratitude* for what one already has. For instance, when the Doctor meets a "human" incarnation of the TARDIS, Idris, he celebrates her life and expresses gratitude to her.[27]
- *Trust*—letting go of the need for certainty. The Doctor trusts his companions, even allowing them to occasionally operate the TARDIS.
- *Creativity*—letting go of comparison and instead following one's own creative process. The Doctor often uses his creative mind to solve problems, defying what he's supposed to do and coming

Continues on next page

up with solutions no one would expect. For instance, he sends a message to Sally Sparrow from 1969 to warn her about the Weeping Angels,[28] or he uses a hologram of himself to confuse a ghost.[29]

• *Playing and resting*, rather than striving for achievement to raise one's self-worth. On many of his adventures, the Doctor finds the time to laugh and enjoy his experiences. For example, when he and Rose find out about encountering potential werewolves, they are both excited about this venture.[30]

• *Practicing mindfulness*—slowing down enough to notice the present moment. The Doctor, knowing this is going to be the last outing with his wife River Song, takes her to the Singing Towers of Darillium and spends time with her, allowing himself to weep and take in every moment.[31]

• *Meaningful work*—letting go of self-doubt and doing what matters, rather than what one is "supposed to." Despite knowing the havoc his longtime enemy Davros will cause him and the universe, the Doctor goes back to save him, stating that it doesn't matter what side one is on, as long as there is mercy.[32]

• *Laughter and dance*—letting go of being in control.[33] Instead of retreating into himself when the Doctor believes he's facing his final day of existence, he travels to the Middle Ages and puts on a show, playing guitar for the crowd.[34]

in the face of uncertainty. Some examples of vulnerability include love, trust, creativity, and joy.[35] The Doctor knows that his wife, River Song, is going to die because their time lines are running in opposite directions. When he meets her,[36] he learns that they've known and trusted each other for many years and then he watches her perish.[37] Even knowing the tragic end she'll face, he continues to meet her throughout time and space and pursue a relationship with her.[38]

Vulnerability and Resilience

Hence, connecting with his core values and engaging in meaningful activities may reflect vulnerability, but it also seems to be helpful. Connecting with companions and activities may have profound effects on psychological resilience. In fact, research on this topic suggests that when people who struggle with depression connect with their core values and perform meaningful deeds, their depression symptoms abate.[39]

Connecting with others can also increase positive emotions, extend life span, and prompt the release of *oxytocin*, the body's own stress-protection hormone.[40] In addition, the willingness and the ability to experience and focus on positive emotions boost human resilience. For example, people who are more likely to practice vulnerability in terms of connecting with positive emotions are more likely to recover from stress quickly, as well as have improved cardiovascular (heart) recovery after being exposed to a stressful situation. Such recovery could lead to improved heart health and serve to protect the individual against the potentially damaging effects of stress.[41]

Healing Broken Hearts

As counterintuitive as it may seem, embracing their vulnerability allows people to be more resilient. In some ways, vulnerability can be a strength; for the Doctor, it could be his best asset. Though he experiences some of the negative reactions to grief, like guilt and isolation, he moves through them. His choice to travel with companions who will eventually leave him and die shows his willingness to experience grief and move through it.

References

Barr, P. (2004). Guilt- and shame-proneness and the grief of perinatal bereavement. *Psychology and Psychotherapy: Theory, Research and Practice, 77*(4), 493–510.

Boelen, P. A., van den Bout, J., & van den Hout, M. A. (2006). Negative cognitions and avoidance in emotional problems after bereavement: A prospective study. *Behaviour Research & Therapy, 44*(11), 1657–1672.

Boelen, P. A., van den Bout, J., & van den Hout, M. A. (2010). A prospective examination of catastrophic misinterpretations and experiential avoidance in emotional distress following loss. *Journal of Nervous & Mental Disease, 198*(4), 252–257.

Bonanno, G. A. (2004). Loss, trauma, and human resilience: Have we underestimated the human capacity to thrive after extremely aversive events? *American Psychologist, 59*(1), 20–28.

Bonanno, G. A., & Kaltman, S. (2001). The varieties of grief experience. *Clinical Psychology Review, 21*(5), 705–734.

Brown, B. (2012). *Daring greatly: How the courage to be vulnerable transforms the way we live, love, parent, and lead.* New York, NY: Gotham.

Cole, S. W., Hawkley, L. C., Arevalo, J. M., Sung, C. Y., Rose, R. M., & Cacioppo, J. T. (2007). Social regulation of gene expression in human leukocytes. *Genome Biology, 8*(9), R189.

Fredrickson, B. L. (2001). The role of positive emotions in positive psychology: The broaden-and-build theory of positive emotions. *American Psychologist, 56*(3), 218–226.

Kanter, J. W., Baruch, D. E., & Gaynor, S. T. (2006). Acceptance and commitment therapy and behavioral activation for the treatment of depression: Description and comparison. *The Behavior Analyst, 29*(2), 161.

McGonigal, J. (2015). *Superbetter: A revolutionary approach to getting stronger, happier, braver, and more resilient.* New York, NY: Penguin.

McGonigal, K. (2015). *The upside of stress: Why stress is good for you, and how to get good at it.* New York, NY: Penguin.

Miller, D. H., Weinshenker, B. G., Filippi, M., . . . & Polman, C. H. (2008). Differential diagnosis of suspected multiple sclerosis: A consensus approach. *Multiple Sclerosis, 14*(9), 1157–1174.

Nakagawa, S., Takeuchi, H., Taki, Y., . . . & Kawashima, R. (2015). White matter structures associated with loneliness in young adults. *Scientific Reports, 5.* http://www.nature.com/articles/srep17001.

Orcutt, H. K., Pickett, S. M., & Pope, E. B. (2005). Experiential avoidance and forgiveness as mediators in the relation between traumatic interpersonal events and post-traumatic stress disorder symptoms. *Journal of Social & Clinical Psychology, 24*(7), 1003–1029.

Prigerson, H. G., Bierhals, A. J., Kasl, S. V., . . . & Jacobs, S. (1997). Traumatic grief as a risk factor for mental and physical morbidity. *American Journal of Psychiatry, 154,* 616–623.

Shear, M. K. (2010). Exploring the role of experiential avoidance from the perspective of attachment theory and the dual process model. *OMEGA: Journal of Death and Dying, 61*(4), 357–369.

Shear, M.K., Monk, T., Houck, P., Melhem, N., Frank, E., Reynolds, C., & Sillowash, R. (2007). An attachment-based model of complicated grief including the role of avoidance. *European Archives of Psychiatry & Clinical Neuroscience, 257*(8), 453–461.

Tugade, M. M., & Fredrickson, B. L. (2004). Resilient individuals use positive emotions to bounce back from negative emotional experiences. *Journal of Personality & Social Psychology, 86*(2), 320.

Notes

1. Christmas special, "The Snowmen" (December 25, 2012).
2. Brown (2012), p. 37.
3. Bonanno (2004).
4. Shear et al. (2007).
5. Bonanno (2004).
6. Shear (2010).
7. Bonanno & Kaltman (2001).
8. Modern episode 9–11, "Heaven Sent" (November 28, 2015).
9. Prigerson et al. (1997).
10. Modern episode 7–13, "The Name of the Doctor" (May 18, 2013).
11. Modern episode 6–13, "The Wedding of River Song" (October 1, 2011).
12. Modern episode 7–5, "The Angels Take Manhattan" (September 29, 2012).
13. Shear et al. (2007).
14. Boelen et al. (2010).
15. Orcutt et al. (2005).
16. Modern episode 4–13, "Journey's End" (July 5, 2008).
17. Cole et al. (2007); Nakagawa et al. (2015).
18. Nakagawa et al. (2015).
19. Miller et al. (2008).
20. Minisode, *The Great Detective* (November 16, 2012), https://www.youtube.com/watch?v=G17_B4uACgg.
21. Minisode, *The Great Detective* (November 16, 2012), https://www.youtube.com/watch?v=G17_B4uACgg.
22. Barr (2004).
23. Boelen et al. (2006).
24. Modern episode 1–2, "The End of the World" (April 2, 2005).
25. Anniversary special, "The Day of the Doctor" (November 23, 2013).
26. Brown (2012).
27. Modern episode 6–4, "The Doctor's Wife" (May 14, 2011).
28. Modern episode 3–10, "Blink" (June 9, 2007).
29. Modern episode 9–3, "Before the Flood" (October 10, 2015).
30. Modern episode 2–2, "Tooth and Claw" (April 22, 2006).
31. Modern episode 4–9, "Forest of the Dead" (June 7, 2008).
32. Modern episode 9–2, "The Witch's Familiar" (September 26, 2015).
33. Brown (2012).
34. Modern episode 9–1, "The Magician's Apprentice" (September 19, 2015).
35. Brown (2012).
36. Modern episode 4–8, "Silence in the Library" (May 31, 2008).
37. Modern episode 4–9, "Forest of the Dead" (June 7, 2008).
38. Beginning with modern episode 4–8, "Silence in the Library" (May 31, 2008).
39. Kanter et al. (2006).
40. J. McGonigal (2015); K. McGonigal (2015).
41. Fredrickson (2001); K. McGonigal (2015); Tugade & Fredrickson (2004).

Are boys expected to give up "softer" parts of themselves in order to become men? How soon will the human race give up organic parts of ourselves on the way to becoming machines?

CHAPTER FIFTEEN

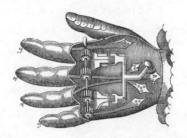

Boys to Cybermen: Social Narratives and Metaphors for Masculinity

BILLY SAN JUAN

"Emotions! Love! Pride! Hate! Fear! Have you no emotions, sir, hmm?"
—First Doctor[1]

> *"Foster a space that welcomes the warrior into therapy by explicitly calling for the strength of the stereotypical male role in a different kind of battle, a 'battle for the mind and heart.'"*
> —psychologist Duncan Shields[2]

As they grow up, boys are often expected to lose their "softer" qualities in order to become tough, strong men. Masculinity, in its stereotyped Western form, is often taught to young boys in an attempt to create an ideal "man" impervious to vulnerability. Many men suffer in their attempt to conform to these impossible ideals.[3] A prime example is the instilled belief that men must deny their emotions,[4] because emotions are viewed as vulnerability and vulnerability is dangerous. These messages are not always conveyed directly, but they can be conveyed constantly. A boy crying on the sports field may be castigated in a variety of ways: *Stop crying. Don't be a baby. Stop acting like a girl.*

Be a man.

Delete your emotions.

Upgrade.

Losing Humanity

The modern world is progressing toward an unpredictable time when advances in cybernetics can change what it means to be human. The Cybermen are robotlike beings, "living brain jammed inside a cybernetic body with a heart of steel, emotions removed."[5] Cybermen are formidable foes for the Doctor and his companions, but they also serve as a prime metaphor for the role that socialized masculinity norms play in everyday male experience. They are partially defined by their ability to regulate emotions through an emotional inhibitor.[6] Blocking emotions does not eliminate them, however. Emotional inhibitors can be hacked with a code,[7] overloaded through a strong feeling of parental love,[8] or overridden through a strong feeling of romantic love.[9] In similar fashion, strong emotions can overwhelm men who adhere to traditional values of masculinity. Instead of an emotional inhibitor being destroyed, this can lead to self-destructive actions. Men may turn to drugs, alcohol, violence, or other unsafe behaviors to cope with feelings they may not be able to truly understand. Emotions, especially those seen as vulnerable, are avoided or deleted. The reason lies in three words the Tenth Doctor whispers to Rose in an attempt to explain why the Cybermen have removed their feelings: "because it hurts."[10]

Emotional inhibition falls into four categories, fitting different themes of masculinity.

Themes of Masculinity

The values by which men are taught to live act as an operating system. These values serve as software by which actions are taken and emotions are interpreted. The values differ slightly based on various factors, but common themes emerge. There are four main themes in the underlying transmission of traditional masculinity norms.[11]

Normative, hegemonic masculine ideals are stereotyped to be the *opposite of stereotyped female behaviors.* This ideology encourages men to achieve social status by devaluing emotions that imply vulnerability and developing a "façade of toughness."[12] Colors, toys, actions, clothing, and interests are divided into dichotomous classes of "boy" and "girl." These gender attitudes, or the beliefs that dictate and constitute appropriate "boy" and "girl" behaviors, are internalized in childhood and adolescence.[13] Consider the fact that nearly all cyber-conversion victims become Cyber*men*, not Cyberwomen, regardless of their original gender.[14]

Masculinity ideals value the acquisition of *status and achievement.* Two primary methods males use to acquire status are prestige and dominance.[15] Prestige is achieved by entities who receive accolades from others. A man builds prestige by developing a positive reputation, such as "wealthy businessman" or "decorated soldier." Dominance is a similar concept; however, it implies an agonistic process whereby influence is exerted by instilling fear. Dominance relies on acts showing physical superiority to attain status or achievement. The word is often used to describe individual athletes in competitive sports, such as boxing or mixed martial arts. The Doctor and the Cybermen exemplify prestige and dominance, respectively. The Doctor's companions normally follow him voluntarily, such as when Donna actively searches to find him specifically so she can join his travels.[16] The Cybermen, on the other hand, often force their victims to upgrade without choice.

Men are habituated to exhibit *emotional self-control*. Men may have difficulty identifying and verbalizing vulnerability, due mainly to the belief they are expected to conceal weakness.[17] Stoicism is seen as a sign of calm and leadership. Every iteration of the Cybermen, from the cyborglike Mondasian Cybermen to the artificially designed Cybermen of Lumic Industries, features an unexpressive face plate with a fixed expression. A fixed expression cannot show variety or reactions.

Masculinity norms value *aggression*. Though anyone can commit violence or be its victim, regardless of sex, physical aggression is clearly associated with masculinity.[18] The adherence to a masculine credo, which includes a focus not only on emotional restriction but also on aggression, status, and sexual functioning, is correlated to men's feelings of competency, independence, and ambition.[19] Cybermen aggress through violence, and their lack of emotion is shown through merciless actions such as the slaughter that occurs during a funeral[20] or their unwillingness to surrender when fighting Daleks.[21]

> *"As long as men are supposed to be 'masculine' and women are supposed to be 'feminine,' many people will suffer in their attempts to conform."*
> —psychologist Rebekah Smart[22]

The Doctor's Masculinity: Positive Psychology/Positive Masculinity
If the Cybermen represent a view of the maladaptive aspects of
masculinity, then the Doctor represents positive aspects which
may come as a result of properly adjusted masculinity narratives. In a shift in modern psychological research and literature, some researchers have begun to look at masculinity in a
manner that emphasizes principles of positive psychology and
seeks to focus on healthier and more constructive aspects of
masculinity. It is important to note that the following qualities
are not unique to men. However, they are qualities that men
often use to define masculinity as a social construct. It is also
important to note that this list merely reflects the myriad of
positive masculine qualities, but is not a complete and comprehensive catalogue:[23]

1. Intimate male relationships are often forged through
   action-oriented activities, rather than more passive
   activities, such as long conversation. Describing the
   findings shown by much research,[24] psychologist David
   Myers has observed that men tend to prefer doing
   activities "side by side" more than communicating
   "face-to-face."[25] For example, watching and/or
   playing sports serve as stereotypical bonding activities
   for men. Fishing, camping, and hunting also serve as
   tropes by which men spend time together to strengthen
   friendships. This can be seen in adventure-oriented
   interactions between the Doctor and the Brigadier,
   such as when the Brigadier saves the Doctor from
   a glowing snakelike creature and quips, "I can't just
   let you out of my sight, can I, Doctor?" The Doctor
   marvels that the Brigadier recognizes him despite
   his regenerated form, at which point the Brigadier
   replies, "Who else would it be?"[26] In similar fashion,

the intimacy between these two characters can be observed in the span of seconds when the Doctor salutes him, a simple action indicating a strong bond because the Doctor rarely salutes anyone and does not like to be saluted.[27]

2. Men with healthy masculinity ideals often value their role as protector for friends and loved ones. A drive to fulfill such a role even motivates healthy behavior for those who want to be capable of protecting others.[28] The Eleventh Doctor proclaims himself to be a protector many times, notably when he asks the Atraxi, "Is this world protected?" and they find the answer in a series of images that show every version of him from the First Doctor up to the most recent.[29]

3. Men tend to be characterized as "good fathers" when they take an active, responsive role in their child's life.[30] The "good father" shows *accessibility* (presence and availability), *engagement* (direct contact and shared interactions), and *responsibility* (taking care of his children).[31] Though initially uninterested in a relationship with his artificially created daughter, Jenny, the Doctor begins to model his method of nonviolence for conflict resolution and becomes her good father.[32]

4. Healthy men are positively socialized to value self-reliance. Though self-reliance includes consideration of opinions or data from other sources, a "healthy man" will help consider others' needs and come to his own conclusion. In several instances, the Doctor acts in a self-reliant manner based on his knowledge and experience. However, he will also listen to input from his companions, such as when Amy helps him find an alternative instead of harming a star whale.[33]

5. Healthy men undertake risks or engage in other forms of daring, but only after careful consideration of consequence and reward.[34] This allows for growth of character through testing their endurance, resilience, and other self "limits." Such a perception of risk-taking may account for why more men than women participate in dangerous activities like skydiving.[35] Nearly every adventure the Doctor undertakes involves some sort of risk or feat of daring. Though some of his incarnations may be a bit more impulsive than others, he usually carefully considers consequence and reward before taking action.

6. Male-oriented organizations often offer humanitarian services in the interest of social good. This is not to suggest that female-oriented organizations do not engage in similar activities. However, this has been noted by researchers as an area of positive expression of masculinity. Organizations such as the Knights of Columbus, Freemasons, and Boy Scouts of America all serve as examples of male-oriented organizations that give men and boys opportunities for stereotypically male-appropriate socialization and service. The Doctor is not necessarily a member of a male-oriented organization and probably would never choose to affiliate with one because joining clubs runs contrary to his nature. (As Groucho Marx said, more than once and in several different ways, "I don't want to belong to any club that will accept people like me as a member.")[36]

7. Men use humor as a means of enjoyment, to forge intimacy with other men, as a strategic tool to manage conflict, and as a means of winning support. Researchers suggest that men may use humor as

a surreptitious method of expressing affection.[37] The Doctor's sense of humor has varied between incarnations; however, it is a quality that endears him to both companions and viewers alike.

8. Traditional masculinity is often embodied in male heroes.[38] These heroes may exhibit incredible strength, may be great leaders, or may have overcome life hurdles to reach their status as "hero." In mythology, Hercules shows great might and becomes more heroic through a series of trials. In the post-9/11 world, Americans elevated firefighters and other first responders to the status of "hero" when the perception of risk involved became greater.[39] The Doctor embodies many traits of a hero: He possesses incredible powers, such as regeneration;[40] he has led both armies and companions;[41] and he has faced a variety of personal tragedies, such as the deaths of companions,[42] wives,[43] and seemingly his entire race.[44]

Silver Nightmares

The Cybermen and the Doctor represent two sides of masculinity. Taken to the extreme, social constructs of masculinity may inhibit beautiful aspects of life related to emotion and even cause biopsychosocial issues for men. On the other hand, in a healthy context, social constructs of masculinity can elevate men to become productive members of an emotionally literate society. Men must make a choice as they are bombarded by so-called masculine constructs throughout their social development. Will they succumb to the idea that emotions are a weakness, an exploitable vulnerability to be hidden at the cost of physical and social health? Will they be upgraded to be emotionally stunted Cybermen?

Or will their hearts grow to beat like the Doctor's?

References

Bem, S. L. (1981). Gender schema theory: A cognitive account of sex typing. *Psychological Review, 88*(4), 354–364.

Boon, K. A. (2005). Heroes, metanarratives, and the paradox of masculinity in contemporary Western culture. *Journal of Men's Studies, 13*(3), 301–312.

Brannon, R. (1985). Dimensions of the male sex role in America. In A. G. Sargent (Ed.), *Beyond sex roles* (pp. 296–316). New York, NY: West.

Cramer, T. (2013, April 18). *PTSD Study: Men versus women*. Inside Veterans' Health: http://www.va.gov/health/NewsFeatures/2013/April/PTSD-Study-Men-Versus-Women.asp.

Eagly, A. H., & Johnson, B. T. (1990). Gender and leadership style: A meta-analysis. *Psychological Bulletin, 108*(2), 233–256.

Farkas, T., & Leaper, C. (2016). The psychology of boys. In W. J. Wong & S. R. Wester (Eds.), *APA handbook of men and masculinities* (pp. 357–387). Washington, DC: American Psychological Association.

Farthing, G. W. (2005). Attitudes toward heroic and nonheroic physical risk takers as mates and as friends. *Evolution and Human Behavior, 26*(2), 171–185.

Geary, D. C., Winegard, B., & Winegard, B. (2016). Evolutionary influences on men's lives. In W. J. Wong & S. R. Wester (Eds.), *APA handbook of men and masculinities* (pp. 211–229). Washington, DC: American Psychological Association.

Hamner, C. H. (2011). *Enduring battle: American soldiers in three wars, 1776—1945*. Lawrence, KS: University Press of Kansas.

Kilmartin, C. (2010). *The masculine self* (4th ed.). Cornwall on Hudson, NY: Sloan.

Kilmartin, C., & McDermott, R. C. (2015). Violence and masculinities. In W. J. Wong & S. R. Wester (Eds.), *APA handbook of men and masculinities* (pp. 615–636). Washington, DC: American Psychological Association.

Kiselica, M. S., & Englar-Carlson, M. (2010). Identifying, affirming, and building upon male strengths: The positive psychology/positive masculinity model of psychotherapy with boys and men. *Psychotherapy Theory, Research, Practice, Training, 47*(3), 276–287.

Lamb, M. E., Pleck, J. H., Charnov, E., & Levine, J. A. (1987). A biosocial perspective on paternal behavior and involvement. In J. B. Lancaster, J. Altman, A. S. Rossi, & L. R. Sherrod (Eds.), *Parenting across the lifespan: Biosocial dimensions* (pp. 111–142). New York, NY: De Gruyter.

Levant, R. (2006). Foreword. In M. Englar-Carlson & M. Stevens (Eds.), *In the room with men: A casebook of therapeutic change* (pp. xv–xx). Washington, DC: American Psychological Association.

Marx, G. (1959). *Groucho and me: The autobiography of Groucho Marx*. London, UK: Gollancz.

Meyers, N. M., Chapman, J. C., Gunthert, K. C., & Weissbrod, C. S. (2015). The effect of masculinity on community reintegration following TBI in Military Veterans. *Military Psychology, 28*(1), 14–24.

Morman, M. T., & Floyd, K. (2006). Good fathering: Father and son perceptions of what it means to be a good father. *Fathering: A Journal of Research, Theory, & Practice about Men as Fathers, 4*(2), 113–136.

Millis, W. (1981). *Arms and men: A study in American military history.* New Brunswick, NJ: Rutgers University Press.

Myers, D. G. (2004). *Psychology in modules.* Holland, MI: Worth.

Potts, A. (2005). Cyborg masculinity in the Viagra era. *Sexualities, Evolution, & Gender, 7*(1), 3–16.

Philaretou, A. G., & Allen, K. R. (2001). Reconstructing masculinity and sexuality. *Journal of Men's Studies, 9*(3), 301–324.

Sadalla, E. K., Kenrick, D. T., & Vershure, B. (1987). Dominance and heterosexual attraction. *Journal of Personality & Social Psychology, 52*(4), 730–738.

Sell, A., Hone, L. S., & Pound, N. (2012). The importance of physical strength to human males. *Human Nature, 23*(1), 30–44.

Shields, D. (2015, November 10). *Culturally competent care for male veterans.* Society for the Psychological Study of Men and Women: http://division51.net/homepage-slider/culturally-competent-care-for-male-veterans/.

Smart, R. (2006). A man with a "woman's problem": Male gender and eating disorders. In M. Englar-Carlson & M. Stevens (Eds.), *In the room with men: A casebook of therapeutic change* (pp. 319–338). Washington, DC: American Psychological Association.

Smith, R. M., Parrot, D. J., Swartout, K. M., & Tharp, A. T. (2015). Deconstructing hegemonic masculinity: The roles of antifemininity, subordination to women, and sexual dominance in men's perpetration of sexual aggression. *Psychology of Men & Masculinity, 16*(2), 160–169.

Snipes, S. A., Hayes Constant, T. K., Trumble, B. C., Goodreau, S. M., Morrison, D. M., Shell-Duncan, B. K., Pelman, R. S., & O'Connor, K. A. (2015). Masculine perspectives about work and family concurrently promote and inhibit men's healthy behaviors. *International Journal of Men's Health, 14*(1), 1–20.

Stuessy, T. (2007). *Risk perception: A quantitative analysis of skydiving participation.* Ann Arbor, MI: ProQuest.

Urbaniak, G. C., & Kilmann, P. R. (2003). Physical attractiveness and the nice guy paradox: Do nice guys really finish last? *Sex roles, 49*(9–10), 413–426.

Wright, P. H. (1989). Gender differences in adults' same- and cross-gender friendships. In R. G. Adams & R. Blieszner (Eds.), *Older adult friendship: Structure and process.* Newbury Park, CA: SAGE.

Young, I. M. (2003). The logic of masculinist protection: Reflections on the current security state. *Signs: Journal of Women in Culture & Society, 29*(1), 2–25.

Notes

1. Classic serial 4–2. *The Tenth Planet* (October 8–October 29, 1966).
2. Shields (2015).
3. Smart (2006), pp. 319–338.
4. Kilmartin (2010).
5. Modern episode 2–5, "Rise of the Cybermen" (May 13, 2006).
6. Modern episode 2–6, "The Age of Steel" (May 20, 2006).
7. Modern episode 2–6, "The Age of Steel" (May 20, 2006).
8. Modern episode 6–12, "Closing Time" (September 24, 2011).
9. Modern episode 8–12, "Death in Heaven" (November 8, 2014).
10. Modern episode 2–5, "Rise of the Cybermen."

11. Brannon (1985).
12. Smith et al. (2015), p. 162.
13. Farkas & Leaper (2016).
14. Even the Cyberwoman in episode 2–13, "Doomsday" (July 1, 2006), looks like a Cyberman.
15. Geary et al. (2016).
16. Modern episode 4–2, "Partners in Crime" (April 5, 2008).
17. Levant (2006).
18. Kilmartin & McDermott (2015).
19. Meyers et al. (2015), p. 2.
20. Christmas special "The Next Doctor" (December 25, 2008).
21. Modern episode 2–13, "Doomsday" (July 8, 2006).
22. Smart (2006), p. 320.
23. Kiselica & Englar-Carlson (2010).
24. e.g., Wright (1989).
25. Myers (2004), p. 165.
26. Classic serial 26–1, *Battlefield* (September 6–27, 1989).
27. Modern episode 8–12, "Death in Heaven" (November 8, 2014).
28. Snipes et al. (2015).
29. e.g., modern episode 5–1, "The Eleventh Hour" (April 3, 2010).
30. Morman & Floyd (2006).
31. Lamb et al. (1987).
32. Modern episode 4–6, "The Doctor's Daughter" (May 10, 2008).
33. Modern episode 5–2, "The Beast Below" (April 10, 2010).
34. Kiselica & Englar-Carlson (2010).
35. Stuessy (2007).
36. Marx (1959), p. 321.
37. Kiselica & Englar-Carlson (2010).
38. Boon (2005).
39. Boon (2005); Farthing (2005).
40. Classic serial 4–2, *The Tenth Planet* (October 8–29, 1966).
41. Modern episode 6–7, "A Good Man Goes to War" (June 4, 2011).
42. e.g., Adric in classic serial 19–6, *Earthshock*, pt. 4 (March 16, 1982); Clara in modern episode 9–10, "Face the Raven" (November 21, 2015).
43. "Four wives, all dead."—Clara in modern episode 8–12, "Death in Heaven" (November 8, 2014).
44. Modern episode 1–2, "The End of the World" (April 2, 2005).

How much humanity do we give up before we stop being human at all?

CHAPTER SIXTEEN

From Human to Machine: At What Point Do You Lose Your Soul?

JIM DAVIES AND DANIEL SAUNDERS

"You lot, you're obsessed. You'd do anything for the latest upgrade."
—Tenth Doctor[1]

*". . . the idea of machinery with a conscious mental inner
life frightens or enrages some people . . . It will soon be
our honor to welcome some of it to the land of the living,
however upsetting that may be to our traditional categories."*
—robotics expert Hans Moravec[2]

In our world, technology-savvy people line up for the latest model of smartphone, and look forward to new features and bug fixes in new versions of software. Not everyone welcomes new tech, though,[3] and some people suffer extreme fears regarding both technology and change.[4] What does the

Doctor have against upgrades? For an expert in technology and a being who has upgraded his body at least a dozen times (and his sonic screwdriver almost as often), it may seem like a surprising position.

It could stem from the fact that in his universe, alluring technology for augmenting human performance often turns out to be a Trojan horse for evil agendas—such as when EarPods, which provide communication and direct brain downloads of news and other current information, are revealed to be a mind control device that causes the entire population to march into the factory where they are to be processed into Cybermen.[5] The Doctor seems to reserve special distaste for technology that replaces significant parts of sentient creatures with cybernetic components. He has called the typical Dalek "a machine creature, a monster"[6] and the Cybermen "a pathetic bunch of tin soldiers,"[7] with each one "a living brain jammed inside a cybernetic body, with a heart of steel."[8] Given the potential advantages of having a body made of durable, replaceable parts, or a mind that can draw on computing power to guide one's actions, are there sound reasons from psychological science to share such a fear? Do cybernetic features pose a threat to our morality?

Cybermorality

One feature of the Daleks or the Cybermen is that they all look like each other, with little or no visible individuality. People are more likely to do selfish acts when they feel they are anonymous.[9] This is true when people are wearing sunglasses,[10] and also when they're wearing masks. In one experiment conducted around Halloween, children were asked to take only two pieces of candy from a bowl. Masked children took more candy than they were supposed to (seemingly feeling more comfortable breaking the rules when in costume).[11]

What about the fact that the Daleks have no faces, and that the Cybermen have faces that can't express any emotion? It could be that this affects their moral attitudes by reducing their overall ability to feel empathy. A study of people who had some of their facial muscles disabled found that those who were less able to smile had more depressive symptoms.[12]

Maybe the fact that the Daleks are working through machinery makes it easier for them to act in an evil way. Studies show that, sometimes, interacting with people through a technological medium reduces empathy. For example, it's easier to "flame" people online, berating them from a distance, because you don't have to face the consequences of their facial expressions and retaliatory anger.[13] Studies of moral psychology show that people are more apt to kill someone (albeit for the benefit of saving others) when they are separated by some kind of technology, such as pressing a button.[14]

People's natural sense of wrongdoing is more activated when the act involves physically putting your hands on someone. That is, pulling a switch to kill somebody feels better, morally, than pushing that person in front of a moving train.[15] This is possibly because we spent the majority of our evolutionary history without technology that allowed us to affect people at a distance, so we didn't evolve to have moral reactions to using technology. To know that pulling the switch might violate the rights of an innocent individual, you have to *think through* the consequences, because most people don't have a gut reaction to it.

A Dalek is an organic creature controlling a robotlike body. Daleks can be seen as being halfway between a creature with a metal body and a creature piloting a small tank.[16] If we look at them as creatures piloting tanks, we can speculate that perhaps this creates a psychological distance between the brain and the victims, making it easier for them to commit murder. But might they see their armored casings as their body?

My Metal Arm Is Me
For fully cybernetic individuals, the case is clearer. Cybermen have their bodies—arms, legs, everything but their brains—replaced with robotic actuators,[17] and this may someday happen to our world's human beings. We can speculate on what it is like to be put in a metal body by thinking of it as amputation to the extreme—amputating just about everything except the brain. A robotic body is like one giant prosthesis. We can imagine what it might be like to be a Cyberman based on what we know about the psychology of amputees and how they adapt to prosthetics.

An argument that the Daleks might identify with their metal shells comes from research on how our minds adapt to the tools we use. After repeated use of a grasping tool (like the kind people use to pick up garbage), people thought their arms actually had gotten longer.[18] When a person uses a tool so often, he or she forgets that the tool is there, and is able to consciously focus on the task at hand, much like one does with the keyboard after learning how to type. We can call this kind of technology *transparent*.[19] The tool feels, to the extent that it feels like anything at all, like a natural extension of our body. All this is to say that objects that are used, or remain in close proximity to our bodies, over time can become extensions of our own body image,[20] and this may apply to the controls and sensory feedback received by the Dalek mutant inside the armor.

When You Really Lose Your Soul

If we want to explain the moral problems that fictional cyborg beings demonstrate, we need to look beyond the fact that they have mechanical bodies.[21] Evidence from the cyborgs we have here on Earth suggests that the mind adapts to tools of all kinds, accepting them as part of who we are. We must instead examine how their minds have been modified by technology.

The Daleks are genetically engineered to have few emotions other than hatred or rage.[22] The Cybermen, on the other hand, have no emotions at all.[23] In both the classic and the new series, their brains have electronic parts that inhibit emotions.[24] Although compassion is not the only emotion that makes us moral, it plays a large role. Social psychologist Jonathan Haidt has found evidence that many of our moral stances are actually based on emotions—anger, disgust, and so on.[25]

Changes to the mind are likely necessary to make it possible to occupy the augmented body. The Tenth Doctor tells Rose that Cybermen need to have their emotions inhibited "because it hurts,"[26] and he disables the Cybermen army simply by reenabling their emotions. By comparison, although the Dalek brain was deliberately engineered by Davros to be genocidal,[27] it's possible that a large degree of alteration would be necessary in any case, to permit years of living as a blobbish mutant sealed into a small metal capsule. If so, then both species show that when augmenting the body requires tampering with core emotions of the brain, a species should beware.

In the end, the Doctor's objection to the metal shells of the Daleks and the Cybermen is that they encase the ruthless, uncompassionate, and the unsensual—that is, they are stripped of everything the Doctor values in human beings. Emotions are a critical component in what we consider to be true humanity. He believes in technology—after all, it is the unimaginably advanced technology of the TARDIS that makes his adventures in time and space possible—but not when upgrading means sacrificing this humanity.[28]

We have good reason to think that the metal bodies of cybernetic individuals would ultimately be considered real bodies by their brains. Minds adapt to new prostheses and see them as a part of their body images. But we have also seen that the tools we use can be a part of the body image, so we can assume that Daleks would also see their metal exoskeletons as a part of themselves. In neither case can we assume that their metal bodies have contributed to their evil.

References

Bains, S. (2007, April 1). *Mixed feelings*. Wired: http://www.wired.com/2007/04/esp/.

Barlett, C. P. (2015). Anonymously hurting others online: The effect of anonymity on cyberbullying frequency. *Psychology of Popular Media Culture, 4*(2), 70–79.

Botvinick, M., & Cohen, J. (1998). Rubber hands "feel" touch that eyes see. *Nature, 391*, 756–760.

Cardinali, L., Frassinetti, F., Brozzoli, C., Roy,A. C., Urquizar, C., & Farnè A. (2009). Tool-use induces morphological updating of the body schema. *Current Biology, 19*(12), R478–479.

Castelnuovo-Tedesco, P. (1989). The fear of change and its consequences in analysis and psychotherapy. *Psychoanalytic Inquiry, 9*, 101–118.

Clark, A. (2003). *Natural born cyborgs: Minds, technologies, and the future of human intelligence*. Oxford, UK: Oxford University Press.

Desmond, D., & MacLachlan, M. (2002). Psychosocial issues in the field of prosthetics and orthotics. *Journal of Prosthetics & Orthotics, 14*(1), 19–22.

Franco, V., Hu, H-Y., Lewenstein, B., Piirto, R., Underwood, R., & Vidal, N. K. (1995). Anatomy of a flame: conflict and community building on the internet. *IEEE Technology & Society Magazine, 14*(2), 12–21.

Ganguly, K., & Carmena, J. M. (2009). Emergence of a stable cortical map for neuroprosthetic control. *PLoS Biology, 7*(7), e1000153.

Giritli Nygren, K. (2012). Narratives of ICT and organizational change in public administration. *Gender, Work, and Organization, 19*(6), 615–630.

Greene, J. (2013). Moral tribes: Emotion, reason, and the gap between us and them. London, UK: Penguin.

Greene, J. D., Somerville, R. B., Nystrom, L. E., Darley, J. M., & Cohen, J. D. (2001). An fMRI investigation of emotional engagement in moral judgment. *Science, 293*(14), 2105–2108.

Haidt, J. (2012). *The righteous mind: Why good people are divided by politics and religion*. New York, NY: Pantheon.

Harris, M. (1983). *The Doctor Who technical manual*. New York, NY: Random House.

Holmes, J. M., Repka, M. X., Kraker, R. T., & Clarke, M. P. (2006). The treatment of amblyopia. *Strabismus, 15*(1): 37–42.

Kirk, J., & Kirk, L. (1997). Computer pains. *Journal of Workplace Learning, 9*(2), 678–72.

Lewis, J. W. (2006). Cortical networks related to human use of tools. *Neuroscientist, 12*(3), 211–231.

Miller, F., & Rowold, K. (1979). Halloween masks and deindividuation. *Psychological Reports, 44*(2), 422–422.

Moravec, H. (1999). *Robot: Mere machine to transcendent mind.* Oxford, UK: Oxford University Press.

Neal, D. T., & Chartrand, T. L. (2011). Embodied emotion perception amplifying and dampening facial feedback modulates emotion perception accuracy. *Social Psychological and Personality Science, 2*(6), 673–678.

Renier, L. A., Anurova, I., De Volder, A. G., Carlson, S., VanMeter, J., & Rauschecker, J. P. (2010). Preserved functional specialization for spatial processing in the middle occipital gyrus of the early blind. *Neuron, 68*(1): 138–148.

Sacks, O. (2012). *Hallucinations.* New York, NY: Vintage.

Sanna, L. J., Chang, E. C., Miceli, P. M., & Lundberg, K. B. (2011). Rising up to higher virtues: Experiencing elevated physical height uplifts prosocial actions. *Journal of Experimental Social Psychology, 47*(2), 472–476.

Spotila, J. R. (2004). *Sea turtles: A complete guide to their biology, behavior, and conservation.* Baltimore, MD: John Hopkins University Press.

Strack, F., Martin, L. L., & Stepper, S. (1988). Inhibiting and facilitating conditions of the human smile: A nonobtrusive test of the facial feedback hypothesis. *Journal of Personality & Social Psychology, 54*(5), 768–777.

VanSwearingen, J. M., Cohn, J. F., & Bajaj-Luthra, A. (1999). Specific impairment of smiling increases the severity of depressive symptoms in patients with facial neuromuscular disorders. *Aesthetic Plastic Surgery, 23*(6), 416–423.

Walters, G. D. (2001). Development of a Fear-of-Change scale for the Psychology Inventory of Criminal Thinking Styles. *Journal of Offender Rehabilitation, 34*(1), 1–8.

Zhong, C.-B., Bohns, V. K., & Gino, F. (2010). Good lamps are the best police: Darkness increases dishonesty and self-interested behavior. *Psychological Science, 21*(3), 311–314.

Notes

1. Modern episode 2–5, "Rise of the Cybermen" (May 13, 2006).
2. Moravec (1999), p. 111.
3. Giritli (2012); Kirk & Kirk (1997).
4. Castelnuovo-Tedesco (1989); Walters (2001).
5. Modern episode 2–6, "The Age of Steel" (May 20, 2006).
6. Classic serial 12–4, *The Genesis of the Daleks* (March 8–April 12, 1975).
7. Classic serial 12–5, *Revenge of the Cybermen* (April 19–May 10, 1975).
8. Modern episode 2–5, "Rise of the Cybermen" (May 13, 2006).
9. e.g., Barlett (2015).
10. Zhong et al. (2010).
11. Miller & Rowold (1979).
12. VanSwearingen et al. (1999).
13. Franco et al. (1995).
14. Greene (2013).
15. Greene et al. (2001).
16. Classic serial 1–2, *The Daleks* (December 21, 1963–February 1, 1964).
17. Classic serial 4–2, *The Tenth Planet* (October 8–29, 1966).
18. Cardinali et al. (2009).

19. Clark (2003), p. 37.
20. Desmond & MacLachlan (2002).
21. Kelly & Davies (this volume).
22. Classic serial 1–2, *The Daleks* (December 21, 1963–February 1, 1964).
23. Classic serial 4–2, *The Tenth Planet* (October 8–29, 1966).
24. Modern episodes 8–2, "Into the Dalek" (August 30, 2014); 6–12, "Closing Time" (September 24, 2011).
25. Haidt (2012). See also Kelly & Davies (this volume).
26. Modern episode 2–6, "The Age of Steel" (May 20, 2006).
27. Classic serial 12–4, *Genesis of the Daleks* (March 8–April 12, 1975).
28. Modern episode 2–5, "Rise of the Cybermen" (May 13, 2006).

The Six Factors—A Good Man?

TRAVIS LANGLEY

Many professionals in psychology examine how we develop our morals,[1] but what are good and evil in the first place? The recently regenerated Twelfth Doctor asks Clara if he's a good man, unsure of the answer himself.[2] The previous Doctor does not think of himself as a good man, telling enemies who abducted pregnant Amy, "Good men don't need rules. Today is not the day to find out why I have so many."[3] Can a person, not just his or her actions, be good or evil? In terms of individual personality, what do these primal concepts really mean?

HEXACO

Akin to how personality psychology founder Gordon Allport launched the study of traits through *lexical studies* (word analyses),[4] some personality psychologists added their H factor to the Big Five first by studying trait adjectives in several European and Asian languages.[5] The trait lists associated with the Big

Five left out many terms related to selflessness or selfishness. Focusing on the positive side of the dimension, they called this new factor Honesty-Humility to give their *six-factor theory* a name that reads like an alien planet or a spell-casting company, *HEXACO*: Honesty–Humility, Emotionality (essentially Neuroticism), eXtraversion, Agreeableness, Conscientiousness, Openness.

Good: Honesty-Humility

A person scoring high in this factor is unlikely to be boastful, deceitful, hypocritical, pompous, or sly. The Doctor seeks truth and yet he tells many lies. Even a person with good intentions may end up on the not-so-good end of the scale. Long before Clara Oswald has no answer when the Twelfth Doctor asks her if he's good, Jamie McCrimmon questions the Second Doctor's priorities: "People have died. The Daleks are all over the place, fit to murder the lot of us, and all you can say is you've had a good night's work."[6]

> **Examples of Honesty-Humility Traits**
> Faithfulness
> Generosity
> Honesty
> Lack of Pretense
> Loyalty
> Modesty
> Sincerity

Evil: The Dark Tetrad

The *dark triad* of psychopathy, narcissism, and Machiavellianism (described in Chapter Nine, "Who Makes a Good Companion?") is a model of variables that, when combined, strike people as selfish and on the evil side—more so when combined with a fourth trait, sadism, to form a *dark tetrad*. These constructs tend to go unrepresented in the Big Five, partially correlating with disagreeableness but not completely. All four selfish, overlapping parts of the dark tetrad correlate with the low end of factor H.[7]

- *Psychopathy* is a broad personality dimension involving lack of empathy, lack of remorse, or lack of consideration as to what is right or wrong.[8] While the Doctor sometimes shows little empathy, insufficient ability to recognize or share the feelings of others, he has a conscience, he cares about right and wrong, and even when he thinks he does not care, he will shift into protector mode as soon as he sees suffering, especially if it involves a crying child.
- *Narcissism* goes beyond merely thinking highly of oneself. This egotistical, grandiose sense of oneself includes inordinate fascination with oneself. The narcissist is in love with himself or herself. Perhaps in reaction to the Fifth Doctor's uncertainty, the Sixth Doctor emerges from his regeneration seemingly the most pompous and egotistical of them all. Narcissism, however, is unlikely to be considered *narcissistic personality disorder* in the case of the person who genuinely has reason to regard his or her own abilities highly.[9]
- *Machiavellianism*, classically thought of as the application of deceit and cunning to get what a person wants out of others, psychologically is more of an attitude about such things. The Machiavellian takes a practical, pragmatic view of morality, with a cynical view of moral concerns. Even though

Jamie does not believe him under the circumstances, the Second Doctor insists that he has never
believed the ends justify the means.[10]

- *Sadism* as a personality trait is not the same thing
  as *sexual sadism*, which means deriving sexual gratification from inflicting pain on others. Someone
  with a *sadistic personality* takes pleasure in other
  people's suffering in many ways, possibly none of
  which include anything erotic. Regardless of which
  form a sadistic tendency takes, whether sexual or
  not, combining it with the dark triad produces a
  personality most people view as evil. A manipulative egotist lacking empathy or conscience seems
  quite dangerous if that person enjoys hurting others.
  The Doctor does not enjoy seeing people get hurt,
  despite moments of anger in which he makes it clear
  that he believes some of his enemies deserve to hurt.
  Usually he's referring to enemies who, themselves,
  relish the pain of others, such as the cruel Dominators,[11] the Kandyman who delights in torturing
  and killing with confectionary,[12] or Angel Bob who
  taunts the Doctor about murder.[13]

Gray Areas

Factor H for good and the dark tetrad for evil both remain
controversial, with plenty of researchers debating their validity
as empirically testable constructs.[14] If good and evil themselves
were easy to define, members of the human race would not
have spent thousands of years arguing over them. We do not
stop contemplating them, nor does the Doctor come up with
a clear opinion of how they fit himself, but their intangible
nature does not make them any less important in our lives.
Dismissively saying "We can't define them" does not make
them go away.

References

Allport, G. W., & Odbert, H. S. (1936). Trait-names: A psycho-lexical study. *Psychological Monographs, 47*(1), i–171.

American Psychiatric Association (2013). *Diagnostic and statistical manual of mental disorders* (5th ed.). Washington, DC: American Psychiatric Association.

Book, A. S., Visser, B., Blais, J., & D'Agata, M. T. (2016). Unpacking more "evil": What is at the core of the dark tetrad? *Personality and Individual Differences, 90*, 269–272.

Cleckley, H. M. (1941/1976). *The mask of sanity: An attempt to clarify some issues about the so-called psychopathic personality.* Maryland Heights, MO: Mosby.

De Raad, B., Barelds, D. P. H., Mlačić, B., Church, A. T., Katigbak, M. S., Ostendorf, F., Hřebíčková, M., Di Blas, L., & Szirmák, Z. (2010). Only three personality factors are fully replicable across languages: Reply to Ashton and Lee. *Journal of Research in Personality, 44*(4), 442–445.

Freud, S. (1909). Analysis of a phobia in a 5-year-old boy. In *Jahrbuch für psychoanalytische under psychopathologische Forshugen*, Bd. 1. Reprinted with translation in *The sexual enlightenment of children* (1963). New York, NY: Collier.

Freud, S. (1940). An outline of psychoanalysis. In *Standard edition of the complete works of Sigmund Freud* (Vol. 23, pp. 141–207). London, UK: Hogarth.

Kohlberg, L. (1981). *Essays on moral development.* San Francisco, CA: Harper & Row.

Lee, K., & Ashton, M. C. (2005). Psychopathy, Machiavellianism, and narcissism in the five-factor model and the HEXACO model of personality structure. *Personality, and Individual Differences* (7), 1571–1582.

Lee, K., & Ashton, M. C. (2012). *The H factor of personality: Why some people are manipulative, self-entitled, materialistic, and exploitative—and why it matters for everyone.* Waterloo, Ontario, Canada: Wilfred Laurier University Press.

Piaget, J. (1932). *The moral judgment of the child.* New York, NY: Harcourt Brace Jovanovich.

Međedović, J., & Petrović, B. (2015). The Dark Tetrad: Structural properties and location in the personality space. *Journal of Individual Differences, 36*(4), 228–236.

Notes

1. e.g., Freud (1909, 1940); Kohlberg (1981); Piaget (1932).
2. Modern episode 8–2, "Into the Dalek" (August 30, 2014).
3. Modern episode 6–7, "A Good Man Goes to War" (June 4, 2011).
4. e.g., Allport & Odbert (1936).
5. Lee & Ashton (2012).
6. Classic serial 4–9, *The Evil of the Daleks*, pt. 5 (June 17, 1967).
7. Book et al. (2016); Lee & Ashton (2005); Međedović, J., & Petrović (2015).
8. Cleckley (1941/1976).
9. American Psychiatric Association (2013).
10. Classic serial 4–9, *The Evil of the Daleks*, pt. 5 (June 17, 1967).
11. Classic serial 6–1, *The Dominators* (August 10–September 7, 1968).
12. Classic serial 25–2, *The Happiness Patrol* (November 2–16, 1988).
13. Episodes 5–4, "The Time of Angels" (April 24, 2010); 5–5, "Flesh and Stone" (May 1, 2010).
14. e.g., De Raad et al. (2010).

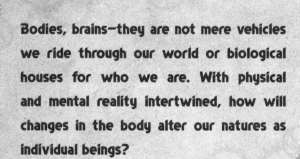

Bodies, brains—they are not mere vehicles we ride through our world or biological houses for who we are. With physical and mental reality intertwined, how will changes in the body alter our natures as individual beings?

Part Five

Natures

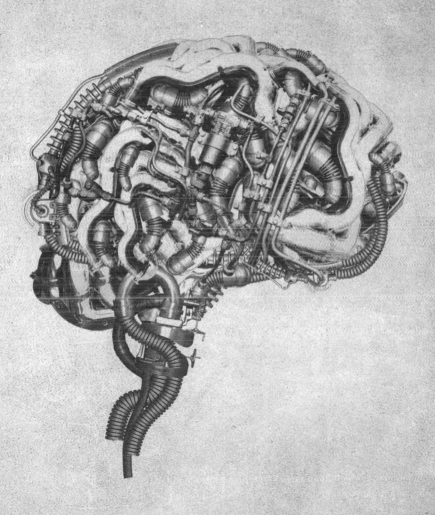

Obviously changes to the brain can alter memory and motor function, but what about dispositions such as grumpiness or generosity, interests in music or other people, or even the accent coming out of an individual's mouth?

CHAPTER SEVENTEEN

Getting to the Hearts of Time Lord Personality Change: Regeneration on the Brain

Sarita J. Robinson

"We all change, when you think about it, we're all different people. . . ."
—Eleventh Doctor[1]

"A musician must make music, an artist must paint,
a poet must write, if he is to be ultimately at peace
with himself. What a man can be, he must be."
——psychologist Abraham Maslow[2]

Neuropsychology is a rapidly developing field of psychology which has started to reveal how the human brain works. Advances in techniques such as neuroimaging have given us windows on the brain that scientists from previous generations did not have. By comparing our understanding of human neuropsychology to an alien such as the one we know as the Doctor, we may be able to explore how his alien brain works and even speculate about the mechanisms involved in the process of regeneration.

Is the brain of an extraterrestrial similar to that of a human? In addition to having many physical differences from humans, most noticeably his binary vascular system with its pair of hearts, the Doctor has some *cognitive* (mental) differences. He processes information from books and computer systems much quicker than is possible for a human and appears to have a certain level of telepathic ability.[3] These differences show us that Time Lords are both physically and psychologically different from humans.

Brain Scans and the Doctor

Does size matter when it comes to your brain? Logically, if someone has a bigger brain, you could expect that person to be more intelligent. However, this does not seem to be the case. One of the greatest scientists of the twentieth century, Albert Einstein, actually had a smaller brain than the typical adult male. After his death, his brain was examined, and some structural differences were observed. For example, Einstein had a larger than average left parietal lobe.[4]

So even though the Doctor might be assumed to have a human-size brain (based on the size of his skull), it could be that the Doctor's brain is structured differently.

Or could it be that the Doctor uses more of his brain? Because humans use only 10 percent of their brains, right?

Wrong!

Although it is a popular myth that we only use 10 percent of our brain power, it is actually untrue.[5] People who have even small amounts of brain damage can have major impairments in

Looking into Skulls

Not until the early 1900s was it possible to look at the brain of a living person. The earliest technique, *pneumoencephalography*, was both dangerous and painful.[6]

After the 1940s, improvements in surgical techniques allowed brain surgeons to carry out operations that could alleviate conditions such as epilepsy. One neurosurgeon, Wilder Penfield, used an electrical probe during those operations to stimulate parts of the brain and then recorded which functions each part of the brain controlled. For example, an electric current in the temporal lobes caused patients (who were kept awake through surgery) to summon past memories.[7]

The Doctor is unlikely to have brain surgery just so that we can poke around in his head. However, a technique called *functional magnetic resonance imaging (fMRI)* allows us to see how different experiences change blood flow and oxygenation levels in the brain, letting us see which areas the brain uses for certain functions.[8] Brain imaging has definitely come a long way in the last 100 years, but further advances are needed as the equipment is cumbersome and expensive.

the way they function. All the parts of the brain are important, with each area responsible for a particular function. Take the occipital lobes (located at the back of the brain), for example; this area is responsible for visual processing. If a brain scan reveals damage to the occipital lobes, we would expect that person to have problems with his or her vision. But using our occipital lobes for processing visual information is only one of the things we do during a typical day. Humans tend to multi-task, and so we must use various areas of our brains for all the different activities we undertake. Even if we just go walking in the park on a summer's day, we will use visual and auditory processing to enjoy the sights and sounds, balance, and other motor skills required to walk. Next, the language-processing areas of the brain would be activated to produce (*Broca's area*) and understand (*Wernicke's area*) speech if we stop for a chat.[9]

As the Doctor appears to be quite psychologically different from us, we have to conclude that his brain must be structured differently. The only way to confirm this would be to do a brain scan. Although some enemies try to steal the Doctor's head,[10] they do not manage to complete scans of his brain.[11] Here on Earth we don't have the benefits of alien technology, and until recently the only way to look into someone's brain was to cut open the skull, as the sidebar "Looking into Skulls" explains.

What Happens to the Doctor's Brain During Regeneration?

During regeneration, the Doctor undergoes a rapid change in his physical appearance as the cells in his body are renewed. He also appears to show changes in his psychological makeup. Although the Doctor can retain his previous memories, the changes in his personality can be as marked as the physical changes. We also know that the process of regeneration can be difficult and painful, leading to emotional upset and physiological problems. In fact, some of the Doctor's behaviors around the time of regeneration are similar to those seen in teenagers. Any parent of a teenager can tell you that the adolescent years are a period of emotional, cognitive, and biological changes. In the Doctor's case, his transformation appears to be compressed into an acute phase lasting a few hours, followed by a longer period of recovery.[12]

Psychologists think that at around age twelve, individuals begin a process called *synaptic pruning*[13] in which the neural connections that are not being used start to die off. For example, if a second language is learned early in life but not used in later years, during adolescence these language connections may be cut. It could well be that the Doctor, around the time of regeneration, undergoes an extreme form of synaptic pruning. In the case of the Doctor, it would appear that he has some control over which synaptic links to keep. Just as the process of synaptic pruning gets a teenager ready for adulthood, the process of regeneration may make the Doctor's brain ready for the challenges he will face in his next regeneration. For example, we know that when the Eighth Doctor regenerates into the War Doctor, he actively regenerates into a form that will be able to face the challenges of the Time War.[14]

During adolescence the process of pruning can go wrong and lead to psychiatric disorders such as schizophrenia, a long-term disorder that can impact how a person thinks, feels, and behaves.[15] It is possible that the Doctor could similarly face the problem of abnormal synaptic pruning following regeneration. The Doctor's regeneration into the Sixth Doctor is especially problematic, with the Doctor appearing unstable and difficult, as demonstrated most dramatically when he attempts to strangle his companion, Peri, in the hours after his regeneration.[16] It is possible that the violent and traumatic event of regeneration can lead to errors in synaptic pruning which take time to resolve.

Interestingly, neuroscientists now believe that the brain can continue to change and be shaped for the challenges we meet even after the teenage years. For example, brain regions involved in the recall of spatial information have been shown to change when London taxi drivers learn "The Knowledge" (the layout of all the roads in London).[17] Specifically, taxi drivers had different neural architecture in an area of the brain well known for being important for memory: the *hippocampus*. So how does the process of regeneration affect the Doctor's brain, and can we guess the possible structure and neurochemical balance of the Doctor in each of his regenerations?

Neophrenology

If no one has taken a picture of the Doctor's brain, can we make any predictions about what it might look like? In the nineteenth century, the study of *phrenology* suggested that the external shape of the skull could be used to ascertain certain characteristics about a person. For example, if a person had a particular bump above his or her right eye, that would tell you something about that person's sense of humor. Phrenology has been thoroughly discredited, but some contemporary neuropsychologists have coined the phrase *neophrenology*.[18] Neophrenology suggests that by looking at a person's brain structure, you may be able to predict differences in his or her mental abilities. Using this reasoning, we should be able to reverse engineer what the Doctor's brain looks like by examining some of the behaviors he displays. The Doctor's brain may look quite different in each regeneration, dependent on the particular skills and abilities peculiar to that Doctor.

1. Disinhibition
The First Doctor physically appears to be physically very old, emotionally very grumpy, and behaviorally not shy about telling people how annoying they are.[19] As we get older, an area at

the front of our brains, the *frontal lobes*, starts to shrink,[20] and so some of the important functions that the frontal lobes control (e.g., planning, judging, actively recalling[21]) start to fail— among them, our inhibitions. It could well be that the Doctor, toward the end of his first life cycle, is starting to show problems with his inhibition control (*disinhibition*) and so becomes rude and unhelpful.

2. Music

The Second Doctor, who has on occasion been described as a clown and can come across as disorganized and bumbling, shows a love of music that sets him apart from other regenerations. In fact, he is often found playing his trusty recorder while trying to concentrate and in times of danger.[22] Psychologists have found that learning to play music can lead to enhancements in certain mental abilities, such as *spatial reasoning*[23] (ability to mentally navigate and visualize objects three-dimensionally from different angles[24]). Even people who do not play an instrument can benefit from listening to music. Research suggests that as little as ten minutes of exposure to Mozart may improve people's reasoning ability.[25] This improvement is thought to occur because the musical and spatial processing areas overlap in the brain, and the music therefore primes areas needed for spatial reasoning. Psychologists who have not replicated these findings suggest that any increases in cognition are due to the music increasing arousal levels, thereby making people more likely to pay attention.[26] Whatever the reason, music does have a positive effect on the brain, and the Doctor's mental abilities are likely to benefit from playing and listening to music during this incarnation.

3. Inventiveness

Made to regenerate by the Time Lords and then exiled on Earth, the Third Doctor has a much reduced ability to travel in time and space. Trapped on Earth in the twentieth century, he is inventive to make the most of the rather primitive technology he has available.[27] This incarnation of the Doctor does enjoy using the available resources to create new devices such as the Whomobile. Is it possible that great inventors have a different type of brain? That could be the case. Researchers have found that when we generate a new idea, there is activation in various areas of the brain, including the left inferior frontal gyrus, anterior cingulate cortex, and precentral gyrus.[28] The inventive Third Doctor may have enhanced functioning in these areas of the brain.

4. Generosity

The Fourth Doctor is outgoing and friendly, with an infectious sense of humor. He is generous, especially with his jelly babies. But what makes a person generous? Some researchers think that differences in hormone levels affect how generous people are. In one study, participants were asked to split a sum of money with a stranger. The researchers found that those who were given a dose of *oxytocin*, the so-called cuddle hormone, were 80 percent more generous than those who were given a placebo.[29] Other hormones, such as testosterone, have been found to reduce generosity.[30]

5. Mental Toughness

The Fifth Doctor enjoys playing cricket.[31] People who have a high degree of *mental toughness* (a resilient attitude, self-belief, and personal motivation) tend to make good cricketers.[32] We know little about the brain structure or neurochemistry of someone who has higher levels of mental toughness. Some studies have suggested a genetic component. Others indicate that the neurotransmitter *serotonin*, known to modify our responses to stress, may be involved.[33]

6. Instability

Immediately after the Doctor's regeneration into his sixth incarnation, it is clear that things have not gone well. Mentally the Doctor is unstable in that he appears impulsive, irritable, bad-tempered, and aggressive. These changes occur because the Doctor is experiencing poor inhibition control (*disinhibition*), suggesting that the areas that regulate self-control over our actions, the *prefrontal lobes*, are in some way not working correctly.[34] As well as aggression, damage to the prefrontal lobes can increase extraversion, which may explain this Doctor's outlandish style with his multicolored coat and bright yellow trousers.[35]

7. Eccentricity

The Seventh Doctor's new personality is eccentric, to say the least. Eccentric behavior can have a genetic component. People who have relatives who suffer from *schizophrenia* have often been found to have mild characteristics of *schizotypal personality disorders*, a condition defined by pervasive eccentricity.[36] These eccentric behaviors could be the result of a lack of dopamine in the prefrontal lobes or occur because people with schizotypal personality traits have a smaller left temporal lobe.[37] Therefore, it is possible that this incarnation of the Doctor has a smaller left temporal lobe or less dopamine than previous regenerations.

8. Memory Loss

The Doctor regenerates into his eighth incarnation when Dr. Grace Holloway performs ill-advised heart surgery.[38] Unfortunately for him, the anesthetic nearly stops his regeneration, and he is left suffering temporarily from a form of amnesia known as *transient global amnesia,* suddenly, though temporarily, forgetting everything about himself.[39] This form of amnesia is not caused by extensive neurological damage to the brain but by migraine or seizures or maybe, in this case, the regeneration process.

8½. Combat Readiness

Little is known about the War Doctor other than that the Sisterhood of Karn gives the Eighth Doctor the ability to control his regeneration so that he can become this warrior.[40] His brain is likely to be designed to overcome the problems people face in war zones, such as mental fatigue. We know that people in combat situations can make errors when they are under strain. A lack of food, water, and sleep can impair cognitive functioning. For example, when a person is dehydrated, the brain actually shrinks and so is unable to carry out complex thoughts.[41]

Although in today's world we are not able to redesign brains to make better soldiers, there are drugs available that can help with mental fatigue. Central nervous system stimulants such as amphetamines can be used to keep pilots awake during long missions, or modafinil, a drug used for sleep disorders, can help keep the brain in a more wakeful state.[42] Another thing that the Doctor could do to increase his resilience to war is to reduce his level of fear. Some researchers believe that the level of fear that we experience is driven by our genes.[43] Maybe the Doctor in this regeneration has reduced the number of his genes that are associated with fear reactions.

9. Accent

Shortly after meeting the Doctor, Rose asks, "If you are an alien, how come you sound like you're from the North?" The Doctor replies, "Lots of planets have a North!"[44] It appears that after his regeneration, he has had a marked change in his accent. Children's accents can change if they move to a new regional area, but for most of us, by the time we hit adulthood, our accents are fixed. However, very occasionally, people have been known to develop a new accent overnight, normally as a result of a brain injury, such as a stroke. This condition is known as *foreign accent syndrome,* in which a brain trauma can lead to a sudden alteration in a person's speech rhythm and prosody. A young Englishman who suffered a stroke suddenly developed a Caribbean accent (specifically similar to the accent found on St. Lucia). In this case, the foreign accent disappeared after seventy-two hours.[45] It could well be that the changes in the Doctor's brain structure during regeneration affect his accent.

10. Neurorehabilitation

Newly regenerated, the Tenth Doctor challenges the leader of the Sycorax to a duel during which the Doctor's hand is chopped off. The Doctor is able to grow another hand as he is within fifteen hours of his regeneration.[46] Unlike humans who have to learn how to use new limbs, the Doctor appears not to need any form of *neurorehabilitation* and can start to use his new hand immediately. Even humans can learn to adopt a hand that is not their own, but they require a period of adjustment during which they must adapt to using their new limbs. In the *rubber hand illusion,* a researcher strokes both the participant's real hand (which is hidden) and the rubber hand, which the participant can see. Over time the participant starts to perceive the rubber hand as his or her real hand.[47]

11. ADHD

When the Doctor turns into "a madman with a box"[48] in his eleventh regeneration, he becomes youthful, lively, and impatient, getting quickly bored and bouncing continually from one task to the next.[49] The impulsivity and hyperactivity he exhibits suggest that he has some traits of *attention-deficit hyperactivity disorder (ADHD)*. Indeed, this regeneration of the Doctor can be quite childish. Children with ADHD can take a few years longer than others to mature into adulthood. Although the precise reason why ADHD occurs in humans is not known, it is thought that there could be differences in the neurotransmitter *dopamine*, a nervous system chemical that performs a variety of cognitive, emotional, and motor functions.[50] This Doctor benefits from the high levels of energy that his hyperactive traits give him.

12. Autism Spectrum

The Twelfth Doctor appears to have unconsciously given himself the face of a man he previously saved in Pompeii to remind himself to show compassion.[51] Whether despite that reminder or because of it, this Doctor appears to have problems with empathy and with understanding complex emotions. In fact, Clara writes a number of cards for him to help him give the right emotional response.[52] This regeneration could give him some of the traits of the neurodevelopmental condition *Asperger's syndrome*. Although the Doctor appears to have learned some compensatory strategies, he does appear to have a less than complete understanding of the social world compared to other Doctors. Psychologists have found that scientists (including mathematicians) are more likely to have Asperger's or *high-functioning autism* compared with academics who are not scientists.[53] In Asperger's, it is thought that there are abnormalities in the brain's white matter and this leads to differences in the way in which different areas of the brain talk to each other.[54]

Beyond Brains and Behavior

Neuropsychology is a relatively young area of psychology, and advances in techniques such as brain imaging are likely to lead to further advances in this field. It is clear from our current understanding of how the human brain works that the Doctor's shares some similarities with ours but in other ways is very alien. One of the most striking differences between the Doctor and humans is his ability to regenerate. Although similar to the process of synaptic pruning in adolescence, regeneration is much more violent and traumatic, leading to exaggerated adolescentlike behaviors in the Doctor. Errors in the regeneration process as well as changes in brain structure as a result of regeneration lead to each Doctor having a markedly different personality in each regeneration. Our understanding of the human brain allows us to guess about the neuropsychological underpinnings of the Doctor's behavior, but neuropsychological techniques must improve before brain and behavior can be more richly explained.

References

American Psychiatric Association (2013). *Diagnostic and statistical manual of mental disorders* (5th ed.). Washington, DC: American Psychiatric Association.

Barkley, R. A. (Ed.). (2014). *Attention-deficit hyperactivity disorder: A handbook for diagnosis and treatment*. New York, NY: Guilford.

Baron-Cohen, S., Wheelwright, S., Skinner, R., Martin, J., & Clubley, E. (2001). The autism-spectrum quotient (AQ): Evidence from Asperger syndrome/high-functioning autism, males and females, scientists and mathematicians. *Journal of Autism & Developmental Disorders, 31*(1), 5–17.

Beaty, R. E., Benedek, M., Wilkins, R. W., Jauk, E., Fink, A., Silvia, P. J., & Neubauer, A. C. (2014). Creativity and the default network: A functional connectivity analysis of the creative brain at rest. *Neuropsychologia, 64,* 92–98.

Beyerstein, B. L. (1999). Whence cometh the myth that we only use 10% of our brains? In S. Della Sala (Ed.), *Mind-myths: Exploring popular assumptions about the mind and brain* (pp. 3–24). Chicester, West Sussex, UK: Wiley.

Blackburn, R. (2014, July 20). Lucy, Limitless, Transcendence: Why the "underused brain" is a film-makers' myth. Belfast Telegraph: http://www.belfasttelegraph.co.uk/news/world-news/lucy-limitless-transcendence-why-the-underused-brain-is-a-filmmakers-myth-30445915.html.

Blakemore, S. J., & Choudhury, S. (2006). Development of the adolescent brain: Implications for executive function and social cognition. *Journal of Child Psychology & Psychiatry, 47*(3–4), 296–312.

Botvinick, M., & Cohen, J. (1998). Rubber hands "feels" touch that eyes see. *Nature, 391,* 756.

Boyd, R. (2008, February 7). *Do people only use 10 percent of their brains?* Scientific American: http://www.scientificamerican.com/article/do-people-only-use-10-percent-of-their-brains/.

Brower, M. C., & Price, B. H. (2001). Neuropsychiatry of frontal lobe dysfunction in violent and criminal behaviour: A critical review. *Journal of Neurology, Neurosurgery & Psychiatry, 71*(6), 720–726.

Buxton, R. B. (2002). *Introduction to functional magnetic resonance imaging: Principles and techniques.* Cambridge, UK: Cambridge University Press.

Carelli, F. (2015). Dissociative amnesia or psychogenic amnesia as results of war's shocking events. *London Journal of Primary Care, 7*(4), 78–79.

Chechik, G., Melijison, I., & Ruppin, E. (1999). Neuronal regulation: A mechanism for synaptic pruning during brain maturation. *Neural Computation, 11(8),* 2061-2080.

DeWitt, I., & Rauschecker, J. P. (2012). Phoneme and word recognition in the auditory ventral stream. Proceedings of the National Academy of Science, 109(8), E505-E514.

Dronkers, N. F., Redfern, B. B., & Knight, R. T. (2000). The neural architecture of language disorders. In M. S. Gazziniga (Ed.), The new cognitive science (2nd ed.). Cambridge, MA: MIT Press.

Friston, K. (2002). Beyond phrenology: What can neuroimaging tell us about distributed circuitry? *Annual Review of Neuroscience, 25*(1), 221–250.

Gardner, H. (2006). *Multiple intelligences: New horizons.* New York, NY: Basic.

Goldberg, E. (2002). *The executive brain: Frontal lobes and the civilized mind.* Oxford, UK: Oxford University Press.

Grafman, J., Schwab, K., Warden, D., et al. (1996). Frontal lobe injuries, violence and aggression: A report of the Vietnam head injury study. *Neurology, 46*(5), 1231–1238.

Huettel, S. A., Song, A. W., & McCarthy, G. (2009). *Functional magnetic resonance imaging* (2nd ed.). Sunderland, MA: Sinauer.

Lieberman, H. R., Bathalon, G. P., Falco, C. M., Kramer, F. M., Morgan, C. A., & Niro, P. (2005). Severe decrements in cognition function and mood induced by sleep loss, heat, dehydration, and undernutrition during simulated combat. *Biological Psychiatry, 57*(4), 422–429.

Lyons, M., Harrison, N., Brewer, G., Robinson, S., & Sanders, R. (2014). *Biological psychology.* London, UK: Learning Matters.

Maguire, E. A., Woollett, K., & Spiers, H. J. (2006). London taxi drivers and bus drivers: A structural MRI and neuropsychological analysis. *Hippocampus, 16*(12), 1091–1101.

Maslow, A. (1943). A theory of human motivation. *Psychological Review, 50*(4), 370–396

McGlashan, T. H., & Hoffman, R. E. (2000). Schizophrenia as a disorder of developmentally reduced synaptic connectivity. *Archives of General Psychiatry, 57*(7), 637–648.

Moreno, J. D. (2006). Juicing the brain. *Scientific American Mind, 17*(6), 66–73.

Penfield, W. (1968). Engrams in the human brain: Mechanisms of memory. *Proceedings of the Royal Society of Medicine, 61*(8), 831.

Poeppel, D., Idsardi, W. J., & van Wassenhove, V. (2008). Speech perception at the interface of neurobiology and linguistics. *Philosophical Transactions of the Royal Society B, 363*(1493), 1071–1086.

Radford, B. (1999). The ten-percent myth. *Skeptical Inquirer, 26*(2), 29–34.

Rauscher, F. H., Shaw, G. L., & Ky, K. N. (1993). Music and spatial task performance. *Nature, 365*, 611.

Romero, J. R., Mercado, M., Beiser, A. S., Pikula, A., Seshadri, S., Kelly-Hayes, M., & Kase, C. S. (2013). Transient global amnesia and neurological events: The Framingham heart study. *Frontiers in Neurology,* 4(article 47): http://journal.frontiersin.org/article/10.3389/fneur.2013.00047/full.

Roque, D., Kottapally, M., & Nahab, F. (2012). A transient loss of British charm: A case of foreign accent syndrome and proposed neuroanatomical pathway (P02. 050). *Neurology, 78* (Meeting Abstracts 1), P02–050.

Rosell, D. R., Futterman, S. E., McMaster, A., & Siever, L. J. (2014). Schizotypal personality disorder: A current review. *Current Psychiatry Reports, 16*(7), 1–12.

Sheard, M. (2012). *Mental toughness: The mindset behind sporting achievement.* Hove, East Sussex, UK: Routledge.

Steelman, V. M. (1990). Intraoperative music therapy: Effects on anxiety, blood pressure. *AORN Journal, 52*(5), 1026–1034.

Stickgold, R., & Walker, M. P. (2010, May 22). *The neuroscience of sleep.* San Diego, CA: Academic Press.

Thompson, W. F., Schellenberg, E. G., & Husain, G. (2001). Arousal, mood, and the Mozart effect. *Psychological Science, 12*(3), 248–251.

Van Duin, E. D., Zinkstok, J., McAlonan, G., & van Amelsvoort, T. (2014). White matter brain structure in Asperger's syndrome. In J. S. Anderson, V. B. Patel, V. R. Preedy, & C. R. Martin (Eds.), *Comprehensive guide to autism.* New York, NY: Springer.

Von Hippel, W., Vasey, M. W., Gonda, T., & Stern, T. (2008). Executive function deficits, rumination and late-onset depressive symptoms in older adults. *Cognitive Therapy & Research, 32*(4), 474–487.

Weissensteiner, J. R., Abernethy, B., Farrow, D., & Gross, J. (2012). Distinguishing psychological characteristics of expert cricket batsmen. *Journal of Science & Medicine in Sport, 15*(1), 74–79.

White, Y. S., Bell, D. S., & Mellick, B. (1973). Sequelae to pneumoencephalography. *Journal of Neurology, Neurosurgery, & Psychiatry, 36*(1), 146–151.

Witelson, S. F., Kigar, D. L., & Harvey, T. (1999). The exceptional brain of Albert Einstein. *The Lancet, 353*(9170), 2149–2153.

Zak, P. J., Kurzban, R., Ahmadi, S., Swerdloff, R. S., Park, J., Efremidze, L., Redwine, K., Morgan, K., & Matzner, W. (2009). Testosterone administration decreases generosity in the ultimatum game. *PLoS One, 4*(12), e8330.

Zak, P. J., Stanton, A. A., & Ahmadi, S. (2007). Oxytocin increases generosity in humans. *PLoS one, 2*(11), e1128.

Notes

1. Christmas special, "The Time of the Doctor" (December 25, 2013).
2. Maslow (1943), p. 382.
3. Classic serial 10–1, *The Three Doctors* (December 30, 1972—January 20, 1973); anniversary special, *The Five Doctors* (November 25, 1983); modern episode 1–11, "Boom Town" (June 4, 2005).
4. Witelson et al. (1999).
5. Beyerstein (1999); Blackburn (2014); Boyd (2008); Radford (1999).
6. Lyons et al. (2014); White et al (1973).
7. Penfield (1968).
8. Buxton (2002); Huettal et al. (2009).
9 DeWitt & Rauschecker (2013); Dronkers et al. (2000); Poeppel et al. (2008).
10. Classic serial 13–5, *The Brain of Morbius* (January 3–January 24, 1976).
11. Classic serial 11–5, *Planet of the Spiders* (May 4–June 8, 1974).
12. Classic serial 4–3, *The Power of the Daleks* (November 5–December 10, 1966); 7–1, *Spearhead from Space* (January 3–24, 1970); 12–1, *Robot* (December 28, 1974–January 18, 1975); 19–1, *Castrovalva* January 4–13, 1982); 21–7, *The Twin Dilemma* (March 22–30, 1984); 24–1, *Time and the Rani* (September 7–28, 1987); *Doctor Who* (1996 television movie); Christmas special, *The Christmas Invasion* (December 25, 2005); modern episode 5–1, "The Eleventh Hour" (April 3, 2010); 8–1, "Deep Breath" (August 23, 2014).
13. Blakemore & Choudhury (2006); Chechik et al (1999).
14. Anniversary special "The Day of the Doctor" (November 23, 2013).
15. McGlashan & Hoffman (2000).
16. Classic serial 21–7, *The Twin Dilemma* (March 22–March 30, 1984).
17. Maguire et al. (2006).
18. Friston (2002).
19. Classic serial 1–1, *An Unearthly Child* (November 23–December 14, 1963).
20. Von Hippel et al. (2008).
21. Goldberg (2002).
22. Classic serial 10–1, *The Three Doctors* (December 30, 1972–January 20, 1973).
23. Rauscher et al. (1993).
24. Gardner (2006).
25. Rauscher et al. (1993
26. Thompson et al. (2001).
27. Classic serial 7–1, *Spearhead from Space* (January 3–24, 1970); 10–1, *The Three Doctors* (December 30, 1972–January 20, 1973).
28. Beaty et al. (2014).
29. Zak et al. (2007).
30. Zak et al. (2009).
31. Classic serials 19–1, *Castrovalva* (January 4–January 12, 1982); 19–5, Black Orchid (March 1–March 2, 1982).
32. Weissensteiner et al. (2012).
33. Sheard (2012).
34. Brower & Price (2001).
35. Grafman et al. (1996).
36. American Psychiatric Association (2013).
37. Rosell et al. (2014).
38. *Doctor Who* (1996 television movie).

39. Romero et al (2013).
40. Minisode, *The Night of the Doctor* (November 14, 2005).
41. Lieberman et al. (2005).
42. Stickgold & Walker (2010).
43. Moreno (2006).
44. Modern episode 1–1, "Rose" (March 26, 2005).
45. Roque et al. (2012).
46. Christmas special, "The Christmas Invasion," (December 25, 2005.
47. Botvinick & Cohen (1998).
48. Modern episode 5–1, "The Eleventh Hour" (April 3, 2010).
49. Modern episode 5–10, "Vincent and the Doctor" (June 5, 2010).
50. Barkley (2014).
51. Modern episode 9–5, "The Girl Who Died" (October 17, 2015).
52. Modern episode 9–3, "Under The Lake" (October 3, 2015).
53. Baron-Cohen et al. (2001).
54. Van Duin et al. (2014).

To what degree might tiny DNA molecules program personality and direct our actions? Can psychology use empirical science to get some answers to the philosophical nature versus nurture debate? The subfield known as behavioral genetics gives it a try.

CHAPTER EIGHTEEN

A New Doctor? The Behavioral Genetics of Regeneration

MARTIN LLOYD

*"I can still die. If I'm killed before regeneration, then
I'm dead. Even then, even if I change, it feels like dying.
Everything I am dies. Some new man goes sauntering away.
And I'm dead."*
—Tenth Doctor[1]

> *"I don't deny the importance of genetics. However, the
> fact that I might be altruistic isn't because I have a gene for
> altruism; the fact that I do something for my children at some
> cost to myself comes from a history that has operated on me."*
> —behaviorist B. F. Skinner[2]

Whether our identities are determined by nature or nurture may be thought of as a philosophical debate, but a subfield of psychology known as *behavioral genetics* probes the relative contributions of both nature and nurture.

Behavioral genetics seeks to understand the origins of the differences between individuals on some measurable trait. Mathematical modeling is used to determine the relative influences of *heritability* (broadly speaking, genetics), *shared environment* (common experiences that make family members similar to one another), and *nonshared environment* (an individual's unique experiences, which serve to make family members different from one another) on the individual differences in a given trait.[3] Shared and nonshared environment are distinguished from one another only in their effect. There is no way to determine automatically whether an experience contributes to shared or nonshared environment, except by whether it makes family members similar or different. Studies used to determine these relative influences examine the similarities between family members with known genetic and environmental relationships, primarily by studying twins and adoptees. While the results vary considerably, depending on the specific trait being studied, it generally appears that about 40 percent of the variance in most personality traits is due to genetic influences and 60 percent is due to the environmental influences.[4] Behavioral genetic studies have always been conducted on humans, but their findings may still be able to explain something about another species: Time Lords.

Time Lords, such as the Doctor, do something that humans do not: On the verge of death, they regenerate. Whether some portion of DNA is retained after regeneration is uncertain. Specific behavioral genetic findings might shed light on why some traits change after regeneration and others remain the same.

The Falconer Formula

In the field of *behavioral genetic* studies, researchers compare the correlations on a particular trait between groups, often identical and fraternal twins. Identical, *monozygotic* twins are virtual clones of each other, sharing 100 percent of their genes. Fraternal, *dizygotic* twins share, on average, 50 percent of their genes. As twins are always the same age, the two groups will not differ substantially in terms of shared environment. Once the correlations on a given trait are determined for both identical and fraternal twins, they are compared using the *Falconer Formula*, geneticist Douglas Scott Falconer's mathematical assessment of the relative contributions of heritability, shared environment, and nonshared environment.[5]

The Falconer Formula would not necessarily apply to the regenerations of a Time Lord. Unlike human twins, who share predictable portions of their genes, regenerations of a Time Lord share easily estimated degrees of experience (environment). In fact, a Time Lord at the end of one cycle and the next iteration at the beginning of a regeneration would share approximately 100 percent of their experiences during that process, though the genetic similarity is unknown. While the same formulas may not apply to Time Lords, human behavioral genetic findings may still prove informative about Time Lord psychology.

That Which Stays the Same

Intelligence

Possibly the single greatest commonality among versions of the Doctor is that the Doctor is always extremely clever. It is rare for any Doctor not to be the smartest person in any given room. In humans, the genetic and environmental influences on intelligence are complex. The reason for this complexity is that the relative contributions appear to change across the life span. This is possible because, again, behavioral genetic studies determine the percentage of the variance within a given population attributable to assorted environmental and genetic factors. Such studies cannot be used to say, for example, that 40 percent of a given individual's intelligence is due to their genetics. The influences within a population can change over time. Overall, about 40 percent of the variance in IQ in children appears to be due to genetics, while genes account for approximately 60 percent of the variance in adults.[6] Conversely, shared environment seems to have a substantial effect on intelligence in children but very little effect in adults, though this finding has not been without controversy.[7] Notably, while studies of adoptees generally find almost no shared environmental influence on adult IQ, results of twin studies have arguably been inconclusive.[8] Regardless, the findings most relevant to the Doctor are those relating to adults, as the Doctor has been an adult throughout the program's history. Even if there were some uncertainty about what qualifies for Time Lord adulthood, the Doctor has reached the end of his natural regeneration cycle[9] and has, in his twelfth incarnation, claimed to be over two thousand years old,[10] so it is safe to say he has reached adulthood.

While adult intelligence appears to have a fair-sized genetic influence, the Doctor has a much higher IQ than most of the population. It is certainly feasible that high IQ might have its own unique set of influences. Indeed, there does seem to be a higher shared environmental influence than is typically found for general intelligence, about 28 percent of the variance, but the variance remains most strongly accounted for by genetics (i.e., about 50 percent).[11] Although the role of shared environment is somewhat larger than for intelligence generally, the influences are not substantially different overall for high intelligence.

Ultimately, variability in adult intelligence appears to be driven mostly by genetics. The Doctor's consistently high intelligence across iterations is therefore an unexpected result, given that regeneration appears to lead to shared experience but perhaps not shared genes. While the behavioral genetic literature allows for a fair-sized contribution from nonshared environment, recall that nonshared environment, by definition, contributes to making people different from one another. In fact, the contribution of nonshared environment is determined, mathematically, by looking at the differences between identical twins.[12] Therefore, the unique experiences of each regeneration would not be expected to contribute to stability in the Doctor's intelligence.

Curiosity

Another trait shared by every Doctor is intense curiosity. After all, after thousands of years, he still elects to spend most of his time exploring all of time and space in a blue box. Curiosity is most strongly related to a personality trait commonly referred to as *openness to experience*, which contains elements, not just of curiosity, but also creativity and perceptiveness.[13] Variability in most personality traits is heavily influenced by genetics, and openness is no exception. In fact, the average heritability estimate for openness is 0.57, which is actually slightly larger than the genetic contributions found for most other personality traits.[14] As a general rule, shared environment has not been found to make a significant contribution. Not only has openness been found to have a significant genetic contribution, it has also been found to share genes with other traits that seem to be consistent across the Doctor's regenerations. Notably, there is about a 64 percent overlap in the genetics for openness and intelligence, and the genetic overlap with creativity is also substantial. The overlap of environmental influences is much smaller, and essentially nonexistent in the case of creativity.[15] Thus, creativity does not show the significant shared environmental influence that would be expected based on its stability across the Doctor's regenerations.

That Which Changes

People vary in their *need for affiliation*, the drive to want personal relationships with others.[16] Even people who regularly travel with companions can vary in terms of how much companionship they want and may differ over the course of a lifetime in how much they seem to like people or how easily they get along with others.

Not Always a People-Person (or People-Time Lord)
In the modern era, the Tenth and Eleventh Doctors are typically warm and welcoming, while the Ninth and Twelfth Doctors can be downright curmudgeonly. This is seen fairly clearly in the Ninth Doctor's refusal to participate in anything "domestic,"[17] though the Tenth Doctor readily joins Rose's family for Christmas dinner shortly after regeneration.[18] The interpersonal warmth displayed by the Doctors to varying degrees is best captured by a personality trait known as *agreeableness*, essentially a measure of how "nice" someone is. Individuals high on agreeableness tend to have better relationships

and more social support in their lives.[19] They also tend to be less prejudiced against minority groups and more accepting of those with disabilities.[20] Those with low agreeableness are more aggressive.[21] They are also more skeptical and more likely to use others to further their own ends.[22] Like most personality traits, agreeableness is substantially influenced by genetics and is only minimally influenced by a shared environment. For a trait that seems to change with the sweeping genetic changes of regeneration, this is to be expected. If the genes are different, a genetically influenced trait would likely change randomly. Nonetheless, the portion of the variance due to genetics is only 0.42 on average, which is actually less than almost any other personality trait.[23] This does, however, suggest a fairly large role for nonshared environment, which may mean that this aspect of the Doctor's personality is, to some extent, a reaction to the experiences of his previous incarnation. Thus, it makes sense for the Ninth Doctor to be somewhat more closed off as a reaction to his guilt over the acts carried out by the War Doctor.

"Am I a Good Man?"[24]

One trait that seems to change, albeit often subtly, from one Doctor to another is his moral reasoning. The Doctors differ in their willingness to employ violent methods. Although it is unclear whether the Twelfth Doctor actually throws the Half-Face Man to his demise,[25] it is hard to imagine other Doctors taking this step. Criminality, in general, has been found to be influenced by both genetics and shared environment.[26] When one looks specifically at violence, however, the influence of shared environment appears to increase. While there remains a strong genetic impact, it is less than has been observed for nonviolent criminality (i.e., 0.50 versus 0.76).[27] A significant role for heritability would be consistent with a trait that changes with regeneration, but high shared environmental influence would suggest stability more than change.

It is well-established that "The Doctor lies,"[28] but some Doctors are more manipulative than others. Deception has also been found to have both genetic and environmental influences. Engagement in fraudulent activities, for example, has been shown to be influenced by an interaction between genes and the environment. Specifically, individuals with a gene coding for high amounts of the enzyme *monoamine oxidase A* (MAOA) were more likely to engage in fraudulent activities, but only when they also had peers who engaged in delinquency.[29] Another version of the gene, this one actually coding for low MAOA activity, has been linked to a number of conditions known to involve deception, including *antisocial personality disorder* and *psychopathy*, especially when there is also childhood maltreatment.[30] While these findings seem somewhat inconsistent, they both point to a genetic effect interacting with an environmental effect. Much like the findings on violence, this muddies the waters somewhat in regard to whether a penchant for deception would be expected to change with regeneration. The genetic effect suggests it would, but this is ultimately complicated by the environmental effects.

Not One of Us

Ultimately, findings from the field of behavioral genetics are not always consistent with how the Doctor changes, or does not change, with regeneration. The Doctor looks radically different from one iteration to another (and it has been established that regeneration could even change a Time Lord's biological sex),[31] suggesting that regeneration changes him on a genetic level. Thus, traits most strongly influenced by genes are the ones that would be most expected to change. This has not necessarily proven to be the case. Most of the psychological traits discussed in this chapter have shown fairly strong genetic effects, including those traits that are stable across regenerations. There are several possible explanations for why the Doctor's regenerations do not conform to the expectations of the behavioral genetic research.

One reason for the Doctor's regenerations not following expected patterns may simply be that the initial assumptions were wrong. The dramatic physical changes that accompany regeneration suggest genetic changes, as physical traits are heavily influenced by genes. Humans look different from each other for reasons that are primarily genetic. Perhaps a Time Lord's genes work differently. Perhaps a Time Lord has *inactive genes* (what we would term "junk DNA") that are randomly activated during regeneration, while others are deactivated. This could differentially affect physical traits, while genes for psychological traits remain stable. If the Doctor's genes for psychological traits were remaining constant, then the psychological stabilities he exhibits (e.g., high intelligence and curiosity) would actually be consistent with the behavioral genetic research.

Another possibility relates to one of the core limitations of behavioral genetic research. Behavioral genetic findings are limited to the population under study.[32] This means that if a study is conducted only on Americans, there is no reason to assume the findings will generalize to populations from Europe or Africa, for example. If heritability and environment differentially affect variability in psychological traits in different human populations, it is even less likely they will function the same way in a population from Gallifrey. After all, though the Doctor may look human, he is ultimately not one of us.

References

Beaver, K. M., & Holtfreter, K. (2009). Biosocial influences on fraudulent behaviors. *The Journal of Genetic Psychology, 170*(2), 101–114.

Bouchard, T. J. (2004). Genetic influence on human psychological traits: A Survey. *Current Directions in Psychological Science, 13*(4), 148–151.

Bresin, K., & Robinson, M. D. (2015). You are what you see and choose: Agreeableness and situation selection. *Journal of Personality, 83*(4), 452–463.

Cloninger, C. R., & Gottesman, I. I. (1987). Genetic and environmental factors in antisocial behavior disorders. In S. A. Mednick, T. E. Moffitt, & S. A. Stack (Eds.), *The causes of crime: New biological approaches* (pp. 92–109). Cambridge, UK: Cambridge University Press.

Daugherty, J. R., Kurtz, J. E., & Phebus, J. B. (2009). Are implicit motives "visible" to well-acquainted others? *Journal of Personality Assessment, 91*(4), 373–380.

DiLalla, L. F., & Gottesman, I. I. (1991). Biological and genetic contributors to violence—Widom's untold tale. *Psychological Bulletin, 109*(1), 125–129.

Falconer, D. S., & Mackay T. F. C. (1996). *Introduction to Quantitative Genetics* (4th ed.). Essex, UK: Longmans Green, Harlow.

Greenberg, J. (1981, September 15). B. F. Skinner now sees little hope for the world's salvation. New York Times: http://www.nytimes.com/1981/09/15/science/bf-skinner-now-sees-little-hope-for-the-world-s-salvation.html.

Gunter, T. D., Vaughn, M. G., & Philibert, R. A. (2010). Behavioral genetics in antisocial spectrum disorders and psychopathy: A review of the recent literature. *Behavioral Sciences and the Law, 28*(2), 148–173.

Haworth, C. M. A., Wright, M. J., Martin, N. W., Martin, N. G., Boomsma, D. I., Bartels, M., Posthuma, D., Davis, O. S. P., Brant, A. M., Corley, R. P., Hewitt, J. K., Iacono, W. G., McGue, M., Thompson, L. A., Hart, S. A., Petrill, S. A., Lubinski, D., & Plomin, R. (2009). A twin study of the genetics of high cognitive ability selected from 11,000 twin pairs in six studies from four countries. *Behavioral Genetics, 39*(4), 359–370.

Kaplan, J. S. (2012). The effects of shared environment on adult intelligence: A critical review of adoption, twin, and MZA studies. *Developmental Psychology, 48*(5), 1292–1298.

Lensvelt-Mulders, G., & Hettema, J. (2001). Analysis of genetic influences on the consistency and variability of the Big Five across different stressful situations. *European Journal of Personality, 15*(5), 355–371.

Page, S. L., & Islam, M. R. (2015). The role of personality variables in predicting attitudes toward people with intellectual disability: An Australian perspective. *Journal of Intellectual Disability Research, 59*(8), 741–745.

Plomin, R. (2003). Genetics, genes, genomics and g. *Molecular Psychiatry, 8*(1), 1–5.

Schermer, J. A., Johnson, A. M., Vernon, P. A., & Jang, K. L. (2011). The relationship between personality and self-report abilities: A behavior-genetic analysis. *Journal of Individual Differences, 32*(1), 47–53.

Shane, S., Nicolaou, N., Cherkas, L., & Spector, T. D. (2010). Genetics, the Big Five, and the tendency to be self-employed. *Journal of Applied Psychology, 95*(6), 1154–1162.

Vukasović, T., & Bratko, D. (2015). Heritability of personality: A meta-analysis of behavior genetic studies. *Psychological Bulletin, 141*(4), 769–785.

Notes

1. Christmas special, "The End of Time," pt. 1 (December 25, 2009).
2. Greenberg (1981).
3. Vukasović & Bratko (2015).
4. Vukasović & Bratko (2015).
5. Falconer & Mackay (1996).
6. Plomin (2003).
7. Kaplan (2012).
8. Kaplan (2012).
9. Christmas special, "The Time of the Doctor" (December 25, 2013).
10. Modern episode 9–8, "The Zygon Inversion" (November 7, 2015).
11. Haworth et al. (2009).
12. Falconer & Mackay (1996).
13. Lensvelt-Mulders & Hettema (2001).
14. Bouchard (2004).
15. Schermer et al. (2011).
16. Daugherty et al. (2009).
17. Modern episodes 1–4, "Aliens of London" (April 16, 2005); 1–5, "World War Three" (April 23, 2005).
18. Christmas special, "The Christmas Invasion" (December 25, 2005).
19. Bresin & Robinson (2015).
20. Page & Islam (2015).
21. Bresin & Robinson (2015).
22. Shane et al. (2010).
23. Bouchard (2004).
24. Modern episode 8–2, "Into the Dalek" (August 30, 2014).
25. Modern episode 8–1, "Deep Breath" (August 23, 2014).
26. DiLalla & Gottesman (1991).
27. Cloninger & Gottesman (1987).
28. Modern episode 5–13, "The Big Bang" (June 26, 2010).
29. Beaver & Holtfreter (2009).
30. Gunter et al. (2010).
31. Modern episode 8–11, "Dark Water" (November 1, 2014).
32. Vukasović & Bratko (2015).

Psychology grew out of two parent disciplines when early researchers applied physiology's methods to some of philosophy's questions, but usually not the question of free will. As modern physiological psychology shows how one brain part after another determines both conscious and unconscious behavior, can a scientist still free room to believe in free will?

CHAPTER NINETEEN

The Time Lord's Brain: Regeneration, Determinism, and Free Will

DAVID KYLE JOHNSON
AND TRAVIS LANGLEY

"So, free will is not an illusion after all."
—Third Doctor[1]

"We must believe in free will. We have no choice."
—author Isaac Bashevis Singer[2]

Most areas of psychology shy away from the classic philosophical debate over *free will versus determinism*: Do we
have free will or are our personality and actions determined
by myriad influences? *Existential psychologists*, who look at the
reasons we ask who we are and why we ask why, criticize other
areas of psychology for being too deterministic, for failing to
consider free will.[3] The Doctor repeatedly opposes tyrants and
others who would deprive people of their ability to choose
(*freedom*), but he does wonder if people can make those choices

without external forces determining which choices we'll make (*determinism*).[4] Growing out of *existentialism* or *existential philosophy*, existential psychology is one of psychology's more philosophically oriented areas. Before adopting methods from physiology, the broader field of psychology itself began as a topic within philosophy, a topic exploring the nature of the mind and questions like whether free will even exists.[5]

Physiological psychology continues to study relationships between physiology and mental processes, identifying many biological influences on behavior. When a drug unknowingly ingested can render someone suggestible and impair memory[6] or a spike through the brain can turn a calm, responsible person into one who is emotional and uncontrollable,[7] how much choice do the people experiencing each of these events have? When regeneration turns the Doctor erratic[8] or even violent enough to choke his own companion[9] and when his changes are so striking that those traveling with him in his universe[10] or fans viewing the program in ours wonder if he is really the Doctor at all,[11] how much choice does he have? If the Doctor's actions are somehow a result of physical changes to his body, is the Doctor really free? Does he have free will? Do we? As in many areas in psychology, physiological psychology and the related modern area of *neuroscience* (which focuses on the nervous system) whittle away at the arguments that favor free will by revealing one variable after another that might determine who we are and what we do.

The Cortical Vortex

Although the idea that mentality is directly related to the brain goes back as far as the ancient Greek Pythagorean

Alcmaeon of Croton,[12] it wasn't until the modern day that this fact became widely accepted. Arguably, one of the most important cases to help establish this idea was the case of Phineas Gage, a railroad foreman who suffered a traumatic accident in 1848 when an explosion gone wrong drove a tamping iron through his head. The resulting destruction of part of his forebrain changed his personality, something that would not have been possible were his psychological makeup not a product of his brain.[13] We see something similar when the Doctor changes. As another Time Lord says about the Doctor's third regeneration, "It will shake up the brain cells a little."[14] In a way, each time the Doctor regenerates, it's as if tamping irons were flying through his skull.

Although Gage eventually partially recovered and the effects of his injury may have been exaggerated, his case nevertheless sent science down a path of discovery that revealed a direct dependence of the mind on the brain. Seeing how specific injuries affected people revealed much about which parts and pathways in the brain played roles in specific aspects of human mentality.

Emotional Responses
Every distinct emotional reaction depends on specific areas of the brain. Trying to reassure a frightened child, the Doctor explains fear in terms of uncontrollable physiological response: "So much blood and oxygen pumping through your brain, it's like rocket fuel. Right now, you can run faster and you can fight harder, you can jump higher than ever in your life. And you are so alert, it's like you can slow down time. What's wrong with scared? Scared is a superpower."[15] When the Doctor calls fear a superpower, empirical evidence would suggest that he refers to the power of the brain's *amygdala* to help us recognize danger, the *hypothalamus* to activate relevant

feelings and drives, and the *pituitary gland* to trigger the release of hormones that will help us take action.[16]

Laughing in the face of death can help a person manage fear, but those rare people who have literally laughed themselves to death (usually through asphyxiation or cardiac arrest[17]) have taught us that laughter is not a fully voluntary function. It results from activity of a series of brain regions that run through the cerebral cortex, now known as the "laughter circuit."[18] A young man terrified by ventriloquist dummies laughs uncontrollably in a mysterious hotel where the Doctor and others must face their greatest fears.[19] People with the condition *pseudobulbar affect* can experience unexpected outbursts of either crying or laughing for several minutes due to errors in neurological functioning.[20]

Motor Control

Much as we might like to think we consciously control our own physical actions, we often do not. When we catch ourselves humming or tapping our fingers and realize we've been doing that for a bit without conscious awareness, we glimpse the control that nonverbal, perhaps subconscious parts of the brain might have. When the Doctor struggles against the Cyber-Planner "Mr. Clever" for control of the Doctor's body,[21] some of his behavior is reminiscent of that shown by *split-brain patients*, people whose brain hemispheres have been surgically separated through injury, surgery (sometimes done to treat grand mal seizures), or some neural disorders.[22] The Doctor cannot keep his own hand from seizing an object and destroying it. "He's got control of the left arm," he says. Split-brain patients often suffer from something similar called *alien hand syndrome*, in which one side of the body literally acts on its own and is not under "their" conscious control. That is, it's not under the conscious control of the verbal left hemisphere, but instead under the control of the largely nonverbal right hemisphere. In one case, a man had trouble getting dressed every morning because as soon as one hand would button his shirt, his other would unbutton it. One young patient's left hemisphere responded to questions by indicating that he wanted to be a draftsman when he got older, while the right wanted to be a race-car driver.[23]

Memory

How the neurons of our brain are wired and fire can direct how we act. So if regeneration makes the Doctor act differently, it's most likely because regeneration rewires his brain, given the Doctor's similarity to humans. Not completely. A partial reorganization of his neurons could explain not only the memory loss that sometimes accompanies regeneration, but the attitude and personality adjustments that come with it as well. Neural death will damage memory, possibly beyond repair. Oxygen deprivation causes cells to degenerate rapidly. This may be why the Eighth Doctor suffers the most severe postregeneration amnesia, because The Seventh Doctor lies in a hospital morgue for hours, not breathing and deprived of oxygen and seemingly dead, before regenerating into the Eighth.[24]

Recognition

And then there is Oliver Sacks's famous man who mistook his wife for a hat. A tumor made parts of his mentality wither away gradually, which often included the symptom of mistaking inanimate objects for noninanimate ones—parking meters for children, his shoe for his foot, and (of course) his wife for his hat.[25] The man did not choose to make those mistakes any more than the Twelfth Doctor choses to suffer some degree of *prosopagnosia*, difficulty or inability to recognize faces or tell two faces apart even when motivated to do so. In one instance, the Doctor has to ask if he is speaking to the same people he was with only moments before because he cannot recognize any of them after only a few minutes.[26] Prosopagnosia can result from brain injury, but about 2 percent of people are actually born with some level of the disorder. Sacks was a sufferer himself. Studies suggest that a malfunction of the *fusiform gyrus* (located in the brain's occipital and temporal lobes) is the culprit.[27] Thus, regenerating into the Twelfth Doctor (his first regeneration of a new cycle, after he should have run out of regenerations[28]) apparently damages his fusiform gyrus.

Concern

In general, antisocial personality disorder and psychopathy—personality conditions involving extreme violations of others' rights, along with lack of empathy or other emotional aspects of a conscience[29]—could possibly be caused by anything from hormone and neurotransmitter imbalances to environmental and cultural influences. The Sixth and Twelfth Doctors may show the greatest difficulty feeling empathy toward others. A rewiring of the Doctor's *prefrontal cortex*, which houses some of our ability to make moral decisions, might be to blame. If that area in the Doctor's brain is damaged or rewired during regeneration, he may have lost his ability to make moral decisions that show concern for others, much as *traumatic brain injury* can result in difficulties processing emotions and make some head injury victims look like psychopaths in their lack of empathy.[30] *Transcranial magnetic stimulation*, using a magnetic field outside the cranium to manipulate the brain inside, can stimulate or inhibit neural activity, with effects that include either enhancing or inhibiting empathy and altering moral judgments, depending on how and where it is applied.[31]

Indeed, an inability to keep the *limbic system* (a set of brain regions responsible for motivation and emotion) in check is

Blindsight

Blindsight is the ability of certain visually blind individuals to respond to visual stimuli that they do not consciously see, enabling them to grab and correctly orient objects or navigate through their environment.[32] Part of the brain sees and provides some awareness of visual cues to the conscious mind, even though the person consciously has no visual experience. To the conscious mind, these individuals often feel they are simply guessing, despite showing accuracy too great for chance.

Of course, not every blind person has blindsight. When Dr. Grace Holloway suffers temporary blindness from looking into a beam that uses a live retina to open the TARDIS's Eye of Harmony,[33] her impairment is to her eyes, not her visual cortex, and therefore her brain would not receive the kind of visual signals necessary for blindsight. Elizabeth Rowlinson, on the other hand, blind until the Seventh Doctor's enemy Morgaine restores her vision, shows considerable awareness of her environment, perhaps through psychic powers but perhaps through some degree of blindsight.[34]

The experiences of individuals with blindsight teach us that unconscious visual pathways in the brain (that don't give rise to conscious visual experiences) are responsible for our ability to interact with the environment.[35] For some professionals, this has prompted reevaluation of the meaning of consciousness itself.[36]

why babies and toddlers are so emotional and selfish. The connections running back from their prefrontal cortex to their limbic system have not yet developed, letting the impulses and emotions that their limbic system generates essentially rule them.[37] It is only through practice that such connections grow, which perhaps explains how the Sixth and Twelfth Doctors each show more concern for others as time wears on.

It's also possible that the Doctor's diminished regard for others stems from an inability to sympathize with them. If so, then perhaps his *mirror neurons*, nerve cells that fire in sympathy with what we observe in others, are damaged during regeneration. When one person witnesses another performing a task, some of the neurons in the witness's brain will fire as if actually performing the task instead of merely observing, mirroring the same way they may be firing in the task performer's own brain.[38] By making the brain mimic what another person's brain might experience when experiencing different emotions, mirror neurons appear to mediate empathy.[39] If the Doctor's mirror neurons are damaged during regeneration, his ability to empathize may be damaged as well.[40]

Hidden Purpose

Repeating the same actions when circumstances are the same suggests that environment determines behavior. When the Twelfth Doctor spends billions of years stuck in a castle repeating the same behavior over and over (as he keeps reliving the same few days without remembering that he has done all these things many times before) rather than reveal a secret other Time Lords want from him, does he have any free will at all?[41] The aforementioned determinism to which the existential psychologists objected suggests that our actions are determined by specific causes. The same circumstances surrounding him and characteristics in him lead the Doctor to repeat the same set of actions, determining the outcome every time. If he truly has free will, his journey through the castle should vary.

Sublimely Subliminal

Subliminal stimuli, information that our brains detect on some level but without our conscious awareness, influence emotions and actions, although not as powerfully as many people believe. For example, research participants in numerous studies have expressed preference for images shown to them too quickly for them to realize they'd seen them[42] or too scrambled for them to know consciously what they were viewing.[43] These tendencies are so weak, though, that it's generally more effective to present stimuli clearly enough that people can recognize them outright.[44]

When the Silence give people commands that they follow even after they forget they've seen the Silence, these commands are technically not subliminal because the witnesses are consciously aware during the initial experience, and yet they function in subliminal ways because people forget where these desires come from.[45] A more apt analogy might be *posthypnotic suggestion*, giving someone the idea to follow a command after a session of hypnosis. Again, though, evidence indicates that hypnosis is not as powerful in the real world as it is within fiction.[46] Whether it's the Master controlling Jo Grant through hypnosis[47] or the Tenth Doctor using hypnosis to calm the Globe Theatre's architect,[48] both of these Gallifreyan hypnotists demonstrate control beyond the scope of human practitioners.

Quantum Choice

The brain is responsible for mentality, the brain produces actions, and the brain remains a vast mystery—in these ways, the Doctor is not unlike us. The way regeneration alters his brain and even his DNA likely accounts for his changes of personality, just as physiological changes can alter us, too. Even the most random-seeming changes that happen to us may depend on choices we make, whether we know it or not. Changes that occur to Time Lords via regeneration are not completely random, either. The Second Doctor has the opportunity to choose his next face,[49] the Eighth Doctor consciously decides to turn into a warrior,[50] and the Eleventh Doctor unconsciously selects the Twelfth Doctor's face to remind himself to save people.[51]

It seems that free will can be neither proven nor disproven. Studies on the variables that influence or cause behavior reveal many patterns by looking at trends, while nevertheless failing to explain every exception. Empirical research cannot prove the *null hypothesis*, the idea that a possible cause exerts no influence in any way whatsoever, and likewise cannot prove absence of any causality. The Third Doctor decides that free will does exist after all, not because of abstract philosophical debate but because of the way he interprets visible evidence after seeing how different a parallel universe's inhabitants can be. Given "an infinity of universes—ergo an infinite number of choices," he decides, "the pattern can be changed." Without free will, each parallel person and event would turn out the same in every reality.[52]

The Doctor chooses to run.

References

American Psychiatric Association. (2013). *Diagnostic and statistical manual of mental disorders* (5th ed.) *(DSM-5)*. Washington, DC: American Psychiatric Association.
Archiniegas, D. B., Lauterbach, E. C., Anderson, K. E., Chow, T. W., Flashman, L. A.,

Hurley, R. A., Kaufer, D., McAllister, T. W., Reeve, A., Schiffer, R. B., & Silver, J. M. (2005). The differential diagnosis of pseudobulbar affect (PBA): Distinguishing PBA among disorders of mood and affect. *CNS Spectrums, 10*(5), 1–14.

Baird, A. D., Scheffer, I. E., & Wilson, S. J. (2011). Mirror neuron system involvement in empathy: A critical look at the evidence. *Social Neuroscience, 6*(4), 327–335.

Blankenburg, F., Taskin, B., Ruben, J., Moosmann, M., Ritter, P., Curio, G., & Villringer, A. (2003). Imperceptive stimuli and sensory processing impediment. *Science, 299*(2514), 1864.

Bramness, J. G., Skurtveit, S., & Mørland, J. (2006). Flunitrazepam: Psychomotor impairment, agitation, and paradoxical reactions. *Forensic Science International, 159*(2–3), 83–91.

Caixeta, L., Maciel, P., Nunes, J., Nazareno, L., Araújo, L., & Borges, R. R. (2007). Alien hand syndrome in AIDS: Neuropsychological features and physiopathological considerations based on a case report. *Dementia and Neuropsychologia, 1*(4), 418–421.

Carr, L., Iacoboni, M., Dubeau, M., Mazziotta, J. C., & Lenzi, G. L. (2003). Neural mechanisms of empathy in humans: A relay from neural systems for imitation to limbic areas. *Proceedings of the National Academy of Sciences, 100*(9), 5497–5502.

Carter, R. (2010). *Mapping the mind* (2nd ed.). Los Angeles, CA: University of California Press.

Celesia, G. (2010). Visual perception and awareness: A modular system. *Journal of Psychophysiology, 24*(2), 62–67.

Dehaene, S. (2009, November 24). Signatures of consciousness. Edge: https://www.edge.org/conversation/stanislas_dehaene signatures of consciousness.

Dvorsky, G. (2013). Scientific evidence that you probably don't have free will. io9: http://io9.com/5975778/scientific-evidence-that-you-probably-dont-have-free-will.

Ferguson, M., & Zayas, V. (2009). Automatic evaluation. *Current Directions in Psychological Science, 18*(6), 362–366.

Geddes, L. (2011, August 24). Empathy enhanced by magnetic stimulation of the brain. New Scientist: https://www.newscientist.com/article/mg21128274.300-empathy-enhanced-by-magnetic-stimulation-of-the-brain/.

Geschwind, N. (1965). Disconnexion syndromes in animals and man. I. *Brain, 88*(2), 237–294.

Goldberg, G., & Bloom, K. K. (1990). The alien hand sign. *American Journal of Physical Medicine and Rehabilitation, 69*(5), 228–238.

Goldstein, K. (1908). Zur Lehre von der motorischen Apraxie [On the doctrine of the motor apraxia]. *Journal für Psychologie und Neurologie, 11*(4–5), 169–187, 270–283.

Gross, C. (1987). Neuroscience, the early history of. In G. E. Adelman (Ed.), *Encyclopedia of Neuroscience* (pp. 843–847). Amsterdam, The Netherlands: Elsevier.

Haynes, J., & Rees, G. (2006). Decoding mental states from brain activity in humans. *Nature Reviews Neuroscience, 7*(7), 523–534.

Hanly, C. M. T. (1979). *Existentialism and psychoanalysis*. New York, NY: International Universities Press.

Hare, R. D. (1996). Psychopathy: A clinical construct whose time has come. *Criminal Justice and Behavior, 23*(1), 25–54.

Harlow, J. M. (1848). Passage of an iron rod through the head. *Boston Medical and Surgical Journal, 39*(20), 389–393.

Hetu, S., Taschereau-Dumouchel, V., & Jackson, P. L. (2012). Stimulating the brain to study social actions and empathy. *Brain Stimulation, 5*(2), 95–102.

Holt, J. (2003). *Blindsight and the nature of consciousness*. New York, NY: Broadview.

Johnson, D. K. (2006). Does free will exist? *Think: Philosophy for Everyone, 15*(42), 53–70.

Jiang, Y., Costello, P., Fang, F., Huang, M., & He, S. (2006). A gender- and sexual orientation-dependent spatial attentional effect of invisible images. *Proceedings of the National Academy of Science, 103*(45), 17-48-17052.

Johnson, D. K. (2010). Is the Doctor still the Doctor? Am I still me? In C. Lewis & S. Smithka (Eds.), *Doctor Who and philosophy: Bigger on the inside* (pp. 41–52). Chicago, IL: Open Court.

Johnson, D. K. (2013). Do souls exist? *Think: Philosophy for Everyone, 12*(35), 61–76.

Kanfer, S. (1997, summer). Isaac Singer's promised city. City Journal: http://www.city-journal.org/html/isaac-singer%E2%80%99s-promised-city-11935.html.

Kaplan, J. T., & Iacoboni, M. (2006). Getting a grip on other minds: Mirror neurons, intention understanding, and cognitive empathy. *Social Neuroscience, 1*(3–4), 175–183.

Langley, T. (2014, August 31). Doctor Who and the neuroscience of morality malfunctions. Psychology Today: https://www.psychologytoday.com/blog/beyond-heroes-and-villains/201408/doctor-who-and-the-neuroscience-morality-malfunctions.

Lewis, J. G. (2013, September 23). Prosopagnosia: Why some are blind to faces. Psychology Today: https://www.psychologytoday.com/blog/brain-babble/201309/prosopagnosia-why-some-are-blind-faces.

Lo, R., & Cohen, T. J. (2007). Laughter-induced syncope: No laughing matter. *American Journal of Medicine, 120*(11), e5.

McCullagh, S., Moore, M., Gawel, M., & Feinstein, A. (1999). Pathological laughing and crying in amytrophic lateral sclerosis: An association with prefrontal cognitive dysfunction. *Journal of the Neurological Sciences, 169*(1), 43–48.

McCullough, M. (2015, January 26). Sciency wiency: Listen. Doctor Who TV: http://www.doctorwhotv.co.uk/sciencey-wiencey-listen-71329.htm.

Mikkelson, D. (2012, June 12). The last laugh's on him: Have people died laughing? Snopes: http://www.snopes.com/horrors/freakish/laughing.asp.

Milston, S. I., Vanman, E. J., & Cunnington, R. (2013). Cognitive empathy and motor activity during observed actions. *Neuropsychologia, 51*(6), 1103–1108.

Ramachandran, V. S., & Blakeslee, S. (1999). *Phantoms in the brain: Probing the mysteries of the human mind.* New York, NY: HarperCollins.

Sacks, O. (1985). *The man who mistook his wife for a hat.* New York, NY: Touchstone.

Shamay-Tsoory, S. G. (2010). The neural bases for empathy. *The Neuroscientist, 17*(1), 18–24.

Spanos, N. P. (1996). *Multiple identities and false memories: A sociocognitive perspective.* Washington, DC: American Psychological Association.

Thomas, B. (2012, November 6). *What's so special about mirror neurons?* Scientific American: http://blogs.scientificamerican.com/guest-blog/whats-so-special-about-mirror-neurons/.

Young, L., Camprodon, J. A., Hauser, M., Pascual-Leone, A., & Saxe, R. (2010). Disruption of the right temporoparietal junction with transcranial magnetic stimulation reduces the role of beliefs in moral judgments. *Proceedings of the National Academy of Sciences, 107*(15), 6753–6758.

Van Inwagen, P. (2000). Free will remains a mystery. *Philosophical Perspectives, 14*(1), 1–19.

Wertheimer, M. (1987). *A brief history of psychology* (3rd ed.). New York, NY: Holt, Rinehart & Winston.

Notes

1. Classic serial 7–4 *Inferno*, pt. 4 (May 30, 1970).
2. Kanfer (1997).
3. Hanly (1979).
4. Classic serial 7–4 *Inferno*, pt. 4 (May 30, 1970).
5. Wertheimer (1987).
6. Bramness et al. (2006).
7. Harlow (1848).
8. As Kanpo Rinpoche predicted in the classic serial 11–5, *Planet of the Spiders* (May 4–June 8, 1974).
9. Classic serial 21–7, *The Twin Dilemma*, pt. 1 (March 22, 1984).
10. Classic serial 4–3, *The Power of the Daleks*, pt. 1 (November 5, 1966).
11. Johnson (2010).
12. Geschwind (1965); Goldberg & Bloom (1990); Goldstein (1908); Gross (1987).
13. Carter (2010), p. 64.
14. Classic serial 11–5 *Planet of the Spiders*, pt. 6 (June 8, 1974).
15. Modern episode 8–4, "Listen" (September 13, 2014).
16. McCullough (2015).
17. Lo & Cohen (2007); Mikkelson (2012).
18. Ramachandran & Blakeslee (1999).
19. Modern episode 6–11, "The God Complex" (September 17, 2011).
20. Archiniegas et al. (2005); McCullagh et al. (1999).
21. Modern episode 7–12, "Nightmare in Silver" (May 13, 2013).
22. Caixeta et al. (2007).
23. Carter (2010).
24. *Doctor Who* (1996 TV movie).
25. Sacks (1985).
26. Christmas special, "Last Christmas" (December 25, 2014).
27. Lewis (2013)
28. Christmas special, "The Time of the Doctor" (December 25, 2013).
29. American Psychiatric Association (2013); Hare (1996).
30. Langley (2014); Shamay-Tsoory (2010).
31. Carr et al. (2003); Geddes (2011); Hetu et al. (2012); Young et al. (2010).
32. Celesia (2010).
33. *Doctor Who* (1996 TV movie).
34. Classic serial 26–1, *Battlefield* (September 6–27, 1989).
35. Ramachandran & Blakeslee (1999).
36. Holt (2003)
37. Carter (2010).
38. Carter (2010).
39. Baird et al. (2011); Kaplan & Iacoboni (2006); Milston et al. (2013).
40. Thomas (2012).
41. Modern episode 9–11, "Heaven Sent" (November 28, 2015).
42. e.g., Ferguson & Zayas (2009).
43. e.g., Jiang et al. (2006).
44. Blankenburg et al. (2003); Dehaene (2009); Haynes & Rees (2006).
45. Modern episodes 6–1, "The Impossible Astronaut" (April 23, 2011); 6–2, "Day of the Moon" (April 30, 2011).
46. e.g., Spanos (1996).

47. Classic serial 8–1, *Terror of the Autons* (January 2–23, 1971).
48. Modern episode 3–2, "The Shakespeare Code" (April 7, 2007).
49. Classic serial 6–7, *The War Games*, pt. 10 (J une 21, 1969).
50. Minisode, *The Night of the Doctor* (November 14, 2015).
51. Realized in modern episode 9–5, "The Girl who Died" (October 17, 2015).
52. Classic serial 7–4 *Inferno,* pt. 7 (June 20, 1970).

Factor File
Five

The Further Factors—Aren't There Limits?

TRAVIS LANGLEY

How many personality factors are there? How many distinct clusters of traits that mostly describe who we are? Two, three, five, six . . . ? How many Doctors can there be? When the showrunners conceived the Doctor's first renewal to solve the immediate problem of actor William Hartnell's health difficulties, they did not know two Doctors would become three, five, sixteen, thirteen . . . Doctors without end? Each way of looking at the array of personality factors may be analogous to looking at the variety of Doctors who can all still be the same man or at the many versions of ourselves we each present throughout our lives while each of us remains one person. The different configurations may all share truth, while none may capture the truth in its entirety. No one description, no one way of looking at things ever can. What about the traits that get left out whenever we focus on those that "mostly" describe a person or character? There may be other ways to interpret those arrays.

The Seven Factors

Early trait researchers left out evaluative terms like *good*, *evil*, *worthy*, and *unworthy* on the grounds that they were ambiguous or that they judged quality instead of describing specific personality characteristics.[1] Others, though, argued that these omissions neglected key areas of individual differences.[2] Some versions of the Doctor and Master may be strikingly similar in Big Five traits, while still differing in their motivation to do good or evil. If the Doctor's companions betray him, he tries to fix whatever has gone wrong for them,[3] but if the Master's companions turn on him, he tries to kill them and tends to succeed.[4] What traits that the Big Five missed might help identify which is the good man? The HEXACO model offers one answer[5] (addressed in Factor File Four: "The Six Factors—A Good Man?"). The Big Seven model offers another one, a seven-factor model based less on morality and more on each individual's evaluation of self-worth.[6]

We commend and condemn ourselves.

The Good: Positive Valence
Not everyone sees goodness in terms of morality. A person may be held in great esteem and have many admirable qualities for a range of reasons. The Doctor speaks highly of his own intelligence,[7] impressiveness,[8] and worth.[9]

> **Examples of Positive Valence Traits**
> Admirable
> Exceptional
> Important
> Impressive
> Outstanding
> Smart

Unconventional

Unusual

The positive and negative valence factors are largely distinct from each other. People with high opinions of themselves might or might not see themselves as also having negative valence traits. Some, like the Doctor, rate themselves negatively because of what they do with their best characteristics and because of what they fail to do.

The Bad: Negative Valence

Characteristics in the negative valence factor come closer to addressing views of oneself as good or evil. After the Time War, the Doctor begins to evaluate himself more harshly and does not see himself as a good man.[10] The Eleventh Doctor tells the Dream Lord, "There's only one person in the universe who hates me as much as you do," showing that his own self-loathing reveals the Dream Lord to be some embodiment of the Doctor himself.[11]

Examples of Negative Valence Traits

Awful

Cruel

Dangerous to Others

Depraved

Deserving Hate

Disgusting

Evil

Vicious

Wicked

Even a person who may be full of self-hatred or believes him- or herself to be bad may still value goodness and strive to do the right thing. "Never be cruel, never be cowardly," the Twelfth Doctor repeats his personal promise to Clara before they part ways, this time adding, "and if you ever are, always make amends."[12]

Infinity inside Us

Other researchers identified greater numbers of distinct personality factors: eight,[13] twelve,[14] thirteen,[15] fifteen,[16] and one of the best-known counts, sixteen.[17] The Big Seven might be genuine or might be an artificial refiguring of the Big Five,[18] and the personality psychologist who developed the 16PF to measure sixteen personality factors recognized that those factors intercorrelated with each other enough to form a configuration of five distinct "global" factors. They're all different and yet they're all the same. They can all look at one person, picking and choosing from that person's countless characteristics, to describe that person in a variety of ways. One person may be the two, the three, the five, the six, the sixteen, and many more. Every cluster both changes and retains some recognizability over time. The person you are at age four both is and is not who you are at age forty. Is the Curator who meets the Eleventh Doctor in a museum really the Fourth Doctor or the Fortieth? "Perhaps I was you, of course, or perhaps you are me," he says on the matter of who they really are, their shared identity, whatever it may be, "or perhaps it doesn't matter either way."[19]

We are who we are.

References

Ashton, M. C., & Lee, K. (2001). A theoretical basis for the major dimensions of personality. *European Journal of Personality, 15*(5), 327–353.

Blumberg, H. H. (2001). The common ground of natural language and social interaction in personality description. *Journal of Research in Personality, 35*(3), 289–312.

Bond, M. H., Kwan, V. S. Y., & Li, C. (2000). Decomposing a sense of superiority: The differential social impact of self-regard and regard for others. *Journal of Research in Personality, 34*(4), 537–5523.

Cattell, R. B. (1944). Interpretation of the twelve primary personality factors. *Character & Personality: A Quarterly for Psychodiagnostic & Allied Studies, 13*, 55–91.

Cattell, R. B. (1956). Validation and intensification of the Sixteen Personality Factor Questionnaire. *Journal of Clinical Psychology, 12*(3), 205–214.

Durrett, C., & Trull, T. J. (2005). An evaluation of evaluative personality terms: A comparison of the Big Seven and five-factor model in predicting psychopathology. *Psychological Assessment, 17*(3), 359–368.

Lee, K., & Ashton, M. C. (2012). *The H factor of personality: Why some people are manipulative, self-entitled, materialistic, and exploitative—and why it matters for everyone.* Waterloo, Ontario, Canada: Wilfred Laurier University Press.

Lovell, C. (1945). A study of the factor structure of thirteen personality variables. *Educational & Psychological Measurement, 5*(4), 335–350.

McCrae, R. R., & Costa, P. T., Jr. (1995). Positive and negative valence within the five-factor model. *Journal of Research in Personality, 29*(4), 443–460.

Psytech (2002). *The 15FQ+ technical manual* (2nd ed.). Psytech: http://www.psytech .com/Content/TechnicalManuals/EN/15FQplusman.pdf.

Tellegen, A. (1993). Folk concepts and psychological concepts of personality and personality disorder. *Psychological Inquiry, 4*(2), 122–130.

Tellegen, A., & Waller, N. G. (1994). Exploring personality through test construction: Development of the Multidimensional Personality Questionnaire. In S. R. Briggs & J. M. Cheek (Eds.), *Personality measures: Development and evaluation* (Vol. 1, pp. 133–161). Greenwich, CT: JAI Press.

Notes

1. e.g., Ashton & Lee (2001).
2. e.g., Tellegen & Waller (1994).
3. e.g., Jo Grant in classic serial 8–1 *Terror of the Autons* (January 2–23, 1971); Clara Oswald in modern episode 8–11, "Dark Water" (November 1, 2014).
4. e.g., Chang Lee in *Doctor Who* (1996 TV movie); Lucy Saxon in Christmas special, "The End of Time," pt. 1 (December 25, 2009).
5. Lee & Ashton (2012).
6. Tellegen (1993); supported by Blumberg (2001), but Durrett & Trull (2005) found the Big Five to account for more variance in traits.
7. "Your leader will be angry if you kill me. I'm a genius."—Second Doctor in classic serial 6–5, *The Seeds of Death*, pt. 3 (February 8, 1969).
8. "I am so impressive."—Ninth Doctor in modern episode 1–2, "The End of the World" (April 2, 2005).
9. "Wise and wonderful person who wants to help."—Fourth Doctor in classic serial 16–5, *The Power of Kroll*, pt. 2 (December 30, 1978).
10. "Good men don't need rules. Today is not the day to find out why I have so many."—Eleventh Doctor in modern episode 6–7, "A Good Man Goes to War" (June 4, 2011).
11. Modern episode 5–7, "Amy's Choice" (May 15, 2010).
12. Modern episode 9–12, "Hell Bent" (December 5, 2015).

13. Bond et al. (2000).
14. Cattell (1944).
15. Lovell (1945).
16. Psytech (2002).
17. Cattell (1956).
18. Ashton & Lee (2001); McCrae & Costa (1995).
19. Anniversary special, "The Day of the Doctor" (November 23, 2013).

FINAL WORD: RUN!

TRAVIS LANGLEY

"Seriously, there's an outrageous amount of running involved."
—Donna Noble[1]

"When I started running, I started dreaming."
—author/marathon runner Bart Yasso[2]

We run through the moments in our lives. What we run to, from, or for may define us, and so might people we run with on our way through those moments—the why and with whom of what we do and when all play parts in defining who we are. The First Doctor runs away from Gallifrey with his granddaughter, and the Second Doctor then becomes known for telling his companions, "When I say run, run. Run!"[3] When the modern series comes along, the Ninth Doctor first appears by grabbing Rose Tyler's hand and saying, "Run!" The running never really stops. Even when we sit still and time seemingly slows down, a clock still ticks somewhere and time keeps running forward.

We've filled a book about the Doctor and his companions, especially the old Time Lord himself. His foes could fill volumes of their own. *Dalek Psychology: To Exterminate or Not to Exterminate* perhaps? We've explored a variety of topics herein—compassion, companionship, morality, mortality, and more—and they've all tied into issues of *personality*, that psychological term for who each person is over time. "Who?" It's part of the first question for the Doctor[4] and possibly the first question to distinguish *sentience* in human beings, the ability to think subjectively,[5] from the thinking processes indicated in other living creatures. The question itself might define us more than any answer will. *Who* the Doctor is keeps changing—not only between regenerations but within each specific Doctor's time. To live instead of being stagnant requires change. We relate to this perhaps because we keep changing throughout our own lives. Change is story.

We run through our memories. Some get lost along the way, and all memories change. Memory is a reconstruction. It's not a perfectly accurate record of what happened but instead a re-creation, omitting details that were never stored, dropping details over time, changing colors and others cues, and shifting to fit our evolving understanding of our own recollections. We don't simply retrieve them. We reweave them every time. Memory is story.

"Every story ever told really happened," the Twelfth Doctor tells Clara. "Stories are where memories go when they're forgotten."[6] In a sense, a fictional event is something that did not happen, and yet those fictions did not spring out of nowhere. Every fiction's creation is itself an event. The Doctor's memories are unreliable (like when the name of the Great Intelligence only "rings a bell,"[7] as one example among many) and so are ours.[8] At times, a reconsolidated memory or outright fiction wields more power than original fact.[9]

The story of *Doctor Who* keeps changing and the program keeps running. Even when it went off the air, the story continued as, among other things, the tale of fans who kept wishing it would come back. Fans become part of the story—as represented by the Doctor's ultimate fan, Petronella Osgood.[10] Interacting with the Doctor and relating to him over time changes her and changes him a bit as well.[11] The Doctor's stories move us, but we move them, too. *Doctor Who* ran for more than a quarter of a century because of its fans, it returned because fans wanted it back, and it keeps going because fans remain part of its story.

We run with the Doctor. The Doctor runs with us—and for us. That's who he is.

> *"We're all stories, in the end. Just make it a good one, eh? Because it was. It was the best!"*
> —Eleventh Doctor[12]

> *"We tell ourselves stories in order to live."*
> —author Joan Didion[13]

References

Bernstein, D. M., & Loftus, E. F. (2009). How to tell if a particular memory is true or false. *Perspectives in Psychological Science, 4*(4), 370–374.

Clark, A. (2000). *A theory of sentience.* Oxford, UK: Clarendon.

Didion, J. (1979). *The white album.* New York, NY: Simon & Schuster.

Loftus, E. F. (2001). Imagining the past. *The Psychologist, 14*(11), 584–587.

Roediger, H. L., III, Wheeler, M. A., & Rajaram, S. (1993). Remembering, knowing, and reconstructing the past. In D. L. Medin (Ed.), *The psychology of learning and motivation: Advances in research and theory* (Vol. 30, pp. 97–134). Orlando, FL: Academic Press.

Spencer, A. (2010, August 13). Interview with Bart Yasso. Marathon Training Academy: http://marathontrainingacademy.com/interview-with-bart-yasso.

Notes

1. Modern episode 4–6, "The Doctor's Daughter" (May 10, 2008).
2. Spencer (2010).
3. e.g., classic serial 4–9, *The Evil of the Daleks,* pt. 6 (June 24, 1967).
4. Modern episode 6–13, "The Wedding of River Song" (October 1, 2011).
5. Clark (2000).
6. Modern episode 9–12, "Hell Bent" (December 5, 2015).
7. In the Christmas special, "The Snowmen" (December 25, 2012), the Eleventh Doctor does not seem to recall that the Second Doctor fought this foe before, first in the classic serial 5–2, *The Abominable Snowmen* (September 30–November 4, 1967).

8. Bernstein & Loftus (2009).
9. Loftus (2001); Roediger et al. (1993).
10. First seen cosplaying as the Doctor in the anniversary special "The Day of the Doctor" (November 23, 2013).
11. Modern episode 9–8, "The Zygon Inversion" (November 7, 2015).
12. Modern episode 5–13, "The Big Bang" (June 26, 2010).
13. Didion (1979), p. 1.

ABOUT THE EDITOR

 **Travis Langley**, PhD, editor of the Sterling Popular Culture Psychology series (*The Walking Dead Psychology: Psych of the Living Dead*; *Star Wars Psychology: Dark Side of the Mind*; *Captain America vs. Iron Man: Freedom, Security, Psychology; Game of Thrones Psychology: The Mind is Dark and Full of Terrors*; *Star Trek Psychology: The Mental Frontier*) is a psychology professor who teaches on crime, media, and mental illness at Henderson State University. He received his bachelor's from Hendrix College and graduate degrees from Tulane University, all in psychology. Dr. Langley regularly speaks on media and heroism at conventions and universities internationally. *Necessary Evil: Super-Villains of DC Comics* and other films feature him as an expert interviewee, and the documentary *Legends of the Knight* spotlights how he uses fiction to teach real psychology. He authored the acclaimed book *Batman and Psychology: A Dark and Stormy Knight*. *Psychology Today* carries his blog, "Beyond Heroes and Villains." He has been a child abuse investigator, expert courtroom witness, and undefeated champion on the *Wheel of Fortune* game show. Keep up with Travis and the rest of this book's contributors through **Facebook.com/ThePsychGeeks**.

As @Superherologist, he is one of the ten most popular psychologists on Twitter. One of his tweets appeared onscreen with the Twelfth Doctor in the "Doctor's Notes' edition of modern episode 9–1, "Heaven Sent" (November 28, 2015). Travis is easy to find at conventions—especially when he cosplays as the War Doctor.

ABOUT THE CONTRIBUTORS

 **Jenna Busch** is a writer, host, and founder of Legion of Leia, a website to promote and support women in fandom. She co-hosted "Cocktails With Stan" with Spider-Man creator and comic legend Stan Lee, and has appeared in the film *She Makes Comics*, as a guest on *Attack of the Show*, NPR, Al Jazeera America, and multiple episodes of *Tabletop with Wil Wheaton*. She's a comic book author, co-host of *Most Craved*, and weekly feminist columnist for Metro. Busch has co-authored a chapter of *Star Wars Psychology*, *Star Trek Psychology*, *Game of Thrones Psychology*, and *Captain America vs. Iron Man*. Her work has appeared all over the web. She can be reached on Twitter @ JennaBusch.

 Erin Currie, PhD, is a geek for all things psychology. As a licensed psychologist and founder of MyPsychgeek, LLC, she provides professional development consulting that focuses on helping people in science, technology, and all geekdom to realize their full potential in their personal and professional lives. Her writing, therapy, and consulting work all combine lessons and metaphors from sci-fi and fantasy with established psychological assessments and techniques (because it's more fun that way). She also wrote for *Game of Thrones Psychology: The Mind is Dark and Full of Terrors*. Find her on Twitter: @mypsychgeek.

 **Jim Davies** is a cognitive scientist at Carleton University in Ottawa, where he conducts research on computer modeling of human imagination. He authored the books *Riveted: The Science of Why Jokes Make Us Laugh, Movies Make Us Cry &*

Religion Makes Us Feel One with the Universe, and has chapters in *Star Wars Psychology: The Dark Side of the Mind*, and *Star Trek Psychology: The Mental Frontier*.

Kristen Erickson is a marriage and family therapist. She received her Master's degree in counseling psychology in 2011. Kristin has served various populations, including children and adolescents in school settings, children with autism spectrum disorders, adults and children suffering from trauma, and adult clients in a drug and alcohol detox/treatment center. She volunteers at ICNA Relief, a free counseling center that serves the Muslim population in Anaheim, CA. Kristin's counseling interests include a holistic approach to therapy, mindfulness, play therapy, cognitive behavioral therapy, and solution-focused therapy.

Wind Goodfriend, PhD, is a professor of psychology at Buena Vista University in Storm Lake, IA. At BVU she is also the director of the trauma advocacy program and serves as the assistant dean to graduate studies. She is the Principal Investigator for the Institute for the Prevention of Relationship Violence. She earned her bachelor's degree at Buena Vista University, then her Master's and PhD in social psychology from Purdue University. Dr. Goodfriend has won the "Faculty of the Year" award at BVU several times and won the Wythe Award for Excellence in Teaching.

David Kyle Johnson, PhD, is an associate professor of philosophy at King's College in Wilkes-Barre and a professor for The Great Courses (his courses include Exploring Metaphysics and The Big Questions of Philosophy). In addition to being the author of *The Myths that Stole Christmas*, he blogs for *Psychology Today*, has written and edited extensively for Wiley-Blackwell's Philosophy and Popular Culture series, has a popular Authors@Google talk on the movie *Inception*, and has published in journals such as *Religious Studies*, *Sophia*, *Philo*, *Think*, and *Science, Religion and Culture* regarding metaphysics and philosophy of religion.

Deirdre Kelly is a cognitive scientist whose main research interests are in moral psychology. In her doctoral thesis, she developed a model of moral decision-making using known empirical evidence of neurologically atypical populations such as psychopaths.

Alan Kistler is the author of the *New York Times* best seller *Doctor Who: A History*. He is an actor and writer living in Los Angeles, and the creator/host of the podcast *Crazy Sexy Geeks*. He is a story consultant and pop culture historian focusing on science fiction and American superheroes. Twitter: @SizzlerKistler.

Martin Lloyd, Ph.D., L.P., received his doctorate in Clinical Psychology from the University of Minnesota. He has worked in various prisons and high-security hospitals, including the U.S. Medical Center for Federal Prisoners and Patton State Hospital. He currently practices as a forensic psychologist in Minnesota and occasionally teaches Forensic Psychology at Gustavus Adolphus College. He hopes his next regeneration is more like the Tenth Doctor.

Jeremy Mancini graduated from Temple University with a degree in psychology. At Temple, he is a post-baccalaureate research assistant in two psychology laboratories. He works as a student support specialist to assist college students on the autistic spectrum. When he is not working, he is indulging in comic books, superheroes, and science fiction. Reach him on Twitter at @Mancini1030.

Katy Manning's career has spanned nearly fifty years and three countries. Her extensive television work began with John Braines's groundbreaking series *Man at the Top*. During this time, Katy was given the role of Jo Grant in *Doctor Who* alongside the unforgettable Third Doctor, Jon Pertwee, a role she revisited some forty years later in *The Sarah Jane Adventures*, starring Elisabeth Sladen with Matt Smith as the Eleventh Doctor. Katy's theater credits extend from London's West End to Sydney's Opera House. She returned to the UK with her critically acclaimed one-woman show about Bette Davis, *Me and Jezebel*. Katy has voiced numerous cartoons, including the award-winning Gloria's House as the ten-year-old Gloria. She has hosted her own interview show and directed two major musicals and several other plays. For over a decade, she has recorded for Big Finish as Jo Grant in *The Companion Chronicles* and as Iris Wildethyme in her own series, and guested on *The Confessions of Dorian Gray*, *Doctor Who Short Trips*, *Dracula*, and *The Lives of Captain Jack Harkness*. Katy wrote and performed *Not a Well Woman* in New York and LA, now recorded by Big Finish. More recently, Katy appeared on *Casualty* and for Bafflegab recorded *Baker's End* with Tom Baker.

Matt Munson can often be found spending time with his local group of fellow Whovians collectively known as "Team Tardis." His earliest memory in life is of watching a Tom Baker episode of *Doctor Who* from behind the couch, spawning a life-long love of *Doctor Who* and all things science fiction. His love for the show was reignited with the introduction of Christopher Eccleston's Doctor, culminating in the completion of a year-long project dedicated to reproducing a full-sized replica of the Eleventh Doctor's TARDIS. Matt serves as an enterprise architect on a flagship project for a Fortune 50 company.

Miranda Pollock, MFA, is an assistant professor of graphic design and director of the gender and women's studies program at Buena Vista University in Storm Lake, Iowa. She earned her bachelor of fine arts degree and her master of fine arts degree from University of Minnesota Duluth. Pollock is a multidisciplinary artist whose work has been published in various journals and books. She has presented at conferences on the role of interactive design in learning environments. Her research interests include design-user interaction, visual storytelling, and design theory.

Stephen Prescott is the creator and host of *A MadMan with a Box* podcast where Whovians from all walks of life discuss and dissect their favorite stories from the show's 50+ year run. With a penchant for minutiae, he possesses an almost encyclopedic knowledge of the show since its 2005 return. He is an avid costumer and prides himself greatly on his Eleventh and Twelfth Doctor costume collections.

 **Sarita J. Robinson**, PhD, is a senior lecturer at the University of Central Lancashire, England. Over the last 15 years, Sarita has investigated the psychobiology of behavior, specifically focusing on how the brain functions (or doesn't) when we face life-threatening events. Sarita's research frequently means she finds herself in high-pressure environments, working with firefighters, people undergoing Helicopter Underwater Evacuation Training, and other stress-inducing survival courses. Sarita is a life-long *Doctor Who* fan who enjoys combining her passion for *Doctor Who* with her love of psychology. In her spare time, Sarita enjoys doing stand-up comedy and public engagement talks.

 **Aaron Sagers** is an entertainment journalist who travels the nation discussing popular culture at fan conventions. He was host and co-executive producer on Travel Channel's *Paranormal Paparazzi*, contributed to multiple books, and authored *Paranormal Pop Culture: Rambling and Shambling through the Entertainment of the Unexplained*. He has interviewed Steven Moffat, Neil Gaiman, several *Doctor Who* companions, and most of the living Doctors. When he isn't playing with action figures or his dog, he spends too much time geeking out on Twitter (@AaronSagers) and Instagram where he shows pictures of action figures and his dog.

 Billy San Juan, PsyD, received his doctorate in clinical psychology in 2015. He currently works as a Psychosocial Rehabilitation Specialist in San Diego, CA. His clinical interests include the incorporation of masculinity as a culture within the context of case conceptualization for therapy. In his spare time, he is a proud member of the Psych Geeks and often speaks on panels incorporating psychology and popular culture. He has also contributed to Psych Geeks works such as *Star Wars Psychology*. You can find him on his professional page at Facebook.com/Billicent or on Twitter @Billi_sense.

Daniel Saunders is a Post-Doctoral Fellow in Cognitive Psychology at the Center for Mind/Brain Sciences in Trentino, Italy. He built his own Dalek out of cardboard, fiberglass, and egg cartons when he was 9, and first heard about the new series on a pilgrimage to Blackpool to see the *Doctor Who* Museum when he was 24.

Janina Scarlet, PhD, is a Licensed Clinical Psychologist, a scientist, and a full time geek. She uses Superhero Therapy to help patients with anxiety, depression, chronic pain, and PTSD at the Center for Stress and Anxiety Management and Sharp Memorial Hospital and is also a professor at Alliant International University, San Diego. Dr. Scarlet is the author of *Superhero Therapy* and has authored chapters in the Sterling Publishing works *The Walking Dead Psychology*, *Star Wars Psychology*, *Star Trek Psychology*, *Game of Thrones Psychology*, and *Captain America vs. Iron Man*. She can be reached via her website at www.superhero-therapy.com or on Twitter: @shadowquill.

William Sharp, PsyaD, is a certified psychoanalyst who teaches at Northeastern University with a private practice in Brookline, MA. His textbook, *Talking Helps*, is one of the few addressing the "impossible profession" of psychoanalytically informed counseling. He enjoys using popular media to explain complex psychoanalytic topics in his psychology courses. You can follow him @DrWilliamSharp for tweets on personality theories, psychoanalysis, psychology, and of course, all things Who.

Suzanne Tartamella, PhD, is an assistant professor of English at Henderson State University. Even without the help of a Doctor and his blue box, she regularly journeys back in time to the early modern period, teaching courses in Renaissance poetry and drama (specializing in Shakespeare), Restoration and eighteenth-century literature, and the early English novel. Her published work includes the book *Rethinking Shakespeare's Skepticism: The Aesthetics of Doubt in the Sonnets and Plays*. Her current scholarly projects focus on the intersections between Renaissance travel and theology in Shakespeare's *Pericles* and *As You Like It*.

INDEX

A

Abnormal synaptic pruning, 247
Acceptance, 181–184
Active compassion practice, 25
Adjourning stage, 163
Adult intelligence, 264–265
Affiliation, need for, 266
Aggression, 218
Agreeableness, 135–136, 158,
    170–171, 266–267
Aitken, Mike, 11
Alien hand syndrome, 276–277
Allport, Gordon, 10, 43, 235
Altruism, 20, 33, 133
Ambiverts, 46, 113
American Psychiatric Association,
    190–191
Amnesia, 252
Amphetamines, 252
Amygdala, 275
Analytical psychology, 105
Angels
    in art, 74–75
    Christian Bible references to, 75
    defined, 75
    as foundational concept of fear,
        81
    male gaze and, 79–81
    modern view of, 76
    in religious art, 76
    as Warrior archetype, 75–76, 81
Anger, 181, 196
Anima archetype, 77
Animus archetype, 77
Antisocial personality disorder, 34,
    268, 278

Anxiety, 21
Approach acceptance, 184
Archetypes
    angels and, 74–78
    anima, 77
    animums, 77
    child-God, 77
    described, 73–74
    Great Mother, 76, 81
    Persona, 111
    Shadow, 78, 81, 111
    trickster, 77
    Warrior or Hero, 75–76, 81
    wise old man, 77
Artificial intelligence (AI), 179
Asperger's syndrome, 254–255
Astrology, 113–114
Attention-deficit hyperactivity
        disorder (ADHD), 254
Attraction, 151, 160–161
Authenticity, 209
Authority/subversion foundation,
    35–36
Autism spectrum disorders, 198,
    254–255
Autonomous ego, 69
Avoidance, 192–195

B

Babyface bias, 144–145
Bargaining, 181
Barnum effect, 114
Behavioral genetics
    described, 261–262
    limitations of, 269
Behaviorists, 56

Betrayal. *See* Loyalty/betrayal
    foundation
Big Seven model, 288–290
Blindsight, 279
Blocking emotions, 216
Bodily-kinesthetic intelligence, 131
Body type, 145–146
Bollas, Christopher, 67
Brain. *See also* Neophrenology
    during adolescence, 247
    amygdala, 275
    cerebral cortex, 276
    dependence of mind on, 275
    emotional responses, 275–280
    frontal lobes, 248–249
    fusiform gyrus, 278
    hippocampus, 248
    hypothalamus, 275
    imaging of, 244–246, 255
    laughter circuit, 276
    limbic system, 278–280
    memory, 277
    motor control, 276–277
    occipital lobes, 245–246
    prefrontal lobes, 251
    recognition, 277–278
    spatial information, 247–248
    synaptic pruning, 247
Briggs, Katherine, 86, 87
Briggs Myers, Isabel, 86
Brown, Brené, 209
Bullying, 33
Burnout, 25

C

Cardinal trait, 10
Care/harm foundation, 32–33
Cause and effect, 65–66
Central traits, 11, 193
Cerebral cortex, 276
Change, 293–294

Character, defined, 63
Cheating. *See* Fairness/cheating
    foundation
Child-God archetype, 77
Childhood trauma, 66, 268
Chronic, defined, 199
Chronic social isolation, 207
Cognitive paralysis, 136
Cognitive therapists, 56
Collective unconscious, 75, 111–112
Companions
    benefits of, 136–137
    dynamics between, 156
    as egos, 59
    as moral compass, 137
    physical benefits of, 137
    qualifications of, 130
    selecting, 128–131
    traveling, 128–129, 136–137
Compassion
    defined, 19
    health and, 21–22
    morality and, 231
    survival and, 20–22
Compassion fatigue, 22–25
Compassion practice, 26
Compassion training, 22
Compassionate caregiving, 20
Compassionate parenting, 20
Complementarity of personality,
    160–162, 164
Complicated grief, 182
Concern. *See* Empathy
Connecting with others, 211
Conscientiousness, 135, 158–159,
    168–170
Conscious mind, 65
Coping behaviors, 107
Correlation, 44
Cortical vortex, 274–275
Costa, Paul, 121, 168
Courage, 14–15

Creativity, 120, 209–210
Criminality, 267
Crystallized intelligence, 169
Cuddle hormone, 250
Cultural rules, 95
Curiosity, 43, 265–266
Cybermorality, 228–230
Cybernetics, 216

D

Dark tetrad, 236–238
Dark triad, 134
Darwin, Charles, 144
Davison, Peter, 11, 12–13, 16
Death. *See also* Fear of death
    acceptance of, 182–184
    altruism and, 33
    awareness of, 179
    grief over, 180, 206
    laughing over, 276
    neural, 277
    oxygen deprivation, 277
    stress-related, 183
    witnessing, 22–23
Death acceptance, 183
Death anxiety, 179
Death drive, 64
Death terror, 182–183
Deception, 268
Decision making, 88
Defense mechanisms, 107
Degradation. *See* Sanctity/
    degradation foundation
Delusional, 193
Denial, 181, 193–195
Depression, 21, 181, 193
Depth psychology, 105–108
Detachment, 195
Determination, 169, 273–274
Diagnostic and Statistical Manual of
    Mental Disorders, 34, 190–191

Disgust, 38
Disinhibition, 248–249, 251
Dissociative symptoms, 199
Dizygotic twins, 263
Dogmatism, 109
Dominance, 157, 217–218
Dopamine, 254
Dream analysis, 105–106, 109
Dreams, 53, 67

E

Eccentricity, 251
Ego, 64, 68–70
Einstein, Albert, 244
Emotional inhibitors, 216–217
Emotional intelligence (EI), 132–133
Emotional self-control, 218
Emotional stability, 47, 157
Emotional support, 137
Emotions, 231
Empathic distress, 25–26
Empathy, 25, 135, 229, 254, 278–280
Energy focus, 88–89
Environment management style, 89
Escape acceptance, 184
Ethical egoism, 39
Eudaimonic happiness, 23, 27
Evolutionary perspective on love
    body type, 145–146
    described, 144
    excitation transfer theory, 146–148
    facial features and, 144–145
    reproductive capacity, 145
    youth and, 145
Excitation transfer theory, 146–148
Existential psychologists, 273
Existential therapy, 179
Existentialism, 274
Experiential avoidance, 207–208
Externalized ego, 69–70
Extraversion, 45–46, 135, 158, 251

Extraversion, Intuition, Feeling,
      Judging (ENFJ), 97
Extraversion, Intuition, Feeling,
      Perceiving (ENFP), 92–93
Extraversion, Intuition, Thinking,
      Judging (ENTJ), 93–94
Extraversion, Intuition, Thinking,
      Perceiving (ENTP), 97–98
Extraversion, Sensing, Thinking,
      Perceiving (ESTP), 95
Extraversion and Feeling
      combination, 93
Extraversion and Intuition
      combination, 93
Extraversion and Judging
      combination, 94
Extraversion and Perceiving
      combination, 95, 98
Extraversion orientation, 88–89, 90,
      96, 112
Eysenck, Hans, 46, 119–120, 168

F

Facial neoteny, 144–145
Factor analysis, 44
Failed constructs, 80
Fairness/cheating foundation, 36–37
Falconer, Douglas Scott, 263
Falconer Formula, 263
Falsifiability, 110
Fear
      angels and, 81
      managing, 276
      as uncontrollable physiological
         response, 275–276
Fear of death
      anxiety over, 179
      avoidance, 178
      at early age, 177
      manifest of, 178
      therapeutic interventions, 179

Feeling and Perceiving combination,
      92, 93
Feeling orientation, 88, 92
Five-factor model of personality. *See
      also* HEXACO model
      agreeableness, 170–171
      conscientiousness, 168–170
      crystallized intelligence, 169
      described, 168
      fluid intelligence, 169
      good and evil, 171
Flashbacks, 192
Fluid intelligence, 169
Foreign accent syndrome, 253
Forming stage, 163
Fraternal twins, 263
Free will, 273–274, 280–281, 282
Free-riding, 36–37
Freud, Sigmund
      dogmatic personality of, 110
      on dream analysis, 53, 105–106
      hypnosis and, 108
      psychoanalysis and, 63
      repetition to avoid suffering, 56
      unconscious mind and, 106–108
Freudian slips, 54
Friendships, 183
Fromm, Erich, 36
Frontal lobes, 248–249
Functional magnetic resonance
      imaging (fMRI), 245
Fusiform gyrus, 278

G

Gage, Phineas, 275
Gardner, Howard, 131
Generosity, 250
Genetics
      agreeableness and, 267
      intelligence and, 264–265
      for openness, 266

Gomez, Michelle, 34
Good and evil, 171, 238
Goodness, 288
Great Mother archetype, 76, 81
Grief, 180–182, 206
Group dynamics, 163
Guilt, 182, 190, 208

H

Haidt, Jonathan, 31, 231
Happiness, 23
Healthy men. *See also* Masculinity
    as good fathers, 220
    as humanitarians, 221
    humor and, 221–222
    intimate relationships of,
        219–220
    as protector, 220
    as risk takers, 221
    self-reliance of, 220
Hedonic happiness, 23
Heritability, 262, 267–268
Hero (Warrior) archetype, 75–76,
    81
Heuristic thinking, 2
HEXACO model, 235–236, 288.
        See also Five-factor model of
        personality
High-functioning autism, 254–255
Hippocampus, 248
Honesty-humility traits, 236
Human condition, 32–33
Human intelligence, 130. *See also*
        Multiple intelligences model
Humanistic therapy, 179
Humanity, 231
Humanness, 16
Humor, to express affection,
    221–222
Hyperarousal, 195–197
Hypervigilance, 196–197

Hypnosis, 108, 281
Hypothalamus, 275

I

Id, 64, 67–68
Identical twins, 263
Identity issues, 12–15
Illusory correlations, 43–44
Imagination, 16
Impaired functioning, 198
Inactive genes, 269
Information processing, 88
In-group loyalty, 37–38
Insomnia, 197
Instant gratification, 23
Intelligence, 77, 131–133, 169,
        264–265. *See also* Artificial
        intelligence (AI)
Intelligence quotient (IQ), 130,
        264–265. *See also* Multiple
        intelligences model
Intelligence testing, 133
Interdependent identities, 148–150
Interpersonal attraction, predictors
        of, 151
Interpersonal intelligence, 132. *See
        also* Emotional intelligence
        (EI)
Interventions, 55
Intimate male relationships, 219–220
Intrapersonal intelligence, 132
Introversion, 45, 158
Introversion, Intuition, Feeling,
        Judging (INFJ), 95–96
Introversion, Intuition, Thinking,
        Judging (INTJ), 91–92,
        98–99
Introversion, Intuition, Thinking,
        Perceiving (INTP), 94–95
Introversion, Sensing, Feeling,
        Perceiving (ISFP), 92

Introversion, Sensing, Thinking,
        Perceiving (ISTP), 96–97
Introversion and Feeling
        combination, 96
Introversion and Intuition
        combination, 91
Introversion and Sensing
        combination, 92
Introversion and Thinking
        combination, 94, 99
Introversion orientation, 88–89, 90,
        96, 112
Intuition and Feeling combination,
        96, 97
Intuition and Judging combination,
        97
Intuition orientation, 88
Inventiveness, 250
Isolation, 180, 195

J

Joviality, 95
Judging orientation, 89, 91
Jung, Carl Gustav, 45, 75, 86, 105,
        110–112
Junk DNA, 269

K

Kelly, George, 80
Kingston, Alex, 14, 15
Kübler-Ross, Elisabeth, 181

L

Latent content, 58, 67
Laughter and dance, 210
Laughter circuit, 276
Liberty/oppression foundation,
        33–35
Libidinal force, 64
Limbic system, 278–280

Linguistic intelligence, 131
Logical-mathematical intelligence,
        131
Loss, coping with, 206
Love
        evolutionary perspective on,
                144–146
        excitation transfer theory,
                146–148
        self-expansion theory, 149–150
Loving-kindness meditation (LKM),
        21, 22
Low conscientiousness, 159
Low extraversion. *See* Introversion
Loyalty/betrayal foundation, 37–38

M

Machiavellianism, 134, 236–238
Madness
        defined, 2
        psychoticism and, 120
Male gaze, 79–81
Male-oriented organizations, 221
Males/men. *See* Healthy men;
                Masculinity
Manifest content, 58, 67
Marital satisfaction, 20
Masculinity. *See also* Healthy men
        aggression, 218
        intimate male relationships and,
                219–220
        male heroes and, 222
        positive qualities of, 219–222
        as protector, 219–220
        social constructs of, 222
        status, 217
        taught to young boys, 215–216
Mathematical modeling, 262
May, Rollo, 110
McCoy, Sylvester, 13–14, 16
McCrae, Robert, 121, 168

Meaning-based happiness, 23
Meaningful work, 210
Meditation, 26
Memory, 294
Men. *See* Healthy men; Masculinity
Mental fatigue, 252
Mental health disorders, 21–22
Mental toughness, 250–251
Mentality, 274–275
Mere exposure effect, 151
Midlife crisis, 99
Mirror neurons, 280
Misattribution of arousal, 147
Modafinil, 252
Model, defined, 149–150
Monoamine oxidase A (MAOA),
    268
Monozygotic twins, 263
Moral compass, 137
Moral development, 39–40
Moral foundations
    authority/subversion, 35–36
    fairness/cheating, 36–37
    liberty/oppression, 33–35
    sanctity/degradation, 38–39
Moral psychology theory
    described, 31–32
    foundations of, 32
Moral reasoning, 267
Morality
    angels and, 76
    cybermorality, 228–230
    emotional foundation of, 34
    goodness vs., 288
    Machiavellian view of, 237–238
    understanding, 39
Mortality. *See also* Fear of death
    artificial intelligence and, 179
    companion's, 178
    death acceptance and, 185
    facing one's own, 178, 179, 183
    regenerations and, 179

Multiple intelligences model, 131–133
Multiple sclerosis (MS), 207
Murray, Henry, 109
Musical intelligence, 131
Myers, David, 219
Myers-Briggs Type Indicator
    (MBTI). *See also* Personality
    theory (Jung)
    ambiversion and, 113
    astrology vs., 113–114
    Barnum effect, 114
    controversy around, 86, 112–114
    critics of, 90
    depth psychology and, 106
    Extraversion, Intuition, Feeling,
        Judging (ENFJ), 97
    Extraversion, Intuition, Feeling,
        Perceiving (ENFP), 92–93
    Extraversion, Intuition,
        Thinking, Judging (ENTJ),
        93–94
    Extraversion, Intuition,
        Thinking, Perceiving
        (ENTP), 97–98
    Extraversion, Sensing, Thinking,
        Perceiving (ESTP), 95
    Extraversion/Feeling
        combination, 93
    Extraversion/Intuition
        combination, 93
    Extraversion/Judging
        combination, 94
    Extraversion/Perceiving
        combination, 95, 98
    Introversion, Intuition, Feeling,
        Judging (INFJ), 95–96
    Introversion, Intuition,
        Thinking, Judging (INTJ),
        91–92, 98–99
    Introversion, Intuition,
        Thinking, Perceiving
        (INTP), 94–95

Myers-Briggs Type Indicator continued
  Introversion, Sensing, Feeling,
    Perceiving (ISFP), 92
  Introversion, Sensing, Thinking,
    Perceiving (ISTP), 96–97
  Introversion/Feeling
    combination, 96
  Introversion/Intuition
    combination, 91
  Introversion/Sensing
    combination, 92
  Introversion/Thinking
    combination, 94, 99
  Intuition/Feeling combination,
    96, 97
  Intuition/Judging combination,
    97
  Thinking/Judging combination,
    91
  Thinking/Perceiving
    combination, 95

N

Narcissism, 134, 236
Narcissistic personality disorder, 236
Negative correlation, 44
Negative self-evaluation, 195
Negative valence, 289–290
NEO (neuroticism, extraversion,
    openness) model, 121–122
Neophrenology
  accent, 253
  ADHD, 254
  autism spectrum, 254–255
  combat readiness, 252
  eccentricity, 251
  generosity, 250
  inhibition control, 248–249, 251
  instability, 251
  inventiveness, 250
  memory loss, 252

  mental toughness, 250–251
  music and, 249
  spatial reasoning, 249
Neural death, 277
Neuropsychology, 243–244, 255
Neurorehabilitation, 253
Neuroticism, 46–47, 136
Neutral acceptance of death, 184
Nonpsychotic mental illness, 46
Nonshared environment
  agreeableness and, 267
  defined, 262
  intelligence and, 265
Null hypothesis, 282

O

Observer, sufferer vs., 21
Occipital lobes, 245–246
Occupational roles, identifying
    selection criteria for, 127
OCEAN. *See* Five-factor model of
    personality
On the Origin of Species (Darwin),
    144
Openness to experience, 121, 135,
    157, 265
Openness traits, 121–122
Oppression. *See* Liberty/oppression
    foundation
Orthogonal personality factors, 45
Oxygen deprivation, 277
Oxytocin, 211, 250

P

Paternalists, 33–35
Penfield, Wilder, 245
Perceiving orientation, 89, 96
Performing stage, 163
Persistence, 169
Persona archetype, 111
Personality, 169

Personality, defined, 85–86
Personality characteristics,
    288–290
Personality disorder, 10
Personality factors, 10, 44–45,
    133–136. *See also* Five-factor
    model of personality
Personality tests, 106
Personality theory (Jung). *See also*
    Myers-Briggs Type Indicator
    (MBTI)
  decision making, 88
  described, 87–88
  energy, 88–89
  environment management, 89
  information processing, 88
  Myers-Briggs Type Indicator
    and, 86–87
Personality traits
  agreeableness traits, 171, 266–267
  cardinal, 10
  central, 11
  conscientiousness traits, 170
  defined, 10, 43
  described, 122
  emotional stability, 157
  extraversion, 45–46
  flexible, 9–10
  honesty-humility, 236
  lexical studies of, 235–236
  negative valence, 289–290
  openness, 121–122
  positive valence, 288–289
  psychoticism, 120–121
  relationship choice and, 156–160
  sadism, 10, 238
  secondary, 11
Phrenology, 248
Physical benefits of companions, 137
Physical proximity, as attraction
    predictor, 151
Physical traits, 43

Physiological psychology, 274
Pituitary gland, 276
Playing and resting, 210
Pleasure principle, 67–68
Pneumoencephalography, 245
Positive correlation, 44
Positive valence, 288–289
Posthypnotic suggestion, 281
Posttraumatic growth, 82, 138,
    190
Posttraumatic stress disorder
    (PTSD)
  avoiding reminders, 192–195
  compassion and, 21
  concentration difficulties, 197
  dissociative symptoms, 199
  duration, 198
  elevated arousal, 195–197
  flashback, 192
  impaired functioning, 198
  negative changes in thought and
    mood, 195
  posttraumatic growth vs., 82
  pretrauma functioning vs., 197
  sleep disturbance, 197
  specifiers, 199
  substance abuse and, 198–199
  symptoms of, 21–22, 191
  tragedy of human design, 190
  trauma without, 189
Practicing gratitude, 209
Practicing mindfulness, 210
Prefrontal cortex, 278–280
Prefrontal lobes, 251
Preloss dependency, 182
Present-focused people, 193
Prestige, 217
Pretrauma functioning, 197
Primary process, 67
Processing information. *See*
    Information processing
Projective tests, 106

Prolonged grief, 182
Prosopagnosia, 277–278
Pseudobulbar affect, 276
Psychoanalysis
    described, 63
    exploratory and insight-oriented
        type of, 56
    to glimpse the unconscious, 60
    misunderstanding of, 54
    as place for self-exploration, 59
    treatment structure, 57
Psychodynamics, 60, 105–106
Psychological screening, 129
Psychological types, 86. *See also*
        Personality theory (Jung)
Psychopathy, 34, 134, 236, 268,
        278
Psychoticism, 120–121, 122, 168
Psychoticism traits, 121
Purity, 38–39

R

Reciprocal liking, as attraction
        predictor, 151
Reckless, 196
Reconsolidated memory, 294
Relationship choice, 156
Relationship satisfaction, 161
Relationships
    attraction and, 160–161
    complementarity of personality,
        160–162
    group dynamics, 162
    stages of, 163
Repression, 107–108
Resilience, 182, 209, 211
Restless sleep, 197
Risk aversion, 158
Romantic attraction, 151. *See also*
        Love
Rubber hand illusion, 253

S

Sacks, Oliver, 277, 278
Sadism, 10, 238
Sagers, Aaron, 12–15
Sanctity/degradation foundation,
        38–39
Schizophrenia, 247
Schizotypal personality disorders,
        251
Schwartz, Joseph, 60
Science
    flawed, 115
    unconscious mind and,
        109–110
Scopophilia, 79
Second Council of Nicaea, 76
Secondary traits, 11
Self-compassion, 209
Self-destructive behavior, 196
Self-expansion theory, 148–150
Self-reliance, 220
Self-worth, 288
Sensing orientation, 88
Sentience in human beings, 294
Serotonin, 251
Severe trauma, 190
Sexual sadism, 238
Shackleton, Ernest, 129
Shadow archetype, 78, 81, 111
Shaky bridge study, 147
Shame, 208
Shared environment
    agreeableness and, 267
    curiosity and, 266
    defined, 262
    intelligence and, 265
Similarity, as attraction predictor,
        151
16PF model, 290
Smith, Matt, 12, 14–15
Social connection, 26
Social cue card, 198

Social dominance, 159
Social isolation, 207–208
Social learning, 95
Social reinforcement, 159
Social support network, 136–137
Societal relationships, 35
Socrates, 56
Spatial information, 247–248
Spatial intelligence, 131–132
Spatial reasoning, 249
Split-brain patients, 276
Stability vs. change, 9, 15
Staring at your enemy psychological
    concept, 78
Stoicism, 218
Storming stage, 163
Stress, 26, 46, 94, 107, 193, 211.
    See also Posttraumatic stress
    disorder (PTSD)
Stressful situations, 136, 139
Stress-related deaths, 183
Subconscious, 106. *See also*
    Unconscious
Subliminal stimuli, 281
Substance abuse, 198–199
Subversion. *See* Authority/subversion
    foundation
Sufferer, observer vs., 21
Superego, 64, 68–69
Superstition, 115
Surgency, 158
Survival, compassion and, 20–22
Survivor guilt, 190, 196
Synaptic pruning, 247
Szasz, Thomas, 2

T

Take-charge behavior, 94
Technology
    to augment human performance,
    228

    minds modified by, 231
    transparent, 230
Tennant, David, 12, 14
Terror management theory,
    182–183
Testability, 110
Therapy
    behavioral and cognitive
        approaches to, 56
    non-insight-oriented approach
        to, 55–56
    treatment structure, 57
Thinking and Judging combination,
    91
Thinking and Perceiving
    combination, 95
Thinking orientation, 88, 96
Thought suppression, 108
Three-factor theory of personality,
    120
Trait clusters, 10, 43, 44–45
Trait theorists, 43
Transcranial magnetic stimulation,
    278
Transference narrative, 56–57
Transient global amnesia, 252
Trauma, 66, 189, 191–193. *See also*
    Posttraumatic stress disorder
    (PTSD)
Traumatic brain injury, 278
Traumatic grief, 206
Traveling companion, 128–129,
    136–137
Trust, 209
Tuckman, Bruce, 163
Two-factor theory of personality, 46,
    119–120

U

The Ultimate Time Lord
    (documentary), 11

Unconscious
    collective, 75
    conceptions of evil, 78
    conscious vs., 54
    described, 64–65
    dreams and, 53
    elements of, 64–65
    Freud theory on, 106–108
    hypnosis and, 108
    layers of meaning and, 67
    methods to delve into, 108–109
    motivating forces of, 64
    nonlinear nature of, 66–67
    as revealed in psychoanalysis,
        60
    ripple effect on life events, 65
    size of, 65–66
Universal personality factors, 45
Us vs. them, 194

V
Van Gogh, Vincent, 120
Vulnerability, 208–211

W
Waist-to-hips ratio, 146
Warrior archetype, 75–76, 81
White matter, 207
Wholehearted individuals, 209–210
Wise old man archetype, 77
Wrongdoing, 229

Y
Yalom, Irvin, 179

Z
Zimbardo, Philip, 194